RECONSTRUCTING SOUTH ASIA

RECONSTRUCTING SOUTH ASIA
An Agenda

Editor
ADLURI SUBRAMANYAM RAJU

GYAN PUBLISHING HOUSE
NEW DELHI-110002

Reconstructing South Asia: An Agenda

Rs. 690

ISBN: 81-212-0928-5

Published in 2007 in India by
Gyan Publishing House
5, Ansari Road, Darya Ganj,
New Delhi-110002
Phones : 23282060, 23261060
Fax : 011-23285914
E-mail : books@ gyanbooks.com
Website: www.gyanbooks.com

Lasser Type Setting by: Rudra Computer Graphics
Printed at : Salasar Imaging System, Delhi

In memory of

Prof. Isaac Sequeira

Former Director of Indo-American Centre for International Studies Hyderabad, India

Contents

SECTION-V: PROSPECTS FOR A SOUTH ASIAN COMMUNITY

Foreword

This volume containing the thoughts of some of the most eminent intellectuals of the South Asian Region examines in considerable depth the possibility of achieving a much sought after ideal of the people of South Asia - a reconstructed or united South Asia.

It represents a challenge of enormous proportions. And yet, considering the achievement by the countries of Europe through the European Union in the recent past, and the advances made nearer home in South-East Asia, something that seems possible and continues to attract the hopes of its people and political leaders alike.

As many of the writers here reiterate, the commonalities that bind the countries of South Asia are many. A common history of a past colonial domination, an even deeper history of common religious and cultural traditions and values, roots of linguistic affinity and shared mythology, and a vibrant economic exchange of goods and services on regular trade routes in pre-colonial times. All strong foundational elements which would conduce towards greater unity.

Yet in the modern world which beckons us towards togetherness for our survival and mutual prosperity, profound questions still keep us apart. These are expertly and with elegance analyzed for the reader by the learned contributors whose knowledge is illumined with the conviction and commitment that a reconstructed South Asia is yet possible. Determination, hard and sustained work by academia and civil society and most of all political will, would necessarily help.

As a committed South Asian myself, I therefore welcome this publication and commend most heartily the dedication and the aspiration of the noteworthy intellectuals who have shown the way to make realizable a long felt goal.

Ranil Wickremesinghe
Former Prime Minister of Sri Lanka

Acknowledgements

It is my foremost duty to acknowledge the monetary support given by the University Grants Commission (UGC), New Delhi, in organizing the seminar. I express my deep sense of indebtedness to Prof. V. N. Rajasekharan Pillai, the then Vice-Chairman of UGC, who was instrumental in making the seminar a success.

I express my sincere gratitude to late Prof. Isaac Sequeira, former Director of Indo-American Centre for International Studies, IACIS (formerly American Studies Research Centre), Hyderabad, for his encouragement and help in organizing the seminar. But for his wholehearted support the seminar would not have materialized. I would like to acknowledge the contribution and support of IACIS staff, particularly Srinivas Rao, Anitha Badrinath, Ann Kumaraswamy, Nageswara Rao, Nagabhushanam, Hanumanth Rao and Prasad.

I express my gratitude to H.E.Sumith Nakandala, Sri Lankan Ambassador to Nepal, Prof. P.V. Rao, Director, Centre for Indian Ocean Studies, Osmania University, and my friends - J.L.N. Rao and G.B. Reddy, who helped me in many ways. I wish to thank Prof. T. Nirmala Devi, Director, Centre for SAARC Studies, Andhra University, who encouraged and supported me in completing this volume. I thank all the contributors for their help.

I would like to thank my parents, my wife and my daughters - Mahitha and Samhitha for their encouragement and cooperation.

Acknowledgements

List of Abbreviations

ADB	Asian Development Bank
ARIF	Alliance for Release of Innocent Fishermen
ASEAN	Association of South East Asian Nations
BIMSTEC	Bangladesh, India, Myanmar, Sri Lanka, Thailand Economic Cooperation
BJP	Bharatiya Janatha Party
CBM	Confidence Building Measures
CEPA	Comprehensive Economic Partnership Agreement
CDM	Clean Development Mechanism
CEC	Committee for Economic Cooperation
CII	Confederation of Indian Industries
DMK	Dravida Munnettra Kazhagam
ECB	European Central Bank
EEZ	Exclusive Economic Zone
EU	European Union
FICCI	Federation of Indian Chambers of Commerce and Industries
GDP	Gross Domestic Product
IEA	International Energy Agency
IGG	Inter-Governmental Group
IOR	Indian Ocean region
IOR-ARC	Indian Ocean Rim Association for Regional Cooperation

ISI	Inter-Service Intelligence
ISGA	Interim Self-Governing Authority
LMU	Latin Monetary Union
LTTE	Liberation Tigers of Tamil Eelam
MFN	Most Favoured Nation
MNC	Multi National Corporation
MRRCs	Maritime Risk Reduction Centres
MZI	Maritime Zone of India
NATO	North Atlantic Treaty Organization
NGO	Non-Governmental Organization
NTB	Non-Tariff Barrier
OCA	Optimum Currency Areas
OTEC	Ocean Thermal Energy Conversion
PILER	Pakistan Institute of Labour Education and Research
PTA	Preferential Trading Arrangement
QR	Quantitive Restriction
R & D	Research and Development
RIS	Research and Information System for the Nonaligned and Other Developing Countries
RTA	Regional Trade Agreement
SAARC	South Asian Association for Regional Cooperation
SALF	South Asian Labour Forum
SLOC	Sea Lanes of Communication
TELO	Tamil Eelam Liberation Organisation
TMS	Trade, Manufactures and Services
UNCLOS	United Nations Convention on Law of Sea
UNCTAD	United Nations Conference on Trade & Development
UNDP	United Nations Development Programme
USAID	United States Agency for International Development
WTO	World Trade Organization

List of Contributors

1. **Imtiaz Ahmed** is Professor of International Relations, University of Dhaka and is currently the Executive Director of Centre for Alternatives. He is also the Editor of *Theoretical Perspectives: A Journal of Social Sciences and Arts* and Co-Editor of two other journals *South Asian Refugee Watch* (Colombo and Dhaka) and *Identity, Culture and Politics: An Afro-Asian Dialogue* (Dakar, Colombo and Dhaka).
2. **Santishree D. Pandit** is Associate Professor - Department of Politics and Public - Administration, University of Pune, holding the additional charge of Director-International Centre, University of Pune. She published several papers and two books.
3. **Gopalji Malviya** is the Professor and Chair in the Deptt. of Defence and Strategic Studies, University of Madras. He has authored four books and contributed more than two dozen articles in various national, international journals, edited volumes and leading dailies.
4. **Manoj Joshi** is the Editor (Views) *The Hindustan Times.* Member of the National Security Advisory Board of the National Security Council. He has published two books: *The Lost Rebellion: Kashmir in the 1990s* (Penguin Books, India, 1999); *New Perspectives on America and South Asia* (New Delhi, Chanakya, 1984) Published several papers in national and international journals.
5. **Rajesh M. Basrur** has taught in Mumbai University (1978-2000) and researched at Simon Fraser University (1994),

the University of Illinois at Urbana-Champaign (1995-96), the Henry Stimson Center (2001), the Brookings Institution (2001-2002), Sandia National Laboratories (2002), and Stanford University (2002-2003). He has published (edited) Security in the New Millennium (New Delhi: India Research Press, 2001); India's External Relations: A Theoretical Analysis (New Delhi: Commonwealth Publishers, 2000); and (edited) Perspectives on India's Defence and Arms Control (Mumbai: University of Mumbai, 1999).

6. **V.R. Raghavan** is a retired Lieutenant General and was the Indian Army's Director General of Military Operations. He is currently, President, Centre for Security Analysis, Chennai, and Director, Delhi Policy Group, New Delhi. He is the author on the history and evolutionof India's army. His monograph, *India's Need for Strategic Balance* and the essays on Limited War and Nuclear Escalation in South Asia, had received wide attention. His book on *Infantry in India* and *Siachen-Conflict without End* has become essential reading in military colleges.

7. **Anant V. Naik** was with Confederation of Indian Industry as Deputy Director - Energy and presently he is with Suzlon Energy Ltd as General Manager - Corporate Affairs. He has been in the energy sector for over 16+ years, having been closely associated with the Coal, Oil and Gas sectors in particular and Power sector to a large extent.

8. **A. Subramanyam Raju** is former Honorary Academic Fellow at the Indo-American Centre for International Studies, Hyderabad and recently joined as Associate Professor of Political Science in the Centre for SAARC Studies, Andhra University, Visakhapatnam. He is also Associate Editor for an international journal *Indian Ocean Survey*. He has published six books and several papers.

9. **V.R. Panchamukhi**, former Chairman, Indian Council for Social Sciences Research, New Delhi and Chancellor, Rashtriya Sanskrit Vidyapeth, Tirupathi. He is working in the field of economics. Some of his books as an editor or edited jointly published by Macmillan (1988, 1995), United Nations

(1991), Sage Publications (1995) and Bookwell (1998). He has published several papers in national and international journals.

10. **Dushni Weerakoon,** Deputy Director and Fellow at Institute of Policy Studies of Sri Lanka, Colombo and Regional Editor for South Asia Economic Journal, Sage Publications, New Delhi. She has published several papers.
11. **J. Laxminarasimha Rao** is a Reader in the Department of Political Science, Osmania University, Hyderabad. He has published several papers in edited volumes as well as in Journals.
12. **I.P. Khosla,** Former Ambassador to India's Ambassador to Bhutan, Bangladesh (as High Commissioner) to Afghanistan, and to the Netherlands. Secretary to government in the Ministry of External Affairs, 1989-92. Retired from service in 1996. Has written extensively on security issues including non-traditional security, as also on other matters relating to India's external interests.
13. **C.K. Lal** is a Columnist and Commentator of Himal Media Group publications *(Himal South Asia, Himal Khabar Patrika* and *Nepali Times).* Occasional Contributor to several other Nepali and English publications.
14. **B. Ramesh Babu** is the Executive Director, Centre for Governance and Development, Hyderabad. He served as the Research Director at the Foundation for Democratic Reforms, Hyderabad. He was the Senior Academic Fellow in International Relations at the American Studies Research Centre, Hyderabad, 1994-1997. Dr. Babu taught at the University of Bombay, for 28 years. He won the Senior Fulbright Fellowship twice. He published ten monographs and books and over 40 articles.
15. **Manoj Soni** is the Vice-Chancellor of M.S.Baroda University, Baroda. Earlier he was a Reader in the Department of Political Science and Director of Sardar Patel Centre, at Sardar Patel University, Gujarat. He specializes in International Relations Studies. In addition to several articles and research reports, his major publication is a 1998

published book on the post-Cold War International Systemic Transition entitled as *Understanding the Global Political Earthquake* by Ashgate Publishing Company, England.

16. **Sanjay Chaturvedi,** Chairman, Political Science and Co-ordinator, Centre for the Study of Geopolitics, Panjab University, Chandigarh. He is one of the Co-editors for a journal entitled *Indian Ocean Survey.* Some of his books: *The Dawning of Antarctica* (1990); *Polar Regions: A Political Geography* (John Wiley & Sons, 1996); *Rethinking Boundaries: Geopolitics, Identities and Sustainability* (New Delhi: Manohar, 2004). He also is the co-author of *Partitions: Reshaping Minds and States* (London: Routledge, October 2004). He has published several articles in national and international journals.

Introduction

A. Subramanyam Raju

South Asia is one of the very few regions in the world with quite a few significant commonalties among its countries. They are close to each other. More importantly, they are linguistically and culturally homogenous. People of the region share common food habits, adopt similar customs and ways of life and dress code.

The South Asian region, where one fifth of the world's population lives, is characterized by low gross domestic product (GDP), low per capita and low literacy rate coupled with high birth and high death rates. About forty four per cent of the world's poor live here. The region is afflicted by a number of problems-social, political and economic. Further, mutual distrust, misunderstanding, suspicion and historical legacy have led to non-cooperation and conflict among the countries of South Asia. Though a number of steps have been initiated to promote greater understanding and cooperation among the sates of the region, lack of common purpose resulted in not having a South Asian identity.

In this context, an attempt is being made to construct a new South Asia by exploring into the problems of the region and finding new ways and means to have a new future for the people of the region. As part of the exercise the volume focuses on the new issues that can give a fresh breath to the region to change the existing scenario.

A New South Asia

The South Asian states are plagued by inter-state conflicts and absence of political will in resolving them. For instance, India has dispute with Pakistan on Kashmir, Siachen, Sir Creek, maritime boundary in the Arabian Sea; with Bangladesh on New Moore island and demarcation of maritime boundary, whereas the dispute between India and Nepal involves about seventy five sq. km of area in Kalapani. Since, the boundaries are the manifestations of national identity in the region, the states are rigid in their stand and disputes continue to remain between India and its neighbours.

The political differences and disputes have stalled the prospects of economic cooperation in the region. For instance, Kashmir is one of the important factors that has led to tensions between India and Pakistan. For India, the Kashmir is not the core issue, whereas for Pakistan, it is an essential prerequisite for improvement of ties. Pakistan wants to improve trade with India only after resolving the dispute. Mir Zafrullah Khan Jamali, the prime minister of Pakistan, in his inaugural address at the twelfth SAARC summit, said that "The ideas of establishing South Asia will remain distant dreams unless we are able to address the political environment in the region in a just and realistic manner."

Since, India is the larger country in the region, the neighbours feel that the former dominates the region and poses threat to their security. Thus, the whole region never perceived a single strategic stance. The countries have been spending more on defence. Every state justifies its actions in the name of national security. The states in the region are increasing their military capabilities whereby creating mistrust and insecurity among the neighbours.

India and Pakistan are the major countries remaining adversaries since the partition in 1947. They procured conventional weapons and stockpiled nuclear explosive materials. These countries have shown in 1998 that they are capable of making nuclear weapons. The sub-continental nuclear adventurism not only reflected the mutual strengths of both the rivals in atomic field, but they also broke the myth of nuclear non-proliferation. In case there is a war, either accidental or incidental, people of South Asia will be exposed to serious problems[4]. In the place of conflict and force, if states opt for mechanisms of cooperation and peace as alternatives, they can coexist with each other. The South Asian countries can retain their armed forces and can establish a common defence arrangement for the whole region.

The world community seems to be uniting around the idea that it should assume greater collective responsibility in a wide range of areas, including human development. There is a sharp increase in environmental degradation, unemployment, poverty, starvation, epidemics, terrorism, ethnic or religious animosities, civil wars, drug trafficking, massive spread of AIDS, etc. All of these issues pose a far more serious and immediate challenge to the security of human beings and the states than the military threats.

The region is home to nearly half of the world's poor and it spends huge money on military establishment. In other words, the states are giving more importance to military security rather than to human security. They ignore the main objective of the SAARC, which envisages "to promote the welfare of the people's of South Asia and to improve their quality of life." The Human Development Report of 1994 rightly observed that "The search for human security lies in development, not in arms." [5] A future South Asia can be seen only when we work towards human development.

It is time to focus on development, building infrastructure, creating an environment that would promote the well being of the people of the region. The South Asian countries must focus on creating a common South Asian market, transforming the region into a free trade area, having single currency and promoting a dialogue between civil societies in the region. At the Islamabad summit the countries had signed the South Asian Free Trade Area (SAFTA) agreement and later in 2005, the agreement was ratified at the thirteenth SAARC summit, Dhaka. These measures could help the region in fighting poverty. The SAARC has the potential to acquire a momentum of its own, which can lead to the transformation of economic relations in the region.

At present the states in South Asia have separate trading, market and pricing systems. Intra-regional trade is occupied with different kinds of restrictions blocking cooperation among these countries. Almost all countries of the region are of the view that their national sovereignty would be at stake through regional cooperation. But now it seems that they are realizing the importance of cooperation among themselves. At the Islamabad summit, many issues were raised and all the countries are willing to address the problems being faced by them.

The South Asian countries are having more trade with other countries than with their nieghbours in the region. Through cooperation, these countries can increase their mutual and regional trade by greater economic activity in the region and thus avoiding imports from third countries and also reducing illegal trade in the region.[6] One major advantage that the trade can achieve is that all the countries can reduce their defence expenditure and spend more on development activities and restore peace in the region.[7] It is high time for these countries to learn from other regions.

The EU and the ASEAN are working very effectively because the states of these organizations share a common security threat. This is not the case with South Asia. For instance, the states of South East Asia were motivated to have ASEAN to face internal and external threat –threats from local communist parties and fear from China to the region.[8] It is not true that disputes stall improvement in trade and regional cooperation. For instance, in Southeast Asia, Malaysia, Indonesia and the Philippines have conflict over territory. But these conflicts did not come in the way in improving their trade relation. The European states, which were involved in the two world wars, realized the importance of economic cooperation and signed a treaty in Rome for establishing the European Community in 1957. Later it transformed into European Union. Thus a question arises: When Europe could unite, why not South Asia?

In South Asia similar factors could not bring all countries together. They, instead of perceiving threat from external sources, perceived threat from within the region. In spite of this, they share many common problems such as poverty, illiteracy, population growth etc having internal and external dimension. If these issues are taken seriously, they will certainly work towards regional cooperation. They can put aside their disputes temporarily and work in improving their economic and trade relations.

Economic reforms in South Asia are demanding more and more facilities and requirements. For instance, many people in South Asia still lack access to electricity in meeting their basic needs. These countries are largely dependent on energy imports. Though these countries have natural resources in abundance, they are yet to be tapped and exploited. Hence, regional cooperation in the energy sector among these countries is most desirable. South Asia is important to world energy market because it contains 1.3 billion people. It consumes about 5.9% of world commercial energy. The energy needs would continue to increase with the ongoing liberalization programmes in the region.

Having energy security as a collective task in the region, a South Asian forum on energy can be established to reduce the costs of research to improve energy efficiency and to promote energy cooperation among the countries of the region. This, in return, will improve relations among the countries of region on win-win situation. While India can benefit from electricity and gas imports from neighbouring countries in achieving faster economic development, Bangladesh, Nepal and Bhutan too can accrue economic benefits from the export of hydroelectric power and natural gas to India. Pakistan's economy too can benefit from exporting electricity to India. Through mutual help and cooperation, all of them can reduce their dependence on energy imports. This in return can help in improving their political relationships. These states can learn a lot from the experience of the European Union. The genius of Jean Monnet, the father of European integration, focused on the key strategic resources, which had traditionally fuelled wars in Europe and later became the basis for integration. Germany and France, who involved in conflicts for several decades, realized the importance of the cooperation. Of course, the European experience may not be applicable to South Asia in toto, as they have to go a long way in pooling their strategic resources. The South Asian states must make greater efforts to have regional cooperation through action rather than rhetoric.

In the 2004 SAARC summit, the leaders of the region agreed to keep the political differences aside and to work for mutual benefits, economic prosperity and regional cooperation. It is noteworthy to mention that the Social Charter envisages removal of poverty, control of population growth, empower women, promote human rights and developing human resources. It is a good sign that the states of the region at last realized that the disputes and conflicts converted the region further backward and worse. They have also realized that cooperation and mutual benefits are the only alternatives left to them.

In this context, the Indo-American Centre for International Studies (formerly ASRC), Hyderabad, organized an international seminar entitled *Reconstructing South Asia: Vision and mission Ahead* on 8-9 July 2004. Main objective of the seminar was to probe into a few questions: Why do we need a South Asian Union? What are the prospects and obstacles for cooperation? Whether the contemporary approach towards political and security cooperation needs to be modified?

Focus of the Volume

The scholars contribute the essays in the volume across the South Asian region. They include former policy makers such as diplomatic and military personnel, academia, media and the corporate world. The contributors discuss holistically and project them for the future course of action. There are sixteen papers, which are divided into five sections.

Section-I: South Asia: Political Issues

1. In the paper titled "Futures Beyond Nationalism", Imtiaz Ahmed maintains that while nationalism found itself reinvented in the era of globalization, mainly in the form of a backlash, sometimes advocating 'two modernities'. There is little hope of its reproduction without the active support of the diaspora and the subterranean international networks or what may be referred to as 'subaltern globalization'. He opines that the limits of nationalism has opened up the Pandora's box of many and diverse futures and like all Pandora's box it is filled with tensions and excitements.

2. Santishree.D.Pandit, in her paper, "Can Democracy be Designed in South Asia-The Politics of Institutional Choices", raises questions such as: What does democracy mean? Is it possible to design democratic institutions in the region? How far do democracies provide conditions for effective anti-poverty policies?

How far do they help to resolve- or to provoke new forms of conflict? While answering them, she argues that there has been a distinction between democratic institutions and democratic politics. It is important to make the distinction, as democratization is not just a process of implanting formal institutions of liberal democracy and a free market but to project norm creation and cultural change. Hence designing democracy for a new South Asia has its own problems and challenges.

Section-II: South Asia: Security Cooperation

3. Gopalji Malviya, in his paper entitled "Evolving Agenda for Peace and Security in South Asia", maintains that in order to reconstruct a peaceful and stable South Asia, certain measures are essential and they should be initiated by the political elite. Confidence Building Measures, dialogue on nuclear issues, proliferation of small arms, and cooperative framework on security issues would be the most appropriate and perhaps the essential tasks that will monitor, manage and establish new standards in governing inter-state relations in South Asia.

4. Manoj Joshi's paper, "A Common Defence Area for South Asia: An Indian Perspective", maintains that after fifty years of war and peace, the nations of the region have began realizing that they do share a common interest in maintaining peace and tranquility as the insecurity of one can quickly spill-over and affect the other. Yet the nations of South Asia are to some degree away from actually cooperating and maintaining security. This paper focuses on the issues that have bedeviled the region and how it can grapple the security concerns in a unified fashion.

5. Rajesh M. Basrur's paper, "India-Pakistan Security Cooperation and the Prospects for a South Asian Security Community", argues that the establishment of regional peace and a structure of cooperation in South Asia are contingent upon the relationship between India and Pakistan. The paper explores the prospects for change in the India-Pakistan relationship through theoretical lenses. It first identifies the variables relevant to the transformation of India-Pakistan relations. A further examination reveals that notwithstanding the numerous structural obstacles to improved relations, there are two areas i.e. nuclear arms control and terrorism in which cooperation is desirable and possible.

Section-III: South Asia: Non Traditional Security Issues

6. V.R. Raghavan's paper entitled "Non-Traditional Threats to South Asian Security" (inaugural address) delas with non-security threats to South Asia. He argues that there are a number of non-traditional security issues such as: economic, environmental, societal, political and military. They are also not exclusive to any one country in South Asia. These are shared by all the states in the region and in fact transcend territorial boundaries. Therefore they can only be tackled within the framework of regional cooperation and collaboration.

7. Anant V Naik's paper on "Energy Security Scenario in South Asia" maintains that the South Asian countries need capital and energy to propel economic growth and improve the quality of life in an environmentally responsible manner. The author feels that the region is endowed with untapped energy resources but their development, efficient distribution and utilization will require co-operation and trade among the countries. Already there are agreements related to supply of electricity between Nepal, Bhutan and India. Multilateral cooperation and sharing energy resources will have far-reaching economic and security benefits for the South Asian countries.

8. A. Subramanyam Raju, in his paper on "Maritime Issues in South Asia", maintains that the South Asian countries do not have a maritime policy and it is time for these states to think in having a common maritime law. The paper analyses various problems being faced by these countries and also the issues, which have become obstacles in forging cooperation among and between them. It describes various contentious issues between India and Pakistan, Bangladesh and Sri Lanka. It also focuses on the problems of the fisherfolk in the region.

Section-IV: Economic Cooperation: Search for New Synergies

9. V.R. Panchamukhi, in his paper entitled "The Process of Integration in the SAARC Region", (valedictory address) analyses why the South Asian countries failed to cooperate with each other. He describes that one of the reasons for non-cooperation is that the countries of the region have many grandiose plans. Problems

like poverty, unemployment, illiteracy, environmental issues etc are not projected enough. He suggests specific sectoral programs. Instead of going for an entire trade sector, he argues, the member countries of the region must select few specific sectors wherein they find advantages of cooperation explicitly. He suggests that there should be a SAARC development fund for conducting feasibility studies on joint ventures. He also talks about the millennium development goals in the region.

10. Dushni Weerakoon, in her paper on "Economic Cooperation in South Asia: Challenges and Constraints", examines the progress of economic cooperation under the aegis of SAARC. The paper identifies the constraints – both economic and political cooperation. On the economic front, much of the concessions negotiated are found to be irrelevant to the trade interests of the countries in the region, while restricted tariff cuts, limited number of concessions and continued use of non-tariff barriers have been identified as further hindrances. On the political front, friction between partners and the failure of the SAARC to insulate its economic agenda on the member countries have been major constraints. The paper examines the potential challenges and constraints of a free trade area for South Asia.

11. J. Laxminarasimha Rao's paper "Envisioning A South Asian Union" argues that as the world economy is getting more and more globalised with increasing international division of labour, politically inspired barriers are progressively becoming meaningless. Creation of community and union would push the negative forces into the background. They can become effective means for greater cooperation at regional level. The paper focuses on the efforts made in the direction of regional cooperation in South Asia and critically analyzes them. It also explores into the means and devices that can envision a South Asian Union in the years to come.

12. In his paper on "A South Asian Single Currency", I.P.Khosla opines that there are definite advantages in having a single currency for South Asia. Transaction costs for trade and monetary movement within the region will be eliminated, thus giving a boost to the flow of both goods and capital. The synchronization

of inflation and macro-monetary policy is a necessary pre-condition for getting onto the approach path to a single currency. He observes that it will lead to greater coordination in growth policies and growth rates, and probably a higher growth curve for the entire region. He formulates that the parallel intra-regional currency would be used as a unit of account for trade and financial transactions within the region, so that over time banks, traders, and others get used to dealing in and accepting it. Once the pre-conditions are met, such a parallel currency can grow in relation to, and over a period replace national currencies to become the single currency.

Section-V: Prospects for a South Asian Community

13. C.K.Lal in his paper on "Imagining South Asia in a Unipolar World" argues that a regional imagining has to be done without appearing to be challenging sub-regional identities. He argues that areas of commonalties have to be identified and steps to be taken in order to accelerate their progress and tools need to be formulated. The paper stresses the importance of thinking big—nothing less than a South Asian Union in future.

14. In his paper on "South Asian Union: Vision, Mission and Agenda", B.Ramesh Babu argues that while countries in other regions of the world have been coming together under a variety of banners for mutual benefit, people in South Asia are living in the past, wallowing in poverty and depriving themselves the benefits and advantages of working together. The treaties, agreements and protocols signed and agreed upon and the positive portends for the future seems to indicate that goals such as free trade area, economic union, open borders, and common currency for the region as a whole are "entirely achievable".

15. Manoj R. Soni's paper on "Envisaging the South Asian Resurgence Systemtic Imperatives for Regional Synergic Management" visualizes transforming a pessimistic geo-strategic environment of South Asia into a resurged and synergized South Asia. This envisagement, however, is not a utopian exercise. It derives its vigor from an analysis of ground realities through a theoretically informed perspective. The paper attempts to anticipate

the implications of a resurgent South Asia and in the process try to re-examine the feasibility of its vision and strategy for regional synergic management.

16. In his paper on "Resurrecting Maritime South Asia: Critical Perspectives on the 21st Century", Sanjay Chaturvedi argues that the SAARC, which lacks a maritime focus at present, should be at the forefront of mapping and building a new maritime architecture of regional and sub-regional cooperation in the Indian Ocean, especially with regard to the Arabian Sea and Bay of Bengal. The paper addresses the problems and prospects of forging new strategic alliances between SAARC and IOR-ARC in pursuit of shared maritime security and prosperity in the region. It critically evaluates on how both the organizations –facing numerous problems at present—could revive and rejuvenate their co-operative mandate and agenda through new maritime visions and strategies.

The chapters in the volume move from state centric to the people centric perspective by focussing on the issues that directly influence their lives and day-to-day activities. The volume tries to focus on the necessity of new institutional choices, an agenda for peace, on security issues including common defense area, on a South Asian Union and a single currency for the region. The issues discussed in the volume would certainly generate a debate among the scholars.

References

1. A Pakistani journalist noted that the biggest hurdles in the way of a tension-free relationship between India and Pakistan are the distorted perceptions, which have been fostered by vested interests on both sides. They are the result mostly of lack of contact and communication at the people-to-people level, which would dissipate if formal and informal exchanges of visits by non-officials were allowed to continue. Some such process has been discernible in recent years. See M.H.Askari, "Obstacles to Normalization", *The Dawn*, 21 May 1997, cited in Moonis Ahmar, *The Road to Peace in South Asia: Lessons for India and Pakistan from the*

Arab-Israel Peace Process, ACDIS Paper, Urbana: University of Illinois, August 1996, p.9.

2. Qazi Hussain Ahmad, Chief of Jamaat-e-Islami, in a seminar argued 'unless the Kashmir issues is resolved the agreements of trade relations with India will amount to hamper[ing] the Kashmir movement and currently Indian hegemony would be established. Although trade could not be rejected with any country for financial benefit, economic ties with India would mean to forget the sacrifices of Kashmir and bargaining on national interests under the new world order, as the Western world wants to make India an elder brother of [the] South Asian region." See *The Frontier Post*, 13 August 1994, cited in Ahmar, *ibid,* p.44.
3. See "SAARC Summit Opens with Cell for more economic cooperation", *Pakistan Tribune*, 11 May 2004.
4. Consequences of a nuclear war could constitute a global climatic catastrophe. For instance, the Hiroshima bomb killed between 100,000 and 200,000 people. A small nuclear war would be impossible to contain before it escalated. The nuclear war between India and Pakistan would lead to irreversible calamity for the entire South Asia. It is noteworthy to quote Teller and Sakharov here: "It is not even impossible to imagine that the effects of an atomic war fought with greatly perfected weapons and pushed by the utmost determination will endanger the survival of man." See Edward Teller, *Bulletin of the Atomic Scientists,* February 1947 & Andrei Sakharov, "A very large nuclear war would be a calamity of indescribable proportion and absolutely unpredictable consequences, with the uncertainties tending toward the worse... All out nuclear war would mean the destruction of contemporary civilization, throw man back centuries, cause the death of hundreds of millions or billions of people, and, with a certain degree of probability, would cause man to be destroyed as a biological species..." See *Foreign* Affairs, Summer 1983, cited in Carl Sagan, "Nuclear war and Climatic Catastrophe: Some Policy Implications", *Foreign Affairs,* vol.62, no.2, Winter 1983/84, p.257.
5. *Human Development Report, 1994*, New York: Oxford University Press, 1994, p.1.
6. Unofficial trade between India and Pakistan through cross-border smuggling and routing through third countries like Dubai and

Singapore amounts to two billion $ per annum. Whereas official trade between them during 2005-06 was about $ 800 million.

7. Aurangzeb Khan opines: "As bilateral trade and both economies progressively integrate and as the benefits become larger and more evident, policy makers will become aware of the importance of sustaining and further consolidating bilateral economic and political ties. As political ties improve, the level of bilateral tension and mutual suspicion may subside...it may prompt both governments to start channeling resources away from their bloated defence establishments to their acutely neglected social, infrastrutures and other developmental spheres." See Aurangzeb ZA.Khan, "Confidence Building Through Free Trade and Joint Ventures" in Sony Devabhaktuni (ed), *Regional Cooperation in South Asia: Prospects and Problems*, Occasional Paper, Washington, Dc: The Henry L.Stimson Center, February 1997, p.47.

8. "Fear of internal and international communism, reduced faith or mistrust of external powers, Indonesia's decision to pursue its active and independent foreign policy through regional cooperation, the desire on the part of Malaysia and Singapore to constrain Indonesia and bring it into a more cooperative framework, considerations of regime consolidation in nearly all member states, and the desire to concentrate on economic development." See Muthiah Alagappa (ed), *Asian Security Practice: Material and Ideational Influences*, Stanford University: Stanford University Press, 1998, p.107.

SECTION-I

SOUTH ASIA: POLITICAL ISSUES

1

Futures Beyond Nationalism

Imtiaz Ahmed

Zeno's paradox of motion - *the flight of an arrow which while in motion is always at rest* - has ignited fresh insights for centuries. It is believed that Zeno (born c. 495 BC) belonged to a school founded by the religious thinker and poet Xenophanes (born c. 570 BC). The latter made a philosophy out of his life-long involuntary exile (driven out first by the Persians and later by the Carthagians and Etruscans), believing in the eternality of the universe while ending up denying the existence of plurality and change. Zeno, as a true disciple, aided no less by Parmenides (born c. 539BC), made a lasting contribution to the certainty of fate faced by Xenophanes in his own lifetime. Zeno concluded that if objects exist disjointedly at a sequence of disjointed moments of time, and if no motion occurs in that disjointed moment, then there is no motion in any given moment. All changes are appearances of things.

Hegel, after many centuries, pondered on Zeno's paradox of motion and came to a qualitatively different conclusion. According to Hegel and given his disciplinary interest in dialectics, the paradox does not lead us to a reality which is stationary or motionless but merely directs us to the fact that there are 'contradictions in reality.' The appearance of sunrise and sunset, despite the reality of them being quite the contrary, would be a good example. Marx, in fact, taking cue from Hegel, went further and stated that 'Science would become superfluous if there was no difference between the appearance of things and reality.' But then the matter remains more complex.

When asked a simple question, what is the composition of water? Pure science tells us that it is H_2O (twice hydrogen *plus* oxygen). But when asked a more relevant question, what about the water in our rivers, washrooms, or even the 'natural mineral water' found in the evian bottles? Ajay Dixit and the author came with a social science definition of water and that is: $H_2O\ P_4$ (twice hydrogen *plus* oxygen *plus* pollution *plus* politics *plus* power *plus* profit).[1] H_2O can only be found in the laboratory, not in our daily use of it. Science too then ends up being in the plural, often with consequences that are qualitatively different.[2]

There are other ways of looking at this issue. For instance, if we were to go by some of the well publicized internationally acclaimed statistics then Kerala (one of India's well-talked about States) is a stunning success of development. It is number 1 in Human Development Index ranking, the literacy rate is 91 percent compared to overall India's 65, and life expectancy at birth is 73 compared to overall India's 61.[3] But then there is a dark side of Kerala not covered by the above set of statistics. When it comes to suicide, Kerala, with 9000 reported suicide deaths a year or 27 per day, is number 1 in India. It has the highest crime rate in India (306.1 crimes committed per 1000 people per year compared to the national crime rate of 176.7 per thousand); the joblessness is the worst in India (36% and 34% respectively of the rural and urban population in the 15-29 age group); and when it comes to atrocities against women, foeticide and alcoholism Kerala again towers above the rest of India.[4] Even the science of collecting and analysing the masses of numerical data can end up with more than one, often shockingly contradictory, outcomes.

Hegel's insightful reflection otherwise replaces Zeno's position of 'no future' with the possibility of having *contradictory* or some could even say, *many futures*. But then the radical verdict got robbed and defeated when Hegel, charmed by the modernist discourse, fell for the meta-narratives and ended up as an organic intellectual of the state. Not surprisingly, when he got a glimpse of

Napoleon's heroic entry into Jena from the window of his study he rushed back to his notes and wrote: 'Today I saw the World-Spirit riding on his horseback.' This was Hegel's contribution to the modernist project of humanizing or should we say secularising the divine. In the process, however, not only the given moment of Napoleon's entry into Jena but also the future of Hegel's reading of Napoleon got trapped into the discourse of modernity.

Modernity, for that matter and somewhat ironically, comes to resemble the Zenoian contention, albeit not in the sense of having 'no future' but rather in making us believe that the future is a consequence of a linear progression and is pretty determined and nothing much can be done about it. Problems crop up, however, when we have contradictory readings of modernity, particularly when it comes to the issue of who is doing what to whom. Architects would certainly view the modernist project differently from those who have little to say and are at the receiving end of the project. Two or three variations can easily be identified.

The first version could be dated from 1637; the year Rene Descartes published his short but profoundly significant volume, *Discourse on Method.* Disturbed by the chaos and despair of the age, indeed, brought about as much by theological controversy as by religious violence, Descartes took the task of restoring faith in humans by making 'reason' the basis for certainty. By way of his novel proclamation: *cogito ergo sum*, 'I think, therefore I am' (Part 4 of the *Discourse*), Descartes replaces the omnipotence of God in earthly matters with, as one critic pointed out, the 'omni-competence of human reason.'[5] Modernity comes into being in the backdrop of the tyranny of authoritarian theology, but only to make itself the foundation and pacesetter of all things. Critics, particularly post-modernists, did not fail to point out that despite the critical bent of mind and the secularisation of life and living modernity ended up no less tyrannical by way of constructing meta-narratives and 'offering foundational accounts of the ultimate order-of-things.'[6]

Accounts of the past in the name of history became linear with sweeping generalisations of the civilizational quest of the humans. 'Ancient,' 'medieval' and 'modern' became a fixity which all societies, all cultures, all polities, and all continents were condemned to experience and live through, the architects by definition, however, remaining at the vantage point of the modern, where others, even the an/architects, only needed to constantly catch them up. Seven years later in 1648, with the Treaty of Westphalia, the modern also became formally territorialized and soon began the territorial glorification of the nation, national state and nationalism that Europe had now involuntarily embraced. Europe and Western civilization became the reference point of past, present and future, once again everything began to be defined in terms of the singular, the 'omni-competence,' indeed, matching the very critique of the tyranny from which modernity came into being.

The second version could also be dated, incidentally some hundred years earlier than the first - from 1492. Mahmood Mamdani aptly describes the period:

The year 1492 was the onset of the European Renaissance and the birth of political modernity. It is also the year Christopher Columbus set sail for the New World and the year the armies of King Ferdinand and Queen Isabella conquered the city-state of Granada, then seen as the last Muslim stronghold in western Christendom. Thus, 1492 stands as the gateway to two related endeavors: one the unification of the nation, the other the conquest of the world.[7]

Modernity, outside Europe or at the receiving end, therefore, came to represent imperialism and colonialism, and also the 'mechanical' imposition of the nation, and for centuries had little to do with the promise of human emancipation that had so much informed and impressed the minds of the Europeans. But thanks to modernity and the colonization of the mind the colonized were quick to learn the wit and wisdom of the masters. Emancipation was sought with the same tools that the masters had used in subjugating them. The person who comes to emphasise this ironic turn of events without a shred of remorse or anxiety is none other than the Martinique-born psychiatrist and Algerian freedom fighter, Frantz Fanon. In *The Wretched of the Earth*, Fanon boldly proclaims: 'The colonized man liberates himself in and through violence.'[8] He then goes on to say:

The violence of the colonial regime and the counter-violence of the native balance each other and respond to each other in an extraordinary reciprocal homogeneity. This reign of violence will be the more terrible in proportion to the size of the implantation from the mother country. The development of violence among the colonised people will be proportionate to the violence exercised by the threatened colonial regime.[9]

Anti-colonial nationalist movements could hardly unseat modernity; on the contrary, violence and polarisation across cultures and religious faiths, the very trademark of 1492, began to haunt the post-colonial national state. The complicity of the national elite cannot be denied, but then, it was as much for personal aggrandizement as it was for jumping into the rat race of catching up with the modern West.

There is also a third version of modernity, which can be dated from the second half of the twentieth century, beginning with Michel Foucault's publication of *Madness and Civilisation: A History of Insanity in the Age of Reason* in 1961 but more aggressively continuing with the Iranian Revolution of 1978. This was largely a twin process. Faced with an intellectual restraint on modernity and the arrival of 'uncertainty' and post-modernity, the declining but still formidable hegemons made an all-out campaign to demonize and rout out the other. Indeed, with the Iranian Revolution, Islam not only became a potential force to be reckoned with but also, and more frighteningly, ended up being labelled as a threat to modernity. Foucault's euphoria with the Iranian Revolution was understandable. On 26 November 1978 he wrote:

It is an insurrection of people with their bare hands who want to lift the tremendous burden that weighs on us all, but especially on them, these ploughmen of oil, these peasants on the borders of empires: the weight of the whole world order. This is perhaps the first great uprising against the planet's systems, the most modern form of rebellion and the wildest.[10]

The Iranian Revolution, very muck like the Bolshevik one, could not live up to the expectations. Challenged by modernity, particularly by the coercive machineries at its disposal, post-revolution Iran became indistinguishable from the various tyrannical regimes that the modern has produced in its own lifetime. Once again we find a post-revolution society committing *hara-kiri* by trying to defend its terrain with the very means against which it had waged a battle. Replication not only kills revolutions but also empowers modernity. The latter has succeeded not only in minimizing (indeed, by way of distorting) the impact of Iran but also in formalizing Islam as the other. By placing its message in the medieval discourse, once again the spectre of the tyranny of authoritarian theology is brought in to demonize and, in the aftermath of 9/11, as many in the Palestine, Afghanistan and Iraq believe, physically rout out Islam.

The versions of modernity could be further developed, particularly with reference to nationalism and the contradictory futures it holds. Let us limit to three areas.

1. The Other Side of the National State

Only in Europe and that again only with the architects do we find 'enlightenment,' 'territoriality' and 'terror' collectively contributing to the birth of the national state. The tyranny of authoritarian theology or more bluntly the tyranny of the Church needs to be credited for the critical spirit and the ascendancy of human reason. The modern demand for the separation of religion from politics or secularism in the original sense of the term can only be understood from the standpoint of the tyrannical existence of the Church and the human struggle to overcome it. The goals were boldly proclaimed: Liberty! Fraternity! Equality! But then this could not be carried very far. The power of human reason, allegedly for unleashing the Faustian demon of limitless freedom, could not help but slide into the Reason of the State. Both territoriality and terror became the foundation of the national state.

The Peace of Augsburg in 1555 provided for the first time compulsory conformity of all the inhabitants of the Holy Roman Empire to either Lutheranism or Roman Catholicism established by their respective rulers. This also marked the beginning of Europe's territorialization of ideas, policies and settlements. The inhabitants were compelled to conform to the rules and regulations not so much of the sovereign authority as of the territory in which the sovereign authority resided. 'Salute to the Nation' replaced the medieval dogma of *vive le roi.* But the premonition from the conflation of territorialization and transformation of sovereign authority could be found as early as 1492. Indeed, the Jews were the first victims of such territorialization of sovereign authority. In 1492 Ferdinand and Isabella signed the Edict of Expulsion mainly to rid Spain of its Jews. Seven years later in 1499 the Muslims suffered the same consequences. The birth of the national state also saw the birth of the suppressed, marginalized, alienated minorities, and with the expulsion of the Jews and Muslims in Spain also the birth of the stateless.

Terror or 'great fear' came to signify the nation. The word incidentally came into use at the dawn of modernity, about 1375.[11] Four centuries later, the newly found French republic sought to reproduce its power through the Reign of Terror (1793-94), which also signaled the arrival of *terrorism* or the government by intimidation as a valid instrument of statecraft. The Reason of the State was no different from the reason that has followed since then. The state or 'the fatherland' was in danger from internal and external enemies and only the age-old policy of terror brought down to the level of the public could now save the republic. In the wake of this violent episode some 10,000 people lost their lives, most of whom were ordinary people who may have felt more attached to the 'tyrannical' Church than the newly formed but no less 'tyrannical' secular state.[12] But this was only the beginning. By twentieth century assassination, incarceration, torture, mass murder, including the killing of six million Jews, twenty-two million Soviets and endless number of people in Dresden, Hiroshima and Nagasaki, all were carried out in the name of saving 'the fatherland' and the national state.

Things could not have been better for those who were at the receiving end. First there was the snubbing of the enlightenment, meticulously put into practice by none other than the architects of modernity. Macaulay's remark in 1835 of trying to make the Indians 'English,' and that again only 'in tastes, in opinions, in morals and intellect,'[13] is the best summation of the modernist project in the colonized world. This paved the way for the colonization of the mind, which proved far more devastating than the physical occupation of India. Take the issue of caste, for instance, as Nicholas Dirks puts it:

[Caste], as we know it today, is not in fact some unchanged survival of ancient India, not some single system that reflects a core civilizational value, not a basic expression of Indian tradition. Rather, I will argue that caste (again, as we know it today) is a modern phenomenon, that is, specifically, the product of an historical encounter between India and Western colonial rule. By this I do not mean to imply that it was simply invented by the too clever British, now credited with so many imperial patents that what began as colonial critique has turned into another form of imperial adulation. But I am suggesting that it was under the British that 'caste' became a single term capable of expressing, organizing, and above all 'systematizing' India's diverse forms of social identity, community, and organization. This was achieved through an identifiable (if contested) ideological canon as the result of a concrete encounter with colonial modernity during two hundred years of British domination. In short, colonialism made caste what it is today (emphasis in original).[14]

The critical quest of the enlightenment otherwise died with colonialism, and this is true as much for the colonized as it is for the colonizers. But in the process of the former replicating the latter there was also a rush on the part of the colonized reliving the tragic and violent life of the colonizers. In no other place was this profoundly exemplified than in the birth of the national state in colonial India. Indeed, in the wake of the birth of the two national states in 1947, aptly referred to as the Partition by many, more than a million people died, equal number of women were raped, widowed and abducted, properties worth in billions in today's estimate were burnt to ashes, and over thirty million people were physically uprooted from their native homes. The matter did not end there. Some twenty-five years later in 1971 came the bloody birth of Bangladesh. Again death figures were in millions, so were the cases of rape, torture and displacement. Such were the price for zealously constructing the national state and catching up with the modern West.

But if the mind is bereft of enlightenment, what remains? Well, if we look at the tumultuous journey of modernity, mostly territoriality and terror. One can certainly see the spectacular presence of both throughout the world. Bosnia, Chechnya, Gujarat, Kashmir, Northern Ireland, Palestine, Rwanda, Sierra Leone, Sri Lanka, and now Afghanistan and Iraq, but these are only few of the innumerable examples. In fact, the world is now so much engrossed with them that it simply cannot fathom the dire consequences that each is capable of unleashing. Human memory is very short and so, despite the three 'great wars' (Napoleonic, World War I and World War II), a countless number of genocides, and the use of weapons of mass destruction in Hiroshima and Nagasaki and all for the sake of the nation and the national state, modernity continues to dazzle us all. Only a totalitarian creed of dehumanisation can boast of such an achievement.

2. The Other Side of National Development

Following the end of World War II came the era of economic nationalism. Although antithetical to capitalism, it proved beneficial to advanced capitalist economies for nearly three decades. According to one estimate, 'by 1973 output in the advanced capitalist countries was 180 percent higher than in 1950– almost three times as great.'[15] This helped to double the output every sixteen years and effectively raise the real wages of the workers. The latter were now twice better off than their parents and four times better off than their grandparents. It also signalled the end of conflict and the beginning of reconciliation between labour and capital in the predominantly modern, industrial, Fordist economies. But capitalism within national boundaries could not be sustained for long, particularly when with the attainment of near full employment labour became more expensive and started cutting down the profits of the capitalist. Aided no less than by elite decision-making and a revolution in new technologies, fragmented production and the development of cheaper transportation, the transnational corporations found it far more attractive to produce beyond the national boundaries and that again in more than one country.[16]

Two things emerged from this development. Firstly, the Keynesian management system with the state as the principal vehicle of the economy lost its charm in the advanced capitalist economies. In its place came the mantra of competitive individualism and market competition. Secondly, in order to invest and maximise the profits the multinational corporations sought states where government regulation, tax regimes and labour costs were low. Opening the economy for foreign investment became an attractive option and there ensued a rat race amongst the less developed economies on this issue. In both developed and less developed economies, therefore, the decline of the national state could not be stopped. But there was a qualitative difference between the two. In the advanced capitalist economies the decline of the national state, as indicated earlier, came as a result of the spectacular development of the economy, whereas in the less developed economies it came as a result of the spectacular underdevelopment or maldevelopment of the economy and the slavish replication of the former. Let us explain this further.

In the post-colonial national state the embracing of economic nationalism, although understood here more as state control of the economy, was a direct consequence of colonial modernity. The state was the only sector that was zealously nurtured and developed during the colonial era, and that again wholly for the exploitation of the colonized. The post-colonial national state, therefore, had no problem in adopting the Keynesian management system, albeit not so much for creating a welfare state and offering the people some purchasing power for reproducing capitalism as for the sake of extending its own power and emptying the state coffers through shameless corruption or what Marx referred to as 'primitive accumulation.'[17] In fact, the aid and investment that came to the less developed economies, apart from reproducing a dependent relationship with the advanced capitalist economies, went mainly to benefit the ruling elite, including a section of the private capital, without effectively contributing to the welfare of the people. And so when the mantra of competitive individualism and market competition got the attention of the post-colonial national state, it was not because of development fostered by economic nationalism, as it has been the case with the advanced capitalist economies, but rather for ending up in *maldevelopment* and the naked pressure of the latter to conform to the new mantra ostensibly for reasons of reform and rectification. Given the qualitative difference in the nature of their respective economies, the maldevelopment of the less developed economies could only deepen with the blind replication of the mantra that may otherwise be appropriate (although there are many who would vehemently disagree) to the dynamics and prosperity of advanced capitalist economies.

But before coming into the precise process and outcomes of maldevelopment it must be pointed out that in some areas the policy of economic nationalism performed extraordinary well. India, for instance, became self-sufficient in the field of nuclear energy, which subsequently helped the state to produce nuclear weapons, although at the same time it ended up having over 400 million people living below the poverty line. The latter is more ironic given the fact that India is the second largest producer and a major exporter of food grains and officially claims itself to be self-sufficient in food! The issue of maldevelopment, however, needs to be further concretised. Let us reflect on environment to make the case.

Floods, famines and large families collectively create an environment not conducive to sustainable living. But the gap between such direct ecological factors (save, of course, the issue of large families) and modern maldevelopment is not that great. There is a growing literature that suggests that much of the environmental problems result from man-made structures. Even in the case of divine's wrath, like floods and droughts, often the dire consequences are the result of human exploitation of the nature. As Vandana Shiva points out:

The drying up of India, like that of Africa, is a man-made rather than a natural disaster.... The manufacture of drought and desertification is an outcome of reductionist knowledge and modes of development which violates cycles of life in rivers, in the soil, in mountains. Rivers are drying up because their catchments have been mined, deforested or over-cultivated to generate revenue and profits. Groundwater is drying up because it has been over-exploited to feed cash crops.[18]

What we have here is a situation where maldevelopment is directly contributing to the collapse of environmental security. This could be further concretised in terms of the three, albeit interrelated, critical variants of environmental security. The first is the lack of *water security*, or more precisely, the lack of having fresh water, which resulted from the drying up of rivers and waterbeds. Often the lack of water security leads to conflicts or 'water wars.' In this sense, rivers without water (i.e. the drought syndrome) play a vital role in reproducing insecurity.

Again, it is important to understand that swelling population, deforestation, overgrazing, including developmental economies or inversely, unsustainable farming practices, all are responsible for water scarcity. Take the case of chemical fertilizer, which not only requires a good deal of water to make it work but also contaminates water, making water even scarcer. Put differently, the use of chemical fertilizer, which has now become a norm in the growth of crops, particularly the high-yielding varieties (HYV), creates conditions of water insecurity.

Water insecurity also results from having more water, often from the overflow of rivers (i.e. the flood syndrome). On the latter, the situation is critical as more and more people, largely because of population pressure, are found residing in floodplains, which tend to flood even with a slight rise in the level of water in the rivers. Embankment is taken to be a quick remedy but experience has lately shown that often it is the embankment that brings more suffering to the people, particularly those living on the other side of the embankment.

The second variant is *land security*, related directly to the degradation of soil and the incapacity of the population to harvest any further. In this connection, it may be pointed out that the farmers are totally at lost in confronting the dilemma that they have lately been put into regarding the use of fertilizer, and that is, without the chemical fertilizer, there is no HYV crop, but then with the chemical fertilizer, there is no sustainable land for long to grow the crop! In fact, land security is threatened by the continued use of chemical fertilizer and pesticide. One researcher has shown that in the past the farmers in South Asia cultivated about 30,000 rice varieties, whereas today, thanks to the modern technique and the desire for conformity, only fifteen varieties are cultivated.[19] In the long run, this could only result in the insecurity of the farmers, which they could choose to transform only by changing their original place of habitat. If the country is small in size, the situation becomes even more precarious because the victims cannot move to the surrounding areas. Consequently, they end up becoming either displaced persons at home or environmental refugees in neighbouring states.

The last variant is the lack of food security, arising partly from a combination of water and land insecurities and partly from the excessive growth of population.[20] It may be pointed out here that food insecurity may grow with an overflow of water in the rivers (i.e. the flood syndrome) as well as with the drying up of the rivers (i.e. the drought syndrome). All of these variants of environmental security soon contribute to a situation where a sizeable section of the people, irrespective of their communal or ethnic affiliations, become, as indicated earlier, displaced persons at home or environmental refugees in neighbouring states. Maldevelopment, otherwise, creates conditions for the partial displacement if not demise of the national state.

3. The Other Side of Globalization

Deleuze and Guattari have already referred to the process of deterritorialization giving rise to a simultaneous process of reterritorialization, although the latter 'subjects men to the new imperial inscription, to the new full body, to the new socius' and as such remain different from the previous territoriality.[21] The matter is not so different when it comes to globalization. But first let us refer to the territorial meaning of the national state and the deterritorialization of it. The concept of Bangladesh, for instance, can no longer be contained or limited within the 55,126 square miles of its territorial boundary but must now include the Bangladeshi diaspora, and a rapidly increasing one, for that matter, in different parts of the world. But this is one side of the matter. In the era of globalization and post-geopolitical phase of international relations Bangladesh has attained the status of a 'large' and more frighteningly, 'menacing' state![22] In fact, the speed with which Bangladeshis are seeking job and migrating abroad, and that again both legally and illegally, has created apprehensions in the minds of the public, politicians and policymakers both within the region and beyond. Indeed, when Bangladesh is viewed in terms of demography and as the eighth largest country in the world, it does have the effect of creating tensions in migrant-receiving societies, particularly those having comparatively less population and communally/racially tensed political structures. And then, given its 'civilizational' links, Bangladesh is readily taken to be sympathizing or even supporting the Islamic cause in the Middle East and elsewhere, which at times creates the notion that it is 'soft' on the so-called Muslim militants or Islamic terrorists. This has particularly been the case with the United States in the post-9/11 period, the latter even categorizing Bangladesh as 'high risk' in its global war on terrorism. If globalization has deterritorialized Bangladesh it has certainly also reterritorialized it, albeit on a different plane mixed with anguish and apprehension. Similar, but not necessarily identical, arguments could be made for other national states as well.

Secondly, there is a sinister side of globalization, which is equally creative when it comes to limiting the power of the national state and reinforcing the power of the post-national non-state. But before we go on exposing this let us first familiarise ourselves with the more popular versions of globalization. This would help us understand the contention better. First is the most commonly known version and that is economic globalization or globalization from top.[23] What it means is that in addition to the internationalization of trade, finance and investment we now have the internationalization of production. That is, multi-national or rather transnational companies now *collect* resources in several countries, *process* them in another several countries and finally, *export* the finished products to the rest of the world. A fully finished product, therefore, no longer has one single birthmark; it has multiple birthmarks since several countries have gone to produce it. A Compaq computer, in that sense, is no longer entirely American, or a Toyota car fully Japanese. The final product of both these items will have components made in several countries of the world. Put differently, unlike the previous internationalization of things, in the globalization phase of capitalism the thing itself is the product of the international or global market. In this newer configuration, the non-state enterprises are often more critical than the state-oriented or state enterprises in the reproduction of capitalism. The need for safeguarding the non-state enterprises, therefore, is as vital as protecting the state enterprises. The outcome has been greater *policing* and diffusion of licit weapons, which often for reasons of pilferage and structural leakage end up in the market as illicit commodities often with dire consequences. More about this issue will be discussed later.

The second version is reverse globalization. This is very much an outcome of the modernist craze, principally the organization of the post-colonial national state in the image of the modern 'Western' state. Two good examples are Bollywood and what goes internationally in the name of Indian cuisine. In a Bollywood movie the lovers would agree to meet in Delhi's Lodhi Garden but in seconds would land up in Vienna or Sydney singing and dancing to a tune or two, and that again, mainly to respond to the desire let loose by the erotic glare of the southerners. By the end of the song, however, they are back in Delhi with little attention to the travel time let alone time difference. But this is only the virtual side of it. Once when flying from Cochin to Delhi after attending an Afro-Asian meeting, a Nigerian friend asked the author: 'Can you help me buy some DVDs in Delhi?' 'Yes, sure, what English movies are you looking for?' author replied. But instantly he responded: 'No, not English movies. I would like to buy some movies of Shahrukh Khan.' The global reach of the Bollywood is impressive, attracting the locals not only of its birthplace South Asia but also of Africa, Europe, Middle East, Southeast Asia and even as far as Australia. It has certainly become the coca-cola of lust and leisure.

The internationalization of the Indian cuisine is another good example of reverse globalization. Curry, masala tikka, biriyani, even dosa and idli are now household names and certainly gastronomic delights across cultures, nationalities and continents. Michael Dummett went on to say, "British eating habits have been considerably affected by the Bangladeshi, and to a lesser extent

Chinese, presence."[24] Indeed, it may not be out of place to point out that in many of the so-called Indian restaurants the chef is a Bangladeshi, adding credence to the fact that the term 'Indian' is more conglomerate when it comes to cuisine and somewhat defies the post-colonial nationality of the Indian state.

There is yet another version of globalization.[25] Critics have already referred to the mushrooming of global networks resisting economic globalization as 'globalization from below.'[26] The latter includes a diverse group of people – environmentalists, NGOs, religious groups, small farmers, labour unions (incidentally of both the developed and developing countries), women's movement, consumerists, African debt relief campaigners, anti-sweatshop activists, and the like, all one way or other either critical of or directly suffering from and struggling against the impact of economic globalization. Here the forces of the seemingly disempowered non-state have creatively joined hands to overcome the exploitation of the empowered non-state, i.e. the forces of economic globalization. The subaltern nature of the resistance movements, particularly the networking, can hardly be minimized.

But then, there is a further subaltern variant to the whole notion of globalization from below. This refers to the deepening of relationship between and amongst the 'dubious groups' and 'shadowy activities' ranging from smuggling of goods and people, illicit production and trading of small arms, money laundering, narco-production and trading, terrorism, and the like, and that again, across and beyond national, ethnic, racial, and even religious affiliations. The subalterns, particularly the poverty-ridden and marginalized population, become easy target of such groups and activities, but more importantly the state of being itself becomes a factor for certain relatively well off individuals to rally support and even clandestinely work for their cause. A protracted nature of poverty and marginality and a lack of substantive global concern also push them to seek informal or even criminal means to reproduce their lives and if possible to redress the situation. The complex networking at this level and in combination with the resistance movements against economic globalization could be best referred to as *subaltern globalization*. Here the subalterns, including their ardent supporters and sympathizers, are no less creative and empowered when it comes to organizing and reproducing their activities at the global level, and that too often by challenging the overly empowered forces of economic globalization.

9/11 is very much a product of subaltern globalization. When it comes to the subaltern network we find the Moroccans, Egyptians, Saudis, Afghans, and certainly some tactical help from the Pakistanis, Germans and even the Americans, all of them collectively contributing to the demonic event. The subaltern network also managed to collect and spend $ 500,000 to carry out the task.[27] But this was enough to kill more than 3000 civilians and cause a material damage of at least $ forty billion, and this is exclusive of the hundreds of billions of dollars lost as a result of the slowing down of global economy immediately after the attack. Globalization seems to have succeeded in creating a spectre out of its own living. Not only do we have the power of the national state dwindle before us but we also have the power of the post-national non-state haunt us in every hour of our lives.

4. What is to be done?

There is a sense of empowered centrality in the Leninist proposition of what is to be done. Although Lenin had it garbed in the colourful wording of democratic centralism, but experience had shown that it simply replaced one tyranny with another. Must praxis then be reformulated for unlocking the futures beyond nationalism? Or, must we replace the archic 'what is to be done?' by the an/archic 'what is to be *undone*?' Undoing the structures that consistently and passionately reproduces modernity could certainly be a starting point. There could be several ways of doing this. Rabindranath Tagore called for 'anti-political politics,'[28] which consisted mainly in recovering the latent power of the *puro samaj* ('the whole society;' not to be confused with the contemporary understanding of civil society) from the domination of the state. Ivan Illich had his faith placed on the recovering of the 'commons,' and went to the extent of championing the cause of silence: "Silence, according to western and eastern tradition alike, is necessary for the emergence of persons."[29] Michel Foucault sought freedom from 'all unitary and totalizing paranoia' by transforming the individual: "The individual is the product of power. What is needed is to 'de-individualize' by means of multiplication and displacement, diverse combinations. The group must not be the organic bond uniting hierarchized individuals, but a constant generator of deindividualization."[30] And then more recently we have Theodore Zeldin pleading for the decentring of the human and the repositioning of the 'person': "humans need to be recognized as persons," he says.[31] And these are all intellectually less imposing free from the Leninist mode of praxis but at the same time far more radical in empowering the person in the business of displacing and disempowering modernity.

The post-national condition can, of course, be further concretised. Let us restrict to three areas, museum, technology and citizenship, each of which went on to construct meta-narratives, indeed, making full use of the foundational dogma of modernity, namely, romanticism, naturalism and liberalism respectively. Freeing them from the modernist structures would certainly help in opening up the many and diverse futures beyond nationalism. Let us take up the issue of museum first.

Museum is one of the most attractive yet indispensable products of the modern age. The Man of Renaissance could not have arrived without a romantic appeal to the primitive and the external, as Francis Bacon so rightly observed in 1594, nearly a hundred years before the birth of the first public museum:[32]

First, the collecting of a most perfect and general library, wherein whosoever the wit of man hath heretofore committed to books of worth...may be made contributory to your wisdom. Next, a spacious, wonderful garden, wherein whatsoever plant the sun of divers climate, or the earth out of divers moulds, either wild or by the culture of man brought forth, may be...set and cherished: this garden to be built about with rooms to stable in all rare beasts and to cage in all rare birds; with two lakes adjoining, the one of fresh water the other of salt, for like variety of fishes. And so you may have in small compass a model of the universal nature made private. The third, a goodly, huge cabinet, wherein whatsoever the hand of man by exquisite art or engine has made rare in stuff, form or motion; whatsoever singularity, chance, and the shuffle of things hath produced; whatsoever Nature has wrought in things that want life and may be kept; shall be sorted and included. The fourth such a still-house, so furnished with mills, instruments, furnaces, and vessels as may be a palace fit for a philosopher's stone.[33]

One could see in Bacon's plea for the libraries, botanical and zoological gardens, research laboratories and museums the unfolding or should we say, the institutionalization of the meta-narratives of the 'universal' Man and Nature. And it was here that the modern taxonomies were constructed and the 'modern' placed at the summit of all knowledge and being. Private collections or 'cabinet' of the aristocrats, however, preceded the public museum. The *studiolo* of Francesco I de' Medici and the *Kunstkammer* of Archduke Ferdinand II in the late sixteenth century attracted attention from faraway places even beyond Europe. But whether private or public the museums displayed the exotic and the rare, collected and looted from all over the world. At times, even the human inhabitants of these exotic lands were paraded before the 'enlightened' public.[34] But if this has allowed the nationalist and simultaneously the imperial consciousness to take roots in Europe it was not long before that the rest of the world, caught up with the desire to become modern and a nationality, started constructing museums in their own backyards. In less than 300 years national museums filled the world and became synonymous with the development of the national state, putting an end to the exotic and the rare of the modern era.

But there is more to the limits of the museum. Selection and sorting out became a political game, with the museum invariably and increasingly ending up partial and fragmented. If the British massacre of Jallianvala Bagh (1919) is a revered object in the museography of the victims of Amritsar, the same cannot be said with respect to the perpetrators. In fact, there is a conspicuous silence of the said massacre in the British Museum. Or, for that matter, Lev Tolstoy would have been horrified to see the life-size painting of the 'villainous' Napoleon Bonaparte majestically displayed at the very entrance of the Smithsonian Museum in Washington D.C. In some cases a whole group of people are obliterated from the gaze of the public to match the statist construction of the nation and the nationalities. The National Museum of Myanmar, for instance, displays the artefacts of seven 'national races' – Shan, Mon, Karen, Kayah, Chin, Kachin and Rakhine, with absolutely no mention of the two million 'stateless' Muslim Rohingyas residing in the Rakhine State.

But limits of the museum also create possibilities particularly if we are ready to contemplate creatively beyond the nation. Take the case of the diamond, *Koh-i-noor*. Originally it weighed 191 carats, but was later recut to enhance its fire and brilliance and made into 109 carats in 1852 at Garrards of London.[35] But this is only one side of *Koh-i-noor*'s life. There is another side full of mystery befitting a Hollywood movie. While it is true that the British acquired and added the *Koh-i-noor* to the crown jewels of Queen Victoria following the annexation of the Punjab in 1849 there is no consensus when it comes to the original master of the diamond. Some believe that Sultan Ala-uddin Khalji got it from the Raja of Malwa (a princely state of India) in 1304 and later on Humayun, the son of Mughal Emperor Babur, got it from the Raja of Gwalior after the Battle of Panipat in 1526. There are others, however, who believe that Emperor Shah Jahan received it from the diggers of the Kollur mine in 1656. And then there are some who trace it to Nadir Shah of Iran, who is said to have added the diamond to his booty following his sacking of Delhi in 1739. And then from Nadir Shah to Ahmed Shah, from Ahmed Shah to Shah Shoja, from Shah Shoja to Ranjit Singh (the Sikh ruler of Punjab), and finally after the death of Ranjit Singh and the annexation of the Punjab to the British.

The mystery no doubt has come to benefit the British, for when post-colonial India requested that the diamond be returned, Pakistan also laid a claim on it. But that was not all. Someone traced it to Bangladesh and laid a claim, and soon Sri Lanka also joined, claiming that historically the diamond belonged to the island! The British could only enjoy this bickering and quickly discard the claim as unworkable. But then there is a way out and the *Koh-i-noor* could easily be brought back to South Asia. All that is required is the making of a *postnational mobile museum*, where *Koh-i-noor* and many other artefacts transferred during the colonial era could be brought back and displayed in each of the South Asian states on a rotation basis. Millions in South Asia would certainly line up to have a glimpse of the things that have contributed so much to the making of modernity and the healthy demise of it. Emotions would no doubt reign high but so would be the cause for celebration across continents.

Secondly, the issue of technology. There are critics who claim that Galileo could not have waged a war against the Church without the birth of the 'cabinet' or museum of scientific instruments.[36] Even the telescope, which was invented by the spectacle-makers of the present-day Netherlands in the beginning of the seventeenth century, became a collectible item for many and Galileo upon hearing this had one constructed for him for his personal use in 1609. The rest of the story now belongs to the history of scientific and technological progress and the spectacle of modernity. The relationship between technology and modernity is a fascinating one,[37] not only with respect to the 'development' of technology and modernity but also with respect to the dehumanized outcome of the latter arising from its relationship with the former. Let us explain.

At the core of technology is the modernist dogma of naturalism, particularly the faith of the latter in value-free knowledge. Set against the epistemological distance between the mind and the outer world, naturalism dispassionately sought to limit truth to 'the brute facts of physical reality,' the ones that can be verified, while treating the unverifiable world of value (morality, aesthetics, religious discourses, and the like) as 'meaningless unreality.'[38] Critics of modernity, as Andrew Wright correctly observed, had no problem in pointing out the consequence of this dualism:

Cut off from any moral constraint, and wedded to a quasi-evolutionary myth of inevitable scientific progress, modern science gives free rein to the cancerous development of technologies of death and destruction whose rapid growth outstrips the civilised world's ability to control them…[The] ultimate irony of modernity is that the self-proclaimed omni-competence of humanity becomes the primary source of the re-enslavement of the human race.[39]

If there is one technological feat that still goes on to symbolise modernity and the power of the national state while providing limitless fodders to the critics it would certainly be the spectacular development of modern weapons technology. Indeed, with the development of the latter there is now conformity in the art and science of terrorizing and killing people. While the history of that is as old as the humans, yet before the advent of modernity different communities in different locations adopted different means, including technologies, for terrorizing and killing people. Let us provide some examples from South Asia.[40]

In ancient India, when punishing offenders, including criminals, rebels and opponents, the rulers and feudal lords used spikes (*shool*). The victim was forced to sit on a sharpened iron spike or *shool*, which used to enter through the lower end of the body and come out through the upper end/head. But there were other, equally ghoulish, methods. Skinning people alive, throwing them in a hungry tiger's cage or under an elephant, or stitching the eyelids of living human beings were common form of royal punishments during the Mughal period. But then we had the Thugs (from Hindi *thagi*, literally deceivers; from fourteenth to nineteenth century AD), who adopted a totally different method of killing people. They strangulated their victims with yellow coloured silk scarf, knotted at one end, which represented the hem of Goddess Kali's robe. The Thugs considered them to be the servants of Goddess Kali and took the murder as a divine mission, while the booty obtained was their earthly reward. And then, following the death of the Mughal Emperor Aurangzeb in 1707 came the Pindaris (from the liquor "pinda" which the members used to drink a lot). The trademark of the Pindari torture was to tie a bag of hot ashes over a man's mouth and nose and then thump his back. This forced the man to divulge the place where he had hidden his valuables but then the ashes also caused his lungs to rot.

The colonial state brought newer methods in the business of terrorizing the colonized. The French introduced the guillotine,[41] while the British made hanging the main instrument of its coercive policy.[42] But then with the development of gunpowder and explosives the British started using cannons and rifles. In fact, following the unsuccessful Sepoy Mutiny of 1857 the British shot hundreds of sepoys from cannons. The Jallianvala Bagh Massacre of 1919 brought a newer dimension to state terrorism and that was random killing of unarmed people by directly shooting at them. It was not long before when the state dissenters, now in possession of guns and rifles, also resorted to firing. The members of the coercive machineries of the state became their main target. But soon the civilians became the main victims of both state and non-state firing.

But then much of this could not have come about without innovations in weapons technology in modern times. Now with a range of small arms (pistols, AK-47, M1 Thompson, grenade launchers, sub-machine guns), missiles and indirect fire weapons (mortars, rockets, SAMs), and bombs and explosives (C4, Semtex, IEDs) in the hands of both state and non-state actors the terror has come to haunt not only the possible victims but also the bystanders and even the perpetrators, and that again, not in one locality but across the globe. Indeed, when it comes to modern weaponries and the art and science of killing it matters little whether one lives in Colombo, Delhi, Falluzah, Guwahati, Kabul, Karachi, Lagos, London, New York, Srinagar, West Bank, or in some other parts of the globe. The fear is the same.[43] Only weapons technology in modern times could claim universal applicability, with the power of transforming the humans into, if we may use a word from Derrida, *hauntological beings*. But the spectre does not end there.

Camus in the middle of the twentieth century made a bold reflection on life and death. He said: "There is but one truly philosophical problem and that is suicide. Judging whether life is or is not worth living amounts to answering the fundamental question of philosophy. All the rest - whether or not the world has three dimensions, whether the mind has nine or twelve categories - comes afterwards."[44] Little did he realize that by the end of the twentieth century there would be numerous of them, with some even having the courage to blow them into pieces while committing suicide. Traditionally, the aim of the terrorist, for instance, was not to commit suicide. Even the Assassins and the Templars (11th to 13th century AD) committed suicide only when challenged. But to make the body itself a part of the weapon and that again with the knowledge that the body would be ripped off while creating havoc in and around the target is something of an innovation, arising no doubt from the 'absurdity' of earthly life in the midst of all the violence and the kind of modern weaponries, particularly explosives, that is now in one's disposal.

The arrival of the suicide-bomber is also the arrival of what we would refer to as, *post-rational terrorism*. Edward Said, while referring to the terrorists of 9/11, provided some sense of this:

I've never condoned or agreed with [Palestinian terrorism], but at least it is understandable as a result of a desperate human being who feels himself being crowded out of life and all of his surroundings, his fellow citizens, other Palestinians, his parents, sisters, and brothers, all of them dying or being hurt, wanting to do something, to strike back....It's not something I agree with but at least you could understand it.

Now, here we're talking about something different, because these people are obviously not desperate and poor refugee camp dwellers. The people who perpetrated the terror of the World Trade Center and Pentagon attacks were obviously middle-class, educated enough to be able to go to flight school in Florida, and could speak English. This is now transcending the political and moving into the metaphysical. And it's a leap that I think is very important to keep one's eye on, because it suggests the kind of cosmic quality – and, I would also say, the demagogical quality – of the minds at work here. They refuse to engage in or have no interest in dialogue or political organization or persuasion of the sort that makes political change and improves one's situation versus this kind of thing which is bloody-minded destruction for no other reason than to do it. Note that there was no claim for this terror bombing. There was no political message behind it. There were no demands. There were no statements. It was a silent piece of terror imposed on a population without discrimination or negotiation.[45]

So spectral has modern weapons technology become that even without actually having any of the sophisticated weaponries (only knives and Mace), as officially disclosed by the US government,[46] a dozen or so terrorists could hijack four aeroplanes full of passengers and transform them into deadly missiles. Now a person, whatever his/her nationality may be, is barred to board a flight even with the technology of cutting nails, lest s/he be tempted to transform the technology into something demonic 'for no other reason than to do it.' This is not madness but to take a leap beyond rationality. The individual has at last become empowered with limitless freedom, albeit not to live but to die and destroy. The stories are not so different in Ahmedabad, Baghdad, Bali, Colombo, Dhaka, Madrid, Nairobi, Oklahoma, Riyadh, and many other places of the world. In all of them modern weapons made a difference and created the demon. And it is here that modern technology creates its own limits not merely by contributing to destruction but by providing the individual the means to become a demon capable of creating hell on earth. If the latter is to be contained and transformed into a non-violent person, there is no reason not to transform technology on a similar path as well.

Finally, the issue of citizenship: Modernity could not have attained its hegemonic status without the liberal quest for citizenship. In fact, if modernity required the national state to fulfil its self-proclaimed destiny, the latter required 'unquestioning allegiance' from those residing within its territorial boundaries, which it hoped to acquire by providing the members social and political rights under the banner of citizenship. But to operationalize citizenship elaborate laws and regulations had to be enacted, and it was not long when the liberal quest itself in marked contrast to its principles began to be thoroughly policed and enforced, with many of the violators even ending up in a state of incarceration. The post-colonial replication of this, particularly in South Asia, has turned out to be tragic if not hilarious.

In the case of Bangladesh, India and Pakistan, save marriage (and that again, a very long cumbersome process; even Sonia Gandhi learned it in a hard way),[47] there can be no legal migration. Both Nehru-Liaquat Pact and two decades later Mujib-Indira agreement have territorialized and frozen the issue of citizenship. Migration in South Asia has meaning only in the sphere of *illegality*. In the case of India, however, there is one novel exception, and that is, the Gurkhas of Nepal who join the Indian Army have the option of claiming Indian citizenship.[48] So much for democracy and people's power over governments and institutions! But more interestingly, although the citizens of these three countries can never legally migrate and exchange citizenship between them, they can all migrate to some developed countries like Canada, US, UK or Australia and become citizens there. In fact, once the author was quite amused to see the national flags of Bangladesh, India and Pakistan of equal length and size hoisted in front of a clothing shop in Luton (UK), although such a thing would be regarded seditious in South Asia itself.

Moreover, in this age of post-nationality and globalization, when the power of national sovereignty has receded considerably, the identification of nationality with citizenship has become less attractive if not out of tune with reality. Some countries have tried to bifurcate the two and play it safe. In Mexico, for instance, members can keep or regain 'nationality,' which bestows property rights and other benefits, without having the right to vote. The latter is a prerogative of citizenship.[49] Some states are trying to introduce an element of inclusiveness even with their physically deterritorialized citizens. Dominican Republic, to cite one case, is debating the feasibility of allotting two seats in its legislature for representatives of New York's Dominican-American population. But such examples are on the margins and are still to prove effective.

A more prominent example is found in the very birthplace of modernity: the gradual elevation of the national state into something of a supra state, now celebrated by the birth and growth of the European Union. Indeed, in the case of the latter, the notion of national sovereignty has subsided into a diffused notion of sovereignty, where the small state of Belgium has as much rights as the bigger state Germany but at the same time *less rights* when it comes to the issue of protecting, prosecuting and punishing its citizens and also other residents within its territorial boundaries. Imaginative international norms flowed from this, including the most current one of setting up the International Criminal Court. Indeed, in the event of genocide or mass killing the state can no longer protect its citizen from prosecution and ultimately punishment in the name of state sovereignty should the citizen be responsible for committing a criminal offence. And in the event of European citizenry (if something of this kind is devised), the Romas or gypsies (historically stateless and barred from becoming citizens) would have the novel option of acquiring citizenship not of this or that state of Europe but of the whole of *Unionized* Europe.

The positive elements of this development, that is, the qualitative transformation of the national state, cannot be overstretched. It has already come under attack both from the Right and the Left, albeit for quite different reasons. The Right has attacked the break up of the national state for it had tended to diffuse the distinction between the majority and minority communities, particularly in the wake of the Europeanization of human rights and greater governmental responsibility. The neo-Nazi attack on the minorities in Europe, whether in France or Germany, often with terrorist methods and means, is one such outcome.[50]

For the Left the supra state is a 'state' after all, with the supra state having an added dimension of being disinterested in the plight around the globe in the midst of its own prosperity and higher quality of living. Sympathizing and even sheltering and supporting the distressed millions around the globe can at times make someone join extreme groups advocating extreme means in order to make a statement of the plight. The alienated migrants from the distressed areas, both old and new, are easily sucked into such groups and activities. One response has been the construction of 'Fortress Europe,' with the newer migrants looked upon as potential troublemakers if not mentally and physically equipped terrorists. But the more Europe is 'fortressed' the more it ends up inviting the wrath of the distressed and those sympathizing with them. Terrorism in this case has come to roost not in the midst of backwardness and instability but somewhat ironically in the midst of power and prosperity. But the European experience does lead us to believe that if citizenship is a construct, it can also be deconstructed.[51] The issue is whether it would be deconstructed to construct new boundaries (as it seems to be the case with Europe now) or deconstructed to transform the terms of reference and create space for deterritorialized, denationalised citizenship to emerge. The author expresses that he would go for the latter, indeed, for no other reason than to claim a place beyond nationalism.

References

1. Imtiaz Ahmed, "Higher Education on Water Resources: The Case of Bangladesh," in Peter P. Mollinga & Jasveen Jairath (eds.), *Higher Education on Water Resources in South Asia: Towards Capacity Building for IWRM*, Hyderabad, India: SaciWaters, June 2002.
2. Briane Greene, *The Fabric of the Cosmos,* New York: Alfred A. Knopf, 2004. See also, Stuart Sim, *Irony and Crisis: A Critical History of Postmodern Culture*, Cambridge: Icon Books, 2002.
3. *The Weekly Magazine Outlook*, Vol. 44, no.27, 12 July 2004, p. 53.
4. *Ibid.*
5. Andrew Wright, *Religion, Education and Post-modernity*, London: Routledge, 2004, p.15.
6. *Ibid.* See also, Michel Foucault, *The Order of Things: An Archaeology of the Human Sciences*, London: Tavistock, 1970.
7. Mahmood Mamdani, *Good Muslim, Bad Muslim: America, the Cold War, and the Roots of Terror*, New York: Pantheon Books, 2004, pp.4-5.
8. Frantz Fanon, *The Wretched of the Earth*, London: Macgibbon & Kee, 1965, p. 67.
9. *Ibid*, p.69. One should not, however, take Fanon to be an advocator of violence. This is clear from his conclusion:Come, then, comrades, the European game has finally ended; we must find something different. We today can do everything, so long as we do not imitate Europe, so long as we are not obsessed by the desire to catch up with Europe.... Let us decide not to imitate Europe; let us combine our muscles and our brains in a new direction. Let us try to create the whole man, whom Europe has been incapable of bringing to triumphant birth.... For Europe, for ourselves and for humanity, comrades, we must turn over a new leaf, we must work out new concepts, and try to set afoot a new man (pp. 253-255).

10. Dominique Lecourt, *The Mediocracy: French Philosophy since the mid-1970s*, London: Verso, 2001, p.41.
11. *Chambers Dictionary of Etymology*, New York: Chambers, 2003, pp.1127-28.
12. Charles Townshend, *Terrorism: A Very Short Introduction*, Oxford: Oxford University Press, 2002, p. 37.
13. Imtiaz Ahmed, "Governance and Flood: Critical Reflections on the 1998 Deluge," in *Water Futures in South Asia*. Special Issue of *Futures: the journal of policy, planning and futures studies*, Elsevier Science, Exeter, UK, Vol. 33, nos. 8/9, October/November 2001.
14. Nicholas B. Dirks, *Castes of Mind: Colonialism and the Making of Modern India*, Delhi: Permanent Black, 2001, p. 5.
15. P. Armstrong, A. Glyn, and J. Harrison, *Capitalism Since 1945*, Oxford: Basil Blackwell, 1991, p.117.
16. K. Cowling and R. Sugden, *Beyond Capitalism: Towards a New World Economic* Order, London: Pinter, 1994, pp. 29-52.
17. Marx's reference to the colonial accumulation of wealth as 'out bargaining and cheating.' See, Imtiaz Ahmed, "Wallerstein's Capitalist Mode of Production: Much Ado About Nothing" (in Bangla), *Rajniti Orthoniti Journal (Journal of Politics and Economics)*, Centre of Political Research, Dhaka, vol.2, June 1992.
18. Vandana Shiva, *Staying Alive: Women, Ecology and Development*, London: Zed Books, 1989, p.179.
19. Jamal Anwar, *Bangladesh: The State of the Environment*, Dhaka: Coastal Area Resource Development and Management Association, 1993, p. 55.
20. Paul R. Ehrlich, Anne H. Ehrlich, Gretchen C. Daily, "Food security, Population, and Environment," *Population and Development Review*, Vol.19, no.1, March 1993.
21. Gilles Deleuze and Felix Guattari, *Anti-Oedipus: Capitalism and Schizophrenia*, London: Continuum, (1972) 2004, pp. 210-217.
22. Imtiaz Ahmed, "Impact of war on terrorism on 'small states': South Asian context with special reference to Bangladesh," *Holiday* (Special Issue), Dhaka, 31 October 2003.
23. Imtiaz Ahmed, "Globalization, State and Political Process in South Asia," in Abdur Rob Khan (ed.),*Globalization and Non-Traditional Security in South Asia,* Dhaka: Academic Press, 2001. See also,

Jeremy Brecher, Tim Costello and Brendan Smith, *Globalization From Below: The Power of Solidarity*, Cambridge, Mass: South End Press, 2000.

24. Michael Dummett, *On Immigration and Refugees*, London: Routledge, 2001, p.15.

25. Imtiaz Ahmed, "Contemporary Terrorism and the State, Non-State, and the Interstate: Newer Drinks, Newer Bottles," in Sridhar K. Khatri and Gert W. Kueck (eds.), *Terrorism in South Asia: Impact on Development and Democratic Process*, Colombo and New Delhi: RCSS and KAF, 2003.

26. Brecher, Costello and Smith, n.23, p.10.

27. Georg Witschel, "Global Terrorism: Trends and Response," *RCSS Newsletter*, vol. 9, no. 1, January 2003, p. 2.

28. "Introduction by E.P. Thompson," in Rabindranath Tagore, *Nationalism*, Calcutta: Rupa & Co, 1992.

29. Ivan Illich, "Silence is a Commons," *The CoEvolution Quarterly*, Winter 1983.

30. "Preface by Michel Foucault," in Deleuze and Guattari, n.21, pp. xv-xvi.

31. Theodore Zeldin, *An Intimate History of Humanity*, London: Vintage, 1998, p. 469.

32. The first public museum was established at the University of Oxford. It consisted mainly of gifts from Elias Ashmole. The gift was made on the condition that a place be built to receive it. The resulting building, which eventually became known as the Ashmolean Museum, opened in 1683. The Ashmolean Museum later moved to another new building nearby, and its original building is now occupied by the Museum of the History of Science. See, *Encyclopaedia Britannica*, Millennium, 4th edition, cd-rom version.

33. Francis Bacon, *Gesta Grayorum*, 1594, cited from Oliver Impey and Arthur Macgregor (ed.), *The Origins of Museums: The Cabinet of Curiosities in Sixteenth - and Seventeenth – Century Europe*, Oxford: Clarendon Press, 1985, p.1.

34. *Ibid*, p.2.

35. *Encyclopaedia Britannica*, n.32.

36. Gerard l'E. Turner, "The Cabinet of Experimental Philosophy," in Impey and Macgregor, n. 33, pp. 216-217.

37. For an insightful reading, see Thomas J. Misa, Philip Brey and Andrew Feenberg (ed.), *Modernity and Technology*, Cambridge, Massachusetts: The MIT Press, 2003.
38. Wright, n.5, p.17.
39. *Ibid*, p.18.
40. For a closer exposition, see Imtiaz Ahmed with Farid Ahmed Bhuiyan, "Weapons Technology and the Reconceptualization of Terrorism," in Imtiaz Ahmed (ed.), *Understanding Terrorism in South Asia: Beyond Statist Discourses*, Colombo: Regional Centre for Strategic Studies, 2005.
41. Joseph Ignace Guillotin (1738-1814) was a physician by profession. Ironically, his name got entangled with a device that became the symbol and chief instrument of the Reign of Terror in the French Revolution. "Guillotine", the beheading device was in fact adopted for humane and egalitarian reasons. Dr. Guillotin belonged to a small reform movement in France that sought to banish the death penalty altogether. At that time executions in France were cruel public events held in town squares and the entire town gathered to watch quartering. Upper class criminals bought their way into a less painful death; decapitation was their exclusive privilege. Guillotin urged the National Assembly to decree that all executions should be carried out in the same manner; he did this as an interim step towards completely banning the death penalty. He did not invent or develop the "guillotine"; in the past such devices were already in use in Germany, Scotland and Persia for executing aristocratic criminals. On the basis of his demand the government commissioned engineers and they had modified the earlier version of the device with the advice of few professional executioners. The first guillotining took place on 25 April 1792, with Nicolas Jacques Pelletie at Place de Greve on the Right Bank. The most famous victims of the guillotine were King Louis XVI and Queen Marie Antoinette. Beheading by the guillotine remained the legal method of execution in France until September 30, 1981 when France abolished the death penalty by law. See, Richard T. Bienvenu, "Guillotine" in *The Encyclopedia Americana* (International Edition), Vol. 13, Danbury: Grolier Incorporated, 1986, p. 580.

42. In England hanging was carried out in public till 1868. From then on executions were carried out within the walls of county prisons. A few witnesses, including reporters were admitted up to about 1910 but thereafter executions were carried out in complete secrecy. Public hanging apparently met the needs of justice but they also served the purpose of terrorizing the common masses. However most executions were carried out in the recognized place, often on market days in the county towns, so as to draw the biggest audience. Crowds, who were supposed to fear and be deterred by the spectacle, actually turned out more for the morbid excitement and a day out. It may be mentioned that the modern expression "Gala Day" is derived from the Anglo-Saxon "Gallows Day". See, "The history of judicial hanging in Britain," http://www.richard.clark32.btinternet.co.uk/hanging1.html
43. A person living in London could expect to be filmed by more than 300 cameras on more than 30 separate CCTV systems every single day, and all for the sake of ensuring security. See, Jessica Williams, *Facts that should change the World*, Cambridge: Icon Books, 2004, pp. 275-279.
44. See Albert Camus, *The Myth of Sisyphus*, London: Penguin Books, 1975, p.11.
45. David Barsamian and Edward W. Said, *Culture and Resistance: Conversations with Edward W. Said*, London: Pluto Press, 2003, pp.112-113.
46. The 9/11 Commission Report mentions that that "One of the callers from United States reported that the hijackers might possess a gun. But none of the other callers reported the presence of a firearm." Furthermore, the Report mentions, "We believe the bombs were probably fake." The spectre of modern weaponries is such that the passengers all believed that the hijackers possessed guns and bombs although there is no evidence of it. See, *The 9/11 Commission Report: Final Report of the National Commission on Terrorist Attacks upon the United States*, New York: W.W. Norton & Company, first edition, undated, pp. 5-13.
47. It is now know that her husband, Rajiv Gandhi, as prime minister of India, had to personally intervene for her to acquire the citizenship. But if we are to believe Sushma Swaraj, one of the

key leaders of BJP, Sonia Gandhi even today is less of a citizen of India!

48. I am thankful to Admiral (retd.) Ramadas for this information.
49. Imtiaz Ahmed, "State and Statelessness in South Asia," *Theoretical Perspectives* (Special Issue), Vols. 9 & 10, 2002-2003.
50. Harry Henderson, *Global Terrorism: The Complete Reference Guide*, New York: Checkmark Books, 2001, p. 38.
51. Mike Bottery, "The End of Citizenship? The Nation State, Threats to its Legitimacy, and Citizenship Education in the Twenty-first Century," *Cambridge Journal of Education*, Vol. 33, no.1, 2003, p.101.

2

Can Democracy be Designed in South Asia - The Politics of Institutional Choices

Santishree D. Pandit

The process of globalization has unleashed forces of internationalism as well as fragmentation. These contradictory forces exist in many parts of the world. This has been the nature of South Asia, which has had forces of fragmentation and discord that has maintained all types of regional cooperation at a state of infantile paralysis. But has this in any way changed that the region will move towards integration. There is need for certain prerequisites, which will be necessary for construction of the ideas, structures and processes in the region. One such issue is the transparency and whether a successful experiment in another region will help us to replicate the same. Can institutions be transplanted just because that they have successfully worked in some other part of the world? This has not succeeded, as one will see the case of Iraq and the American experiment to transplant institutions, which they think are wonderful and the best the western liberal democracy. Here these institutions have not been able to take roots. Going slightly down the lane of history, one would realize that the attempt of civilizing the colonies by the British did not succeed in many of them. Except for India where the credit goes to the political culture of the country and the British transplantation helped for the atmosphere was conducive. But this has not been the case with the other British colonies, many have become theocracies and military dictatorships.

Is there a choice for many from the forces of globalization? Globalization is not new, but the present era has distinctive features. Shrinking space, shrinking time and disappearing borders are linking people's lives more deeply, more intensely, more immediately than before. The paradigm shift will be in :

- New markets- foreign exchange and capital markets linked globally, operating 24 hours a day with dealings, with dealings at a distance in real time.
- New actors- the World Trade Organization (WTO) with authority over national governments, the multinational corporations (MNC) with more economic power than many states, the global networks of non-governmental organizations (NGO) and other groups that transcend national boundaries.
- New rules- multilateral agreements on trade, services and intellectual property backed by strong mechanisms and more binding for national governments, reducing the scope of national policy.

Globalization and regional integration offer great opportunities for great human advance, but this requires stronger governance. In South Asia it requires greater political will, for it is this that has kept all cooperation as a region at the lowest. This requires a growing dependence of people's lives that calls for shared values and a shared commitment to the human development of all people, especially of people in the region. It is necessary that this region is lagging all other regions and it is the most impoverished and the least gender sensitive region.[1]

The challenge of globalization in the new century is not to stop the expansion of global markets. The challenge is to find the rules and institutions for stronger governance- local, national, regional and global- to preserve the advantages of the global market and competition, but also to provide enough space for human, community and environmental protection with sustainable just development. Resources to ensure that globalization works for people-not just for profits but for their welfare as well. A regional framework will make us ensure that globalization in a better way. This will help for the better working of globalization with :

- Ethics- less violation of human rights, not more
- Equity- less disparity within and between nations, not more
- Inclusion-less marginalization of people and countries, not more
- Human Security-less instability of societies and less vulnerability of people, not more
- Sustainability-less environmental destruction, not more
- Development- less poverty and deprivation, not more

Effective institutions can make the difference in the success of market reforms for the individual countries in the region. Without land-titling institutions that ensure property rights, poor people are unable to use valuable assets for investment and income growth. Without strong judicial institutions that enforce contracts, entrepreneurs find many business activities very risky. Without effective corporate governance institutions that check managers' behaviour, firms waste the resources of stakeholders. And weak institutions hurt the poor especially. For example, estimates show that corruption can cost the poor three times as much as the wealthy.[2]

Any vision for the region has to envisage the challenge of building effective institutions, which are critical to the region's mission of fighting poverty. " How do we account for the persistence of poverty in the midst of plenty? If we knew the sources of plenty, why do not poor countries simply adopt policies that make for plenty?... We must create incentives for people to invest in more efficient technology, increase their skills and organize efficient markets. Such incentives are embodied in instiutions."[3]

In understanding what drives institutional change, this paper aims not to define what should be done in an ideal world, but what can be done in today's world. The evolution of nations in the region teaches that building institutions takes time and that the process within each country may stall or reverse because of political conflicts or economic and social pressures. It offers lessons about the process of change and the importance of norms and culture in particular countries. Institution building is a cumulative process, with several changes in different areas building up to complement and support each other. The paper identifies the hurdles that exist in the region that may rupture this process. Every small change can build momentum for future changes. The whole is greater than the parts, and even a moderate progress in the parts can contribute to a better system to promote growth and reduce poverty.

But so far the whole has been marginalized and two of the major parts have played the *"Tu Tu Main Main" game*. Hence the issues that have fractured and ruptured the regional process may still continue, if the largest two states do not consciously decide to reverse the process. It has to be a conscious decision and a deliberate process for progress to take place. Until now it has been that each refutes the other's suggestions and this as led to incompatible relationship on issues of border, the state of Jammu and Kashmir and terrorism. If the process of reversal does not happen, then will incompatibility lead to velvet divorce or a bloody rivalry?

From Geopolitics to Geo-economics

The issue is that in the region the grammar of commerce has not overtaken the (il)logic of conflict. Are the economic issues becoming autonomous of the political and military issues? May be, they have in some parts of the world but definitely not in South Asia. Natwar Singh, the then Indian minister for external affairs, suggested that India and Pakistan could emulate the Sino-Indian model. Quick was the reply reflecting the "Tu Tu Main Main" culture. This reflects in the half century relationship has been anything but friendly. There is an incompatibility between issues of geopolitical importance, especially the issue of Jammu and Kashmir. It is far from resolved. This has led to a nuclear race and balance that has brought strategic parity for the smaller neighbour. The region is the most militarized region in the world.

The reasons for the shift from geopolitics to geo-economics are the causes of trade, technology and immigration.[4] Edward N. Luttwak added that in some cases, the logic of commerce would result in fierce competition. In others the same logic would lead to alliances between economic entities in any location to capitalize ventures, vertically integrate, horizontally co- develop, co- produce, or co-market goods and services. But competitively or cooperatively, the action on all sides would always unfold without regard to frontiers.[5] The South Asian region is still at the very preliminary stage of thinking alike for a co-prosperity zone. There is a geopolitical obsession and this seems to have blinded all geo-economic rationality.

Enter Economism and Exit Politics

The fear with policy makers is that economic cooperation first may create insecurity for the ruling elite. The lack of democratic governance within states in the region has further heightened the insecurity of the ruling elite. The fear that the political issue that is used as a scapegoat to divert attention from pressing economic issues. Once the economic issues take center stage, the fear is that the political scapegoats and the legitimacy of maintaining such huge nuclear arsenals may become redundant.

The politics of economism is a strategy of defining certain institutions and issues as 'economic' and using the doctrine of economic neutrality to produce a boundary between the economic and political spheres. With the doctrine of economic neutrality is a discourse according to which economic issues are somehow apolitical, beyond political power struggles.[6] Economy is a social and historical construction. One way to look at the construction of the economic sphere is to see it as an ideological concealment of the political reality behind it. This concealment certainly happens but to regard the economic sphere merely as an 'imposed illusion' may be somewhat misleading. If enough people act as if something called an economic sphere with an autonomous and natural logic exists, the sphere becomes in some sense real, even if socially constructed and historically specific.

Apart from presenting the ' economic' as its own sphere, removed from the reaches of democratic control, the politics of economism also tends to subordinate other social spheres to its normative supremacy.[7] Democratic norms have generally not been considered valid within the economic sphere nor in international or transnational relations that transgress state boundaries. In other words, both the politics of economism and the politics of sovereignty have affected the sphere of validity of democratic norms.

In any regional integration the socially constructed sphere of the economic, both domestic and foreign, is growing and taking over some of the social relations that were previously considered under the control of institutions that constitute the political sphere. The truism that the domestic sphere is losing its importance for the processes that have been considered external to the domestic sphere, both economic and political, are taking over some of the functions that have previously been considered to belong exclusively to the sovereign state. This is a long way for the region where basic differences have ruptured any cooperation.

Democratic Deficit

There has been a democratic deficit within states in the region, except one or two states. This has created an unequal situation. The role of external powers has further worsened this as they have aided and abetted these undemocratic forces. The lack of trust and intractable conflicts have heightened the fracture in regional cooperation. The marginalization of the developing states in the global decision making process increases the necessity to reconsider their governance structures. Their own internal politics and lack of political will to improve the human development of the people seems evident.

For democracy to widen and deepen it is necessary for politics and political institutions to promote human development and safeguard the freedom and dignity of all people. Globalization is forging greater interdependence, yet the world becomes more fragmented between the rich and the poor, between the powerful and the powerless, and between those who welcome the new global economy and those who demand a different course. The 9/11 and 13/12 terrorists attacks cast a new light on these divisions, returning strategic military alliances to the center of national policy making. The debate has been on the danger of compromising national security for human rights.

Terrorism has made democratic states look more vulnerable and as soft states. The problems of terrorism exist in the region and there have been no similarity of views. The reasons for much of this are seen in poverty and child mortality, which is one of the highest in the region. There is a democratic deficit at the global level and in international monetary institutions, but this also the case in the region. Most of the relations have been based on mistrust. What is needed is the bridging of the gulf between potential and reality is a matter of time and political will. The slow pace of change is not a problem it is the basic direction. In a more interdependent world, politics and democratic political institutions are even more central to human development.

The connection between democracy and human development are not straight and automatic. The problem arises when a small elite dominates economic and political decisions, the link between democracy and equity is broken. Equity and Justice are important issues for human development. When democratic institutions function badly, poor and vulnerable people tend to suffer most. But just as human development requires much more than raising incomes, governance for human development requires much more than having effective public institutions. Good governance requires fostering fair, accountable and transparent institutions that protect human rights and basic freedoms. The spread of democracy, the integration of national economies, revolutions in technology- all point to greater human freedom and greater potential for improving people's lives. The paradox in most countries is that freedom and democracy seem to be under greater threat in the region.

Transplanting of Democratic Institutions

Democracy that empowers people must be built from within, it cannot be imported from outside. These institutions come in different shapes and forms. The democracy a nation-state chooses to develop depends on its history, culture and circumstances, states will necessarily be differently democratic. But in all states, democracy is about much more than a single decision or a hurriedly organized election. It requires a deeper and a continuos process of political developed embedded in values and culture.

Promoting democratic politics means expanding capabilities such as education, to enable people to play a more effective role in politics, and fostering the development of civil society groups and other informal institutions to help democratic institutions better represent people. Democratic governance is valuable in its own right. It can advance human development better than other systems of government. Democracy is the only political regime that guarantees political and civil freedoms and rights to participate in the system's decisions that shape one's life are fundamental rights. They are part of human development in their own right. Democracy plays a role on protecting people from economic and political catastrophes such as famines and descents into chaos.

Democracies contribute to political stability, providing open space for political opposition and handovers of power. It also triggers a virtuous cycle of development. States that guard political freedom empower people to press for policies that expand social and economic opportunities, and as open societies help communities shape their own priorities. Gender sensitive policies also promote human development and women development.

Civil society is another category that has its problematic with East Asian and South East Asian societies. The idea that culturally these societies are used to soft dictatorships has been stated. [8] Lee Kuan Yew's warning to the US that they should "not to foist their system indiscriminately on societies in which it will not work". [9] This was refuted in subsequent article that values like human rights and democracy are universal and not unique. [10] Democratic values are not alien to Asia and there are references in Indian and Chinese traditions, much before its statement in Western philosophy by John Locke.

Rulers, who legitimize authoritarianism in the name of Asian values, have marginalized the linkage between the rules of effective governance and the concept of legitimacy. What is really needed is a global democracy, which will recognize the connection between how we treat each other and how we treat nature, and it will pursue policies that benefit future generations. Global interdependence calls for more participation and accountability in the global decision making. Empowering people to influence decisions that affect their lives and hold their rulers accountable for their actions is no longer constrained by national boundaries. In an increasing globalizing world these democratic principles have an international dimension because global rules and actors often affect individuals' lives as well as that of the nation-state. It is democracy and protection of human rights should be the priority not hides the lack of it behind the façade of culture.

Poverty and Democracy

Poverty and democracy, the two categories, impact each other. The South Asian region is the most impoverished region in the world. Does this in anyway impact on democracy? If so has the region been able to address this problem? It is really the human development indices that growth has meant other things, more than just economic growth.. "What I was arguing that helping one-meal family, enabling a woman without a change of clothing to afford to buy a second piece of clothing, is a development miracle."[11] The global gap between haves and have-nots, between know and know-nots, is widening. This can be seen in South Asia, where there are islands of development and large areas of underdevelopment.

Building Institutions

The best thing that can be done is to build effective institutions, which will also suit the markets as well as provide democratic governance in the region:

- Design them to complement what exists- in terms of other supporting institutions, human capabilities and available technologies. This is necessary for the availability and cost of supporting institutions, existing levels of corruption, human capacity and technology determine the impact of a particular institution. That is why institutions that achieve their goals in the developed world may not do so in developing countries.
- Innovate to design institutions that work and drop those initiatives that do not. In states with similar incomes and capacities, innovation can create stronger institutions because of differences in local conditions- differences ranging from cultural milieu, social norms to geography. Experimentation, which has some, costs must be recognized, can nevertheless help identify new and effective structures.

States in the region can gain from expanding successful public innovations. But they must have the courage to drop failing experiments.

- Connect communities of market players through open information flows and open markets. Is it possible for the region to exchange goods and services outside existing networks and communities creating a demand for market supporting institutions. Exchanging of information through open debate creates a demand for institutional change by holding people to account, by changing behaviour and by supplying ideas for change from outside the community. Linking civil societies in networks of information and prosperity is thus a challenge for policy makers in the region for building accountable democratic institutions for the region.

References

1. Maqbul-ul-Haq, *UNDP Human Development Report of South Asia-1997*, Karachi:Oxford University Press, 1998.
2. Dirk Berg-Schlosser and Norbert Kersting (ed.), *Poverty and Democracy*, London: Zed Books, 2003.
3. Douglas C. North, "Institutions", *Journal of Economic Perspectives*, Vol. 5, no.1, 1991, pp. 97-112.
4. Edward N. Luttwak, "From Geopolitics to Geo-Economics", *The National Interest*, Summer 1990.
5. *Ibid.*
6. R. Swedberg, "The Doctrine of Economic Neutrality of the IMF and the World Bank", *Journal of Peace Research*, Vol. 23, no.4, 1986, pp. 377-89.
7. N.Lechner, " The Transformation of Politics" in F. Aguero and J. Stark (eds.), *Faultlines of Democracy In Post- Transition Latin America*, Miami: North-South Center Press, 1998.
8. Fareed Zakaria, "Culture is Destiny: A conversation with Lee Kuan Yew", *Foreign Affairs,* March/April 1994.
9. *Ibid.*
10. Kim Dae Jung, Is Culture Destiny? The myth of Asia's Anti-Democratic Values, Foreign *Affairs,* November- December 1994.
11. Muhammad Yunus, *Human Development Report 1999* , Oxford: Oxford University Press, 1999.

SECTION-II

SOUTH ASIA: SECURITY COOPERATION

3

Evolving Agenda for Peace and Security in South Asia

Gopal ji Malviya

Historically, the conflict in South Asia could be traced in three broad causes. First, there are legacies of colonialism; secondly, the conflict, which arose as the newly independent countries of the sub-continent sought to develop their national identities and strengthen their security; and thirdly, the fact that lack of an adequate conflict control mechanism, allowed disputes between states to escalate. The types and levels of conflict, which took place in the sub continent, now ever vary with the changing circumstance, both internal and external, that affected the region.[1] The postcolonial states in South Asia have been engaged in domestic turmoil, civic strife inter-state border and territorial disputes that snow balled into conflicts and wars in the region. In the last fifty five years has been a witness to their difficult and agonizing experiences of the state building exercises in the region that saw the endeavors to evolve viable democracies and a difficult path of social and economic developments.

The South Asian states' experiences with a host of traditional and non-traditional security issues that emanates from domestic insecurities, internal strife, political instability, lack of civil society and communal, ethnic, racial, and regional aberration poses daunting challenges to the statecraft and governance. Also this spill over of domestic conflicts into inter-state rivalries has led to intense and persistent hostilities. South Asia is, perhaps, the classic example that features the entire array of internal vulnerabilities and external conflicts. The crisis of the South Asian States is therefore the crisis of governance. In order to reconstruct a peaceful and stable South Asia, certain measures are essential and need to be initiated by the political elite. Confidence Building Measures (CBM), dialogues on nuclear issues, proliferation of small arms, and cooperative framework to address terrorism, militancy and other security issues would be most appropriate. Perhaps an essential task that will monitor, manage and establish new mechanism in governing inter-state relations for a lasting peace in South Asia.

Concepts of reconstruction of the region for lasting peace and security rest on the premise that conjoint efforts by nations can ensure national security more effectively that the dynamics of conflict.[2] The military approach to crisis and conflicts as evident in the recent escalation has a finite value and hence the need to seek and establish a common ground is a pre-requisite to any resolution of the core problems. Cooperative security does not preclude efforts to national defence nor can it mitigate the competition for power and influence. In fact it enhances the prospects of the process of sustained dialogue and encourages understanding in areas that are worthwhile in cooperation and promote for the basic stability of the region.

The South Asian canvas of the new security agenda provides the basis of analysis of the host of challenges and threats that confront the nation states of the region. On a common denomination, the range of military-strategic threats faced by all the nation states have been primarily due to the state centric issues of insecurity with the intensity of regional rivalries, inter state border disputes, communal antagonisms, and unresolved boundary issues. The second form of security threats and challenges emanate from human issues of insecurity that features cross border movements of refugees, illegal migrants along with infiltration of terrorists, insurgents and human trafficking etc. The third form of insecurity has emerged from transnational challenges to security emerging from drug trafficking, environmental pollution, rapid depletion of water resources, loss of bio-diversity wealth, energy resources depletion, its cumulative impact on the society and state system in South Asia. Hence, these transnational security issues require multi-national approach to address.

Regional Threat Perceptions

In the context of a review in the agenda of peace and security of South Asia, the need to locate the issues and dynamics of the changing scope of military strategic and non-military issues of security is significant. The vast canvas of security issues depicted below constitute the prime agenda of the emergent issues in South Asian security scenario:

Jihadi and other Brands of Terrorism
Nuclear Cloud over South Asia
Military Strategic Issues in the South Asia
Political Threats to Security
Economic Threats to Security
Social and Cultural Threats to Security
Ecological Threat to Security
Threat of Proliferation of Small Arms

There is no selective or single interpretation of peace and security in South Asia. A host of micro-security issues and macro strategic issues that emanates from the region are significant for security analysis. However, a few areas that is essential and could constitute the agenda for peace and security are discussed here.

Terrorism – New War

The sequence of events in South Asian strategic landscape has provided an imperative analysis and generated meaningful debate on the emerging security environment. The events that has followed September 11, 2001 (Black Tuesday) has provided basis for 'Paradigm Shift' in the perceptions of national, regional and International security. Even the concept and definition of National Security is being restructured, South Asia stands as a threshold of momentous changes that has totally transformed the strategic thinking and policy directions. The shift has come at a time when relentless pursuit of cross-border terrorism engineered from regional to global dimensions. The term 'rebels', 'ultras', 'militants', 'insurgents' and 'terrorists' are in use, rather loosely, by various militant groups that are engaged in a large-scale organized violence in different parts of South Asia. Irrespective of their objectives, ideologies, and doctrines these groups adopt the crude methodology and means of new form of war to paralyze the administration and disrupt the law and order machinery. They are also referred to as 'freedom fighters' to justify the *jihad.* Some intellectuals in Islamic world consider this widespread indiscriminate violence as a struggle against aggressions and oppressions. They feel that wherever there is an oppression, injustice, or denial of freedom to worship, any form of struggle to liberate them is *jihad.* These intellectuals have devised this convenient explanation to justify on-going violence in parts of South Asian region.

The landmass in and around South Asia has for long been the cradle for Islamic militancy, it has provided safe heavens for the terror entities. The operations of these terror outfits (*Tanzeem*) have been largely seen as the manifestation of the radical militant Islam that proposes to demolish the 'enemies of Islam'. South Asia has emerged as a critical mass of the new war, since the terror operations of this Jihadi brand of terrorists are quite focused in this region.[3]

Ethnic crisis in Sri Lanka has the bloody history of two decades. Maoist insurgency in Nepal has shaken the ruling pillars of the state and affected socio-economic fabric of the country. Ethnic and terrorist violence in Pak-Afghan border has to a large extent created turmoil in the country. Cross-border terrorism blend with its *jihadi* colour has paralyzed peace and economic development in Jammu & Kashmir for the last quarter of the century. The on-going low-intensity conflict in terms of prolonged period, nature of arms used, number of casualties and overall magnitude of military operations from both sides of the border, it would seem that there is an on going undeclared war. Yet, it is called as a 'low-intensity conflict'! Bangladesh is fast emerging as the most favoured sanctuary for various terrorist and militant groups. Bhutan too has similar experiences. This provides a true picture of South Asia in the grip of uncontrolled and devastating violence. Use of military can never eliminate this menace, perhaps it can only contain to an extent.

It is now clear that the duration of war on terrorism will be measured not in months or years but in decades. It will be too late for the South Asian states, if they fail to address these security issues now. The only alternative before the ruling elites of the South Asian states is to create a cooperative mechanism with transparency and accountability for effective measures to control and eliminate all kinds of terrorism. The agenda, therefore, would require sustained efforts, total commitment and political will to eliminate myriad dangers from South Asian soil. Whether South Asian states are ready to initiate such measures?

Nuclear Issues

It may be exaggerated, but the fear is real; will there be a nuclear flare up in South Asia? Despite the assurance by the nuclear-weapon states that they will not be the first to initiate a war, the continuing stand off between the nuclear power states in the face of diplomatic efforts to diffuse the crisis, has kept the fear alive. This region is seen as the eminent danger of 'nuclear flash point', apart from uncontrolled conflicts that have extended to a dangerous proportion leading to a deteriorating security scenario. The nuclear imperative that has now descended on South Asia has serious consequences for security and stability of the region. The induction of nuclear weapon in a region that has had persistent level of crisis and adversity imposes sufficient space for escalation. Therefore, the need is to strengthen nuclear deterrence, stability and endeavour to reduce the risk in the region, also need to evolve credible working safety measures that de-escalates the crisis and disengages the nuclear forces. The best approach would be to reduce the fear of 'first strike' in the adversaries' mind. A combination of 'no first-use', de-alerted arsenal and meaningful confidence building measures would be a preferred option.

Nuclear weapon status of South Asia would inevitably make more complex the management conflict and military risks. Nuclear weapon in the sub-continent is a reality. Hence, a range of measures is required to be put into place, both to make the conflict threshold stable and to reassure the states in the region. Nuclear CBMs would be a first such measures. Nuclear weapon states in the region need to demonstrate their commitment to prevent an arms race and their ability to manage nuclear capability with responsibility.[4] Nuclear safety should be the emphasis of such measures. The countries could also make allowances for the need for mutual technical assistance in the event of inadvertent nuclear accidents. Minimizing the risk of an accidental or unauthorized nuclear exchange may serve an initiate a de-escalation breakthrough. Further, prior notification should be given before missile test launches with provision for joint tracking. These are some of the practical de-alerting measures appropriate to South Asia. A crucial element of stabilization measures would be command and control related risk reduction measures featuring the adoption of credible administrative and technical missile launch procedures. Such measures would provide due notification to the other side of missile launches, sustain and maintain control of post test launch courses such as in-flight self destruct and detargetting commands, should the test missile stray off course. The adoption of these measures would sustain the present 'induction without overt deployment' strategy, providing substantial reaction time and fire break before a crisis flares up. Finally, there is crisis resolution ability. This refers to the ability to resolve a crisis as soon as it erupts. While crisis prevention is likely to be difficult in the current situation, crisis management and crisis resolution has been adroitly handled in South Asia in the past. Nuclear missile risk reduction measures are vital for crisis resolution given the weaponised deterrence of the two countries. Elementary logic would inform us that if the risk of use of nuclear weapons is to be reduced, the potential for arms conflict across its full spectrum must be drastically reduced. This is turn would require discussion on military doctrines, defence expenditure, conventional force reduction, and philosophy of use of force besides creating far greater transparency in military postures.[5]

Role of Civil Society

Civil society is a network of relationships among state, society, political, economical and social institutions and a cluster of interest groups such as political parties, religion, social and cultural groups.[6] Civil societies seek to create conditions where the nations need each other so much that either there is no room for conflict or minimized and controlled. Post-colonial South Asian states have pursued a modern agenda in building nation state and popular interactions are for the most part, shaped by 'state driven choices'. The single-minded approach of the nationalist discourse in building a nation state has marginalized civil society. The drive for preserving a state sovereignty, national security and search for national identity has resulted in emasculating people to people contacts in this region. Though it is a western concept but linked with the concept of democracy. "Civil society is a new terrain of democratization. In recent times, concept of civil society has emerged as the primary focus for the expansion of participative democracy in both authoritarian and liberal democracies".[7]

There is a need for a post modernist discourse strengthening the civil society and generating a new public culture, which in turn promote and encourage people to people contacts in South Asia. Thus generating trust, confidence, understanding and harmony that are needed for lasting peace and cooperative security in South Asia. Civil society is the new terrain of democratization. South Asian sates are multi-ethnic and multi cultural society. Hence, a participative democracy could expand the role and significance of civil society.

The main objective of civil society is to strengthen social, cultural, economical and political institutions, which protects and safeguards individual rights from any kind of authoritarianism at the state and society. A democracy enjoying plural mandate could result in a mature civil society. While guaranteeing the sanctity of pluralism, a mature civil society rejects the ideological totalitarianism, elitist monopoly and majoritarianism coercion.

Civil society does not exist in South Asia because prevailing geo-political and geo-strategic environment does not permit this. The region lacks any political culture suitable needed for a civil society. Deliberate attempts have been made to weaken the civil structure by the forces of status quo and power hungry ruling elite.[8]

The fragile societal forces also provide the ruling class to exploit them. These are primarily variety of hurdles for a viable civil society in South Asia. They are: Lack of political culture; Lack of accountability; Religions fundamentalism; Element of militancy/ terrorism; State terrorism; Controlled media; Class differences; Economic fragility; Poor governance; and Rampant corruption.

As the creation of civil society is rather slow and gradual, South Asian states have not witnessed any concrete efforts in this direction. The realization of the fact among the states in South Asia that political solution is the only way of resolution of any dispute that is possible through dialogue and understanding. Hence, South Asian states have to bring their house in order and learn to live with peace and tranquility with neighbours that are required for harmony.

State Craft and Good Governance

The all-enveloping crisis of governance in South Asia is apparent from inability of the state to govern, in contra distinction to rule, which has strengthened the phenomena of in human governance, transcending other regional contentions. Manifestation of poor governance is plainly apparent; they are exemplified by the wasteful use of scarce resources. Unresponsive administration at its cutting edge, pervasive corruption at all levels, little policy coherence to address the issues and concerns impinges upon South Asian states. These manifestations of poor governance include lack of decentralization and devolution, unimaginative dealing with minorities, decay of established institutions and self-centered ruling elite. There is also a paucity of documentation of what constitutes the ruling elites understanding of the threat to national security, issues and concerns of comprehensive security.[9]

The main problem of governance in democratic and plural societies is meeting their population rising expectations molded by their exposure to electronic media. Multi-cultural and multi - ethnic character of these societies requires adequate space being provided for diverse community to live in harmony. Regrettably the compulsion of electoral politics dictates the use of communal, caste and class division by the political masters to consolidate their respective vote banks. This is bound to generate social conflict and violence in society. This electoral politics lies at the roots of crisis of governance and security. Money and muscle power, obviously, become the important ingredients for this phenomena. The problem is also perceived to be with politics and politicians who have reduced the agenda of governance in pursuit of power. The dilemma before the State is that it cannot reform itself while remaining party to its sustained mis-governance.

Dissent, violence, militancy and terrorism on one hand, and politician criminal nexus on the other hand, blend with lawlessness and rampant corruption has caused enfeeblement of government, especially its police and criminal justice system in South Asian states. If a concerted campaign is to be launched against drugs and arms smuggling, child and women trafficking or other transitional crimes, serious efforts are bound to fail. This is precisely because the profiting mafia has higher reaches with ruling establishments; hence, these issues cannot be addressed as long as it is linked with the crisis of governance. The very machinery of governance, thus, insidiously becomes a source of insecurity.

Link between governance and internal source of conflict is important on any reckoning and particular relevance to the development of South Asia.[10] It is generally believed that under a democratic government, country provides a 'safety valve' that could dampen or minimizes internal sources of conflict. But in South Asian states reality is different. There is also a link between democracy and human development, because a good government must guarantee its citizens certain basis liberties for promotion of their progress and the expansion of the social opportunities.

Democratic process could felicitate the framing and enactment of law that reflects popular aspirations but effective implementation and enforcement of the same remains with the mighty ruling elite. It is here that good governance could do the best. Unfortunately, South Asian states have been failing to act in this direction. The need for good governance and consequently for de-politicizing pressure on all branches of administration is being increasingly highlighted in the region.

The question of governance is, indeed, of much relevance to the cooperative security concept to address the various sources of conflict and to deal with them effectively. Establishment of co-ordination between government and civil society is essential in South Asian states that would help to mobilize resources for development and facilitate monitoring of the process of executing programmes.

Role of Media

Public perception persists that authentic cooperation is yet to emerge, as there are no tangible or visible benefits of public information and awareness generation in South Asian states about cooperative security initiatives. It is important that cooperation in technical areas such as telecommunications, meteorology and environment that constitute integrated programme of action are of specialized nature and does not attract wider interest beyond the respective specialized constituencies.[11] South Asian states have not yet developed a public information system. There is an urgent need to widely disseminate knowledge about the issues and concern of original cooperation through a well thought of programme of public information. Media alone can help the masses in developing positive regional consciousness. South Asian media is more of event oriented rather than process oriented. Media bears a great moral responsibility of making concerted efforts in sensitizing the government and the general public about the issues and concerns of South Asia, which is otherwise missing due to lack of any cooperative efforts in this direction.[12] It is the time for media in South Asia to transcend national boundaries and work across frontiers by ensuring that they do not entrap each other within the paranoia to which they catered. Media in South Asia reflected the deep divide between the societies, political, ethnic, religious, cultural and social. The media also adopted an ambivalent attitude towards regional cooperation and tended at times to aggravate the bilateral constrain that exists between the neighbouring countries and to reinforce old prejudices and new suspicious.

Specific measures could be discussed to overcome any obstacle in order to provide free flow of information in the region to make factual news content, accurate and unbiased interpretation. By such measures media can create a wider awareness among the people of South Asia and facilitate mutual understanding. Cooperation in the field of media will facilitate enrichment of the profession of the journalism through collaborative training programme, research and exchange of media practitioners. Such cooperation would also enhance a public access to the relevant and reliable information of each other's countries. Which would in turn minimize prejudices that, inhibits progress in regional cooperation. It will foster public participation collaborative efforts to improve the quality of life and accelerate development process in South Asia.

Electronic media, operating from high altitude with no territorial respect, has tremendous potential as unifying force amongst the South Asian states. Hence, a 'media without walls' would be an appropriate measure towards unique regional cooperation at all levels. Electronic media has an infinitely larger reach than newspapers, hence, a wider impact on the public perception. Broadcast channels of South Asian states are owned by the governments and project only state centric views on sensitive issues. Print media in South Asian states tend to reinforce rather than questioning. News coverage remains narrow negative and high selective. Press focuses on political security and social tensions and highlight conflict over cooperative issues in the region. Soft news process of social change and other developmental or constructive events that society experiences go virtually unnoticed. Newsgathering becomes more difficult due to strict visa regime imposed on journalists in respective states.

The promotion of adversarial image by the media – print or electronic–is a major hurdle in building constructive civil society in South Asia.[13] While English language papers do give insight to security issues, foreign policies and international affairs, press in other languages does not focus on these issues rather confines to local and narrow issues. This keeps the large masses of society ignorant of real issues and events in the world politics and regional context. Therefore, society by and large remains unaware of the liberal and moderate approaches and concepts that count more towards a well-developed and well-informed society in South Asia.

It is high time that the South Asian initiatives on formulation of a regional communication are needed. While adequately covering events on the news value, will shift the focus of mutual perceptions from conflict to cooperation, an act as a catalyst as well as carrier of multi-dimensional information, knowledge and understanding.

Role of CBM

CBM in inter-state relations could be traced deep and sound through the corridors of history over the years and around the world. These CBMs have developed as powerful tools towards building peace, harmony and for avoiding conflict in the conduct of inter-state relations. No concept in the filed of conflict resolution, peace and security has assumed so much of importance in recent times as CBMs. Though a western concept, which can mean from goodwill, gestures, initiatives and acknowledgements to resolve differences and disputes by creating harmonious and congenial environment for any interaction at all levels. One cannot undermine its significance in building trust and understanding. Unfortunately, South Asia does not have structures for a meaningful implementation of CBMs, which is a fundamental challenge to the application of the concept. The peculiar politico-strategic environment in strife-torn South Asia has prevented any successful mechanism developing effective measures in the region.

Ideally, the best measures are incremental building on earlier successes and developing the same. Certain measures to facilitate CBMs such as official transparency, strong civil society, people to people contact and a political leadership enjoys confidence at home to be able to take bold steps. These initiatives could form the following measures: transparency; communication, doctrinal, early warning and notification, periodic consultation and monitoring nuclear risk reduction and conflict prevention, management and de-escalation.

The real question, however, relates to how useful the CBMs are in relation between adversarial and competing states. Nevertheless, these measures may yield positive results, if sustained efforts are initiated. Concept of CBMs need time to get institutionalized and to be accepted by the people of the region.

The following are suggestive CBMs that may help to reconstruct South Asian peace and security: to promote viable, assertive, positive and meaningful role of education, media and civil society required to support the process of confidence building in South Asia; viable role of Non-Governmental organizations required so as to facilitate people to people contacts and also to encourage exchange of professionals; need to institutionalize interstate cooperation in the nuclear field, particularly in the area of nuclear energy; holding of nuclear dialogue between nuclear states for establishing a nuclear restraint regime in South Asia, which is essential for peace and stability in the region; positive reporting of media about conflicts in South Asia and also to establish media channels in South Asia; and to promote greater interaction between media, civil society and academia for building confidence in South Asia.

There is a need and scope to strengthen the apparatus of the state, which could address not only military centric national security, but also human security aspirations of South Asia.

Peace and stability in South Asia has further jolted by the loss of strategic autonomy in post-9/11 scenario. The recent politico- strategic environment in South Asia has gradually eroded the ability and fractured the statecraft. The extra regional powers though ignored South Asia earlier, are now actively engaged in providing prescriptions blend with diplomatic pressure and economic package to suit their design in South Asia under the pretext of "global war against terrorism". The strategic engagement of these extra regional powers does not augur well for future of South Asia. This is bound to complicate the prospects and stability in South Asia instead of providing lasting solutions.

Unresolved dispute may turn into minor conflicts, and sustained, low intensity conflicts may lead to a major war, and this may result in nuclear catastrophe. Hence, the worldwide perception of South Asia as a 'region of nuclear flash point'. The realistic possibility towards conflict resolution and peace building could be achieved through a cooperative framework evolved by the South Asian states for sustained economic development and peaceful future. A more effective way to ensure security is to create positive process that can lead to peace and disarmament in the region. It is essential to create an irreversible process with such a momentum, that all states cooperate for their common survival. Acceptance of common security agenda for efforts to reduce risk of war, limit arms, and move towards disarmament means, as the organizing principle that cooperation will replace confrontation in resolving conflicts of interests in South Asia.[14]

Cooperative security assumes heightened importance in an environment in which disintegration of political structure raises questions about the ability of some states to proved basic necessities to its people. Hence, providing priority to element of human security. Cooperative security orientation could focus national, regional and global security dimensions.

References

1. Bhabani Sengupta and Amit Gupta, "Changing Patterns of Regional Conflicts in South Asia", in Bhabani Sengupta (ed.), *Regional Cooperation and Development in South Asia*, Vol. I, New Delhi: South Asian Publishers, 1986, pp. 247-49.
2. P.R Chari, "Security Studies in India: Recent Trends and Future Directions", in Dipankar Banerjee (ed.), *Security Studies in South Asia: Changes and Challenges*, New Delhi: Manohar, 2000, pp. 52-53.
3. See Gopal ji Malviya, "Self-styled Zealots of a New War", Book Review, *The Hindu,* 16 September 2003.
4. V.R.Raghavan, "Post-cold War Security Studies in India: Continuity and Change", in Banerjee, n.2, p. 89.
5. Jasjit Singh, "Talk away the Flashpoint", *New Indian Express*, 18 June 2004
6. Naeem Ahmed, "The Role of Cooperative Security and CBMs in South Asia", in Moonis Ahmar (ed.), *The Challenges of Confidence Building in South Asia*, New Delhi: Har-Anand, 2001, p. 266.
7. Rita Manchanda, "Confidence Building Measures and Regional Dialogue Retrospect and Prospect: What Role for NGO?", in Dipankar Banerjee (ed.), *Confidence Building Measures in South Asia*, Colombo: Regional Centre for Strategic Studies, 1999, p. 169.
8. Ahmed, n.6.

9. P.R. Chari, "Governance and Security", *The Hindu*, 3 November 2001.
10. Gamnai Corea, "Globalization, Governance and Environment", *RCSS Newsletter*, April 2001. p. 3.
11. Kant Kishore Bhargava, et al.(ed.), *Shaping South Asia's Future Role of Regional Cooperation*, New Delhi: Vikas,1995, p. 29.
12. *Ibid.*
13. Ahmed, n.6, p.279.
14. Common Security: A Programme for Disarmaments, The Report of the Independent Commission on Disarmament and Security issues (named the Olaf Palme Report), pp.7-8, cited by Chari, n.2, p. 51.

4

A Common Defence Area for South Asia: An Indian Perspective

Manoj Joshi

During the heyday of the British Empire, the security of the region was directed by British officials who saw their task in global terms. British relations with European powers—be it Russia, France or Germany— decided its security perspectives in this region. Being the only global power in the world at the time, Britain saw the security of India and the Indian Ocean in a holistic fashion. The key here was the need to maintain the lines of communications between Britain and India via the Suez or the Cape of Good Hope.

Britain thought long and hard about the security of its interests in the region. For the British Foreign and Commonwealth Office, Pakistan was the logical vehicle of British interests since it was a large Muslim nation whose armed forces were officered by British personnel. For this reason, the Commonwealth Office strongly backed the Pakistani claim to Kashmir.

The conflict in Kashmir put paid to any notion that India and Pakistan could cooperate on issues relating to security. Instead as time went on, they were locked into a larger global problem – Pakistan became part of the US-led alliance system, India stayed neutral and sought Soviet assistance in building up its armed forces.

The Sino-Indian border conflict brought in another element into the equation and instead of a common security area, the region became a cockpit for Cold War rivalries.

There were two episodes of external aggression during the Cold War that sought to posit the region as a single security area. The first was the Chinese invasion of India in 1962. The Indian defeat did bring huge temptation for Pakistan to act against India, but it did not. In part this was the result of US and British pressure on Pakistan.

The second episode was the Soviet invasion of Afghanistan. While India did not join the condemnation of the Soviet Union, it told the Soviet leaders that it was unacceptable and urged them to pull out. However, larger forces, in the shape of a United States determined to bleed the Soviet Union, ensured that the region became a battleground.

The end of the Cold War has not had the impact that it could have had because of the India-Pakistan problem, laced with the desire of China to keep the South Asian pot boiling. However, after the 1998 nuclear tests, changes are visible in this area as well. These changes have been accelerated by the 9/11 events that played a major role in persuading Pakistan to turn its back on the jihadi component of its security policy. The push towards making South Asia a free trade area, global trends in the war against terrorism are now taking the region to the point where it can once again contemplate considering ideas on cooperative security.

It would not be an exaggeration to say that South Asia is one of the most insecure regions of the world. In addition to three nuclear powers, India, Pakistan and China vide Tibet, it has a host of insurgencies and private armies. There are problems of irredentism, antagonistic ethnic sub-nationalisms, religious strife and presence of weapons of mass destruction.

There are certain givens in India's relations with other South Asian nations. India is larger than all of them combined and borders each of them, while none of the others border each other. This introduces a unique dynamic that has seen each of these countries, with the exceptions of the smaller Bhutan and Maldives, having difficult relations with New Delhi for varying periods of time. In part this has been due to the not unnatural tendency of smaller countries to resent a more powerful neighbour. In part it is because of insensitive Indian policy. But more than Indian economic or military might, the point of resentment is often the massive Indian cultural footprint in the region.

India's relation with each of the South Asian states has been distinctive. It has had an antagonistic relationship with Pakistan from the very outset and helped create Bangladesh, a factor that has added to the antagonism with Pakistan, and paradoxically, Bangladesh itself. For quite some time, it had an uneasy relationship with Sri Lanka, but ever since India turned its back on Tamil militancy, the Sri Lankan governments have been more appreciative and supportive of India's role. Nepal is another country with whom India has had a peculiar relationship. The Indo-Nepal border is virtually unpoliced and both countries permit a free movement of citizens. Nevertheless, there have been periods of tension – 1988-89—being the worst. Subsequently there has been considerable unhappiness in India over what was seen as Inter-Service Intelligence (ISI) operations in Nepal targeting India. Currently, the Nepalese government sees India as an ally in combating the threat of Maoist insurgency.

India shares close ties with Bhutan. The fact that several north-eastern groups had sanctuary in southern Bhutan was not seen as an Indo-Bhutanese problem by New Delhi. On the other hand, the Bhutanese action in eliminating these sanctuaries has been seen as a model of sorts in a neighbour, even one so small and vulnerable as Bhutan, going out of its way to address the security concerns of its bigger neighbour.

The Indian operation to secure Maldives against a coup staged by mercenaries was widely applauded in the region and the world. Given the geography, only India had the capacity to assist Maldives in its time of need.

A measure of India's insecurity vis-à-vis its neighbours have been the decision to fence the India-Pakistan and India-Bangladesh borders, beginning in 1988. This is an enormous exercise, costing several thousands of crores because it requires not just the fencing, but floodlighting as well as constructing border roads.

From the Indian point of view, there are a variety of threats that have generated insecurity in the region – external intervention, be it the US or Chinese support to Pakistan, support and aid provided to religious extremists by Islamabad. But as we know that the issue is more complex and also involves Indian policies and action. For this reason we will take up a more detailed look at the Sri Lankan crisis where national chauvinism, irredentism, religious and ethnic strife and Indian policy combined to create a major crisis.

Case Study of Sri Lanka

Sri Lanka's Tamil minority makes up seventeen per cent of the population of the island, being concentrated in the north and some parts of the east. While most of these, called Jaffna Tamils, have been there for thousands of years, there are some four per cent Indian Tamils who were brought to work in the plantations.

In the aftermath of independence, the political competition between the United National Party and the Sri Lanka Freedom Party made the alleged domination of Tamils in the bureaucracy and educational institutions into a cause for reverse discrimination against the community. S.W.R.D. Bandaranaike, who was later assassinated by a Buddhist monk, began an aggressive 'Sinhala only' policy. His widow, Sirimavo, who became prime minister in 1960 began to rigorously enforce anti-Tamil measures which did not abate even after her defeat in the 1965 elections. But she was re-elected in 1970 at the crest of an even more extreme anti-Tamil wave. The island was re-named Sri Lanka and in 1972, after defeating a Trotskyite uprising, she amended the constitution to give Sinhala the status of the official language and Buddhism as the state religion.

This pushed the mainstream Tamil parties, the Ceylon Workers Party, representing the plantation Tamils and the Federal Party representing the Jaffna Tamils into creating a Tamil United Front, which later became the Tamil United Liberation Front, but still espoused the path of parliamentary democracy.

But at the same time, younger politicians began thinking in terms of more militant politics. Nadraja Thangavelu aka

Thangadurai, Selvaraja Yogachandran aka Kuttimani set up a Tamil Eelam Liberation Organisation (TELO), attracting the Jaffna youth. Other outfits like the Tamil Students League (TSL) and the Tamil Youth League also came up. Sivakumaran of the TSL attempted to assassinate a Sri Lankan minister in 1970 and the mayor of Jaffna, Alfred Duriappah in 1971 and later committed suicide when trapped after a bank robbery.

It took another decade for the militancy to take root. While the young Jaffna Tamils used Tamil Nadu for shelter, the government of the state, at the time the Dravida Munnettra Kazhagam (DMK) did not have much sympathy for the militancy. In 1973 when the Sri Lankans seized of boatload of dynamite belonging to TELO, Kuttimani fled to India, but was extradited by the DMK government and sent to jail. In July 1975, a young 17-year old Velupillai Pirabhakaran succeeded in assassinating the Jaffna mayor Duriappah. He later founded the Tamil New Tigers who later became the Liberation Tigers of Tamil Eelam (LTTE).

Another of set of militant groups were founded in UK, but most of them learnt their craft on the ground. Indian intelligence agencies came into the picture after 1983 when the ambush of a Sri Lankan army patrol on the Jaffna-Palali road led to the massacre of a number of Tamil leaders in Welikade prison, including Kuttimani. But other inputs for the militants came from the Popular Front for the Liberation of Palestine. Indian aims were twofold. First, they wanted to keep the militant assertion of Tamil identity away from Indian shores. Second, they saw this as part of India's battle to keep foreign influences, read US and its allies, from the region.

An Indian Peace Keeping Force landed in Sri Lanka as part of the Indo-Sri Lanka Accord. The Indians were there to round up the arms that were to be surrendered by the LTTE, aid in the creation of a united North-eastern province where Tamils would be dominant and assist the election process through which a new government would emerge. But the LTTE had no intention of following this scenario and they undermined the process, eventually compelling the IPKF to use military force to coerce them. This process was well underway when the new Sri Lankan president

Ranasinghe Premdasa fell into the LTTE trap and began a covert aid programme to ease the pressure on the LTTE, and demanded an Indian withdrawal.

Finally, with their task incomplete, the Indian forces withdrew from the island in March 1990. The LTTE used a fourteen-month ceasefire thereafter to reestablish itself in the north and the east. It also established a logistical network across the Palk Straits to Tamil Nadu. India made efforts to check this particularly after the assassination of EPRLF leader Padmanabha in Chennai in June 1990. There were cordon and search operation and surveillance of the 1,000-strong fishing fleet and a promise of central support. But things did not happen till Rajiv Gandhi's assassination in May of 1991. Thereafter, the Indian side cracked down on the LTTE infrastructure and instituted a much more rigorous sea-patrol system using hired trawlers that could navigate the shallower parts of the sea that were could not be accessed by naval vessels.

In the ensuing years, particularly after the assassination of Sri Lankan president Premdasa, its hard line national security minister Lalith Athulathmudali and defence minister Ranjan Wijeratne, India's hands off policy, combined with a tough anti-LTTE stance, has convinced the Sri Lankan authorities that India has no desire to interfere with the island's sovereignty. The Indian side has refused to be party to the Norway-brokered LTTE-Sri Lankan negotiations, despite requests from both sides. A new situation has been created by the emergence of the DMK as a coalition partner of the new United Progressive Alliance government, but it is unlikely to radically change things.

The Lessons of Sri Lanka

There are several lessons to be derived from this experience. First, that exporting your problem to another country is not a sustainable strategy. India tried to ensure that the problem would not visit its shores, but they did, though fortunately, they were quickly dealt with. Pakistan has begun learning the lesson somewhat later.

The second lesson is that given the traditions and history of the region, domestic constituencies are not enthusiastic supporters of external intervention. One of the key lessons India learnt was that it was not possible to raise security concerns over Sri Lanka to the Indian populace, at least to the extent where it could get a domestic consensus on intervening in the island.

In the case of Pakistan, it has been somewhat different. Because Kashmir is seen as disputed, a domestic consensus on backing militancy has been there, but of late there are questions being raised about this. Third, and this is a lesson for Sri Lanka which is that it is not possible to coerce a domestic minority beyond a point.

Fourth, that making peace requires a lot of helping hands. In the case of Sri Lanka, Norway's role has been significant, but so have India's behind-the-scenes efforts.

Fifth, that there are karmic consequences of actions. India, for example, paid the price for supporting the LTTE, just as Sri Lanka has done. Pakistan is now paying the price for backing jihadi terrorists.

Larger issues

When we look at the larger framework for South Asia, several issues emerge. The first is the question of sanctuary and shelter. At various points in time South Asian countries have provided sanctuary and shelter to insurgents from neighbouring countries. This may have been an involuntary process such as the case of Bhutan and ULFA, or a matter of policy in the case of India in 1971 and in the early eighties in relation to Sri Lanka, or Pakistan with regard to Sikh and Kashmiri militants subsequently.

Countries have argued that they are supporting freedom fighters or aiding those struggling against repression. Unfortunately, there are instances, such as in the case of Bangladesh, even this excuse is not used. The only thing that Bangladesh has to say is either that nothing is happening, or that elements outside the control of government are involved.

But this trend is slowly changing. This has arisen from a self-awareness that supporting such groups does more harm than good. A case in point is Pakistan. For more than a decade, it has supported what it calls the freedom struggle in Kashmir. In the process, it has encouraged groups preaching jihad to carry out terrorist acts in India. Pakistan pursued this track despite clear evidence that the people involved were also those involved in terrorist activities in Pakistan, particularly of the sectarian variety. But in the past one-year, many such actors have turned against the Pakistani state.

A critical shift has come in the wake of 9/11. UN Security Council resolution has put paid to the issue and made it clear that in most cases, supporting insurgents could be tantamount to supporting terrorism.

The second is the question of the existence of Weapons of Mass Destruction in the hand of two of the South Asian states makes this an important factor in the insecurity of the region. The state in the region, indeed in the world have a right to expect that India and Pakistan will manage their nuclear status with responsibility and care. Though it really involves two of the states, but it is not possible to exclude China from any discussion. Chinese help has been central in enabling Pakistan to develop a nuclear capability and obtain a delivery system. However, the problem here is that China does not recognize the legitimacy of Indian and Pakistani nuclear status.

Nevertheless, the Indian-Pakistani tensions make their nuclear status dangerous. In the Lahore summit of 1999, the two sides signed an Memorandum of Understanding on nuclear confidence building measures that ranged from providing information on nuclear accidents or unauthorized launches of missiles to discussion on nuclear doctrines.

The third issue is the poor health of democracy and good governance in the region. All the states of the region are now formally democracies, but they are at different levels of development. Democracy, we must emphasize is not just a matter of free and fair elections, but also of providing good governance which includes the rule of law, especially, equal protection of the law to minorities.

A linked issue is moderately competent and corruption-free administration to provide for a system that can create the physical and governmental infrastructure to meet the economic and social needs of the people. In some ways, it is the only mechanism through which competing sub-nationalisms and ethnic competition can be managed in a benign fashion.

Conclusion

There is generally greater awareness in the region that the way to go is cooperation rather than conflict. But there is not yet sufficient awareness or perhaps political will to end support for insurgents and terrorists.

Simultaneously, the countries of the region must through bilateral mechanisms seek to understand and address legitimate concerns of their neighbours. In this context, the Bhutanese action against insurgent camps in its southern jungles is a model of sorts. Bhutan's security was not directly affected, yet it chose to act. From the Indian perspective there is need for the countries of the region to realize that India, though by far the largest country, too, has security concerns that need to be addressed. As time has shown that nothing that any neighbour can do or can pose any mortal threat to India, barring the use of nuclear weapons. But they can cause a lot of grief and push the Indian polity into a hostile mode.

India has the capacity of doing a lot of mischief in the region, but has largely restrained itself in the past decade or so. In 1990, for example, the government took the decision not to permit any tit-for-tat responses to ISI-sponsored bomb blasts in India. Since then there has also been a policy of offering unilateral concessions in the trade front. A more economically and physically secure India can and must be even more generous. The massive disparity between India's economic size and that of the neighbours requires New Delhi to be more sensitive about their concerns.

Only if and when small and big disputes are resolved and the region's economies are more integrated, will it begin seeing itself as a common security area. The first stage for this awareness has already come with the countries of the region becoming more sensitive to the issue of supporting insurgent groups. As far as India and Bangladesh, Nepal, Sri Lanka and Maldives are concerned, there are no significant problems. But Kashmir remains a major problem. India and Pakistan have now begun to talk in earnest to resolve this issue. In the interim, perhaps the SAARC should come up with an Asean Regional Forum type of a body where security issues are discussed multilaterally. This would be a first step in articulating hidden and not-so-hidden worries of the states of the region.

5

India-Pakistan Security Cooperation and the Prospects for a South Asian Security Community

Rajesh M. Basrur

The history of regional cooperation in South Asia has been a chequered one. The rise of regional organisations in the post-World War !! era – notably the European Union (EU) and the Association of South East Asia Nations (ASEAN) – gave rise to the hope that something similar might be achieved in South Asia. After all, Europe had been at war during the preceding century, and the states of Southeast Asia had frequently been at loggerheads in the post-colonial period. The establishment of the South Asian Association for Regional Cooperation (SAARC) in 1985 was regarded as a necessary step in building regional cooperation. Despite the constant tensions of South Asian politics, SAARC was created in 1985 in an effort to find common ground among the states of the region. Among the underlying factors that gave birth to the organisation was the awareness that a hostile environment is ultimately counter-productive because it prevents cooperation for mutual benefit, especially in areas relating to economic development. Quite early, however, the difficulties involved became clear. Trade remained marginal, and inter-state disputes dogged efforts at collaboration. A recent review of the SAARC experience shows that not much has changed.[1] Progress toward enhanced regional trade has been slow and political quarrels – notably the India-Pakistan dispute (though it is not the only one) – continue to hinder the organisation's development. The prospect of a South Asian security community seems remote as things stand.

The growth of meaningful security cooperation in South Asia turns largely upon a substantial change for the better in India-Pakistan relations. Without a transformation in India-Pakistan relations, there is very limited scope for the emergence of regional security cooperation, let alone the establishment of a regional security community. The prerequisite for this is a sharp turn in policy by both countries, i.e., for a shift from what has been hitherto a zero sum game, in which one's loss is seen as the other's gain, to a positive sum game, in which both gain. This not to say that there has been no beneficial cooperation between them in the past. The Indus Treaty of 1960 is a striking example of what is possible. The fact remains, however, that the general tenor of the relationship has been negative despite repeated efforts to negotiate a solution, most recently in the Agra summit of 2001. A systematic analysis of the factors which constrain cooperation and those which facilitate it will be discussed below.

The next section will set out the analytical framework for assessing the prospects for cooperation. This will clarify the requirements for policy change. The basic framework is that of "levels of analysis," which facilitates a comprehensive study of the problem by the examination of relevant variables at three analytical levels: the international system, the state, and the individual. This will be followed by a scrutiny of each level in the context of India-Pakistan relations. Subsequently, a brief review of relations between India and other states will also be taken up in order to provide a complementary perspective. Finally concluding observations will underline the difficulties that confront regional security cooperation in South Asia, but will at the same time identify those areas which offer room for optimism.

Analytical Framework

In an illuminating paper, Jakob Gustavsson critically examines as many as six different models of foreign policy change that explain varying degrees of transformation in policy ranging from the incremental to the fundamental.[2] All the models posit three steps: (i) background factors conducive to policy change; (ii) cognitive factors and factors relating to the decision making process; and (iii) the connection between these two and a foreign policy outcome in the form of a typology of foreign policy change. Gustavsson integrates and refines the models by identifying the basic sources of change (background factors) as international and domestic factors, which are inputs influencing a decision maker, who channels his/her own cognitive learning into the decision process. The decision process produces an output, which circles back to the background factors by way of feedback, thus producing a continuous and dynamic model of change. Gustavsson adds a crucial element: the availability of a "policy window," or a moment of opportunity, which determines the timing of change. He sees this policy window as the space created by crisis situations, which alter the calculus of policy change, making the latter more feasible than in normal times.

In essence, Gustavsson's model does not differ significantly from a levels-of-analysis approach. This approach begins with the question: who or what constitute the main "actors" in international politics? There is no unanimity among those who have undertaken specifically to examine the problem. Arnold Wolfers focuses on two major actors: the individual and the state;[3] Kenneth Waltz adds a third, the international system;[4] and Robert Jervis brings in bureaucratic processes.[5] In addition, as David Singer notes, "many others are available."[6] It may be argued, for instance, that international organisations do not fit neatly into any of the categories noted above. However, in the discussion that follows, the author confines to the three levels preferred by Waltz, viz., the international system, the state, and the individual. What Gustavsson's approach does is clarify the flow from the systemic and state-level factors to the individual level, where decisions are (normally) made. Regarding the policy window, it may be added that, apart from crisis-driven change in policy, change may also occur in another way. When the disharmony between an existing policy paradigm and a changing international setting reaches a point of serious disequilibrium, a policy window may be said to have opened up. This is akin to Thomas Kuhn's conception of paradigm change in the sciences, when existing ways of doing things are found to be increasingly inadequate as evidence of anomalies mounts.[7] Thus, for example, Mikhail Gorbachev's monumental decision to transform Soviet policy toward the United States was not propelled by a crisis, but rather by the accumulated inadequacy of Soviet policy (and the Soviet system itself) in coming to terms with a changing world. A change in India-Pakistan relations, and in South Asian regional security cooperation, may occur, accordingly, either as a consequence of crisis or as policy makers' response to the accumulated weight of dysfunctional policy.

India-Pakistan Relations

System-Level Factors

The international system is a set of interacting states with a certain degree of autonomy, and consequent effects on state policies. It tends to bring out like behaviours on the part of states regardless of state-level factors such as who is in power or what political and economic interests are at play. For instance, balance-of-power politics – the tendency to balance the power of a strong state by the counter-accumulation of power by one or more states – tends to follow repetitive patterns irrespective of internal politics. Most basic to such politics is the anarchic character of the international system.[8] Because there is no sovereign authority above states, each state tends to accumulate power for security, and, not wishing to risk relying on others, to put self-interest before common interests. Both these realities make inter-state cooperation difficult (though not impossible). Additionally, in an adversarial relationship, the military resources of each are a threat to the other. As a result, even if they do not intend to use force, hostile states tend to acquire more and more instruments of power in an action-reaction relationship that takes the form of an arms race.

Leaving aside the Kashmir dispute, power politics plays an important role in spawning tensions between India and Pakistan. India's sheer size is a source of insecurity for Pakistan, which seeks to boost its military strength through a high level of arms spending. India in turn feels compelled to counter the perceived threat from such high spending by enhancing its own capabilities. The Indian need to confront a second threat – from China – adds to the problem. The result is a tendency toward arms racing, now extended to the realm of nuclear weapons. It is readily evident that, from this perspective, the Kashmir dispute is of secondary significance. The primary need for both countries is a stable strategic relationship in a nuclearized environment. While Kashmir is important, the lives of millions of their citizens are far more so. Besides, even if the Kashmir dispute were to be resolved, the structural basis of the India-Pakistan dispute would still remain: Pakistan would still be uncomfortable with Indian dominance of the region. It would still be worried about being swamped politically, economically, and culturally, as is Bangladesh, with which India has no serious territorial dispute.

Nuclear weapons have brought an unprecedented form of interdependence to India-Pakistan relations. Conventional war, with its attendant risk of escalation to nuclear conflict, is no longer a feasible option. It follows that arms control and nuclear confidence building are essential to the security of both countries. But, as with the Cold War, nuclear weapons have not brought stability. On the contrary, mutual hostility has been intensified. Like the United States and the Soviet Union, India and Pakistan have sought to overcome the constraints imposed by nuclear weapons by testing the limits of force projection. Pakistan has attempted to use a sub-conventional strategy in initiating the Kargil conflict (1999) and in supporting terrorist groups active in India, while India has tried through Operation Parakram (2001-02) to exercise coercive diplomacy and pressurise Pakistan into withdrawing its support for cross-border terrorism. Both have been partly successful. Pakistan has been able to ensure that Kashmir remains high on the global and bilateral political agenda, while India has been able to expose Pakistani complicity in terrorist violence and bring international pressure to bear against it. But both have also been unsuccessful in altering the terms of their engagement. In the process, their relationship has assumed more ominous proportions, thus creating the widespread perception that the spectre of nuclear conflict hovers close by. At the same time, the two antagonists have made several attempts to negotiate a political solution from time to time but are still continuing.

One possibility that might create a policy window is a nuclear crisis. It is widely feared that a future India-Pakistan confrontation might lead to conventional war, which could escalate to the level of nuclear conflict. Given the tendency of both countries to exercise restraint well short of a nuclear face-off, this seems unlikely. Both have refrained from deploying their nuclear weapons even at the height of tension. But the possibility remains. Other possibilities include an accidental launch, or a launch command given by a local commander able to bypass the centralised command and control systems both countries are believed to have in place. This seems far-fetched at present, but is possible should India and Pakistan at some point of time decide to deploy their weapons. A nuclear disaster, if it occurs, is likely to bring policy reversal. But ironically, so long as the risk of nuclear war remains relatively low, so does the probability of extensive arms control and political compromise of a significant nature.

Another systemic source of positive change could be the emergence of a common threat, which would produce the incentive for the adversaries to forge unity in a typical balance-of-power reaction. Historical examples include the coming together of France and Germany in the face of the Soviet threat and the unifying effect on the Middle East of Saddam Hussain's invasion of Iraq. But the prospect is an unlikely one. The possibility of a major state (China is the only one in close proximity) seriously threatening India and Pakistan is remote. Besides, both countries possess nuclear deterrence capability, which is sufficient to keep any state with nefarious designs on either at bay.

However, if we go beyond the state-centrism commonplace in the study of security policy, we may view terrorism as a threat to both countries. An obvious objection is that, to the contrary, terrorism has been an instrument of Pakistani state policy, and has therefore been the *source* of much of the India-Pakistan tensions of recent years. But that may be changing. The Pakistani distinction between "freedom fighters" active in Kashmir, and "terrorists" attacking targets in Pakistan was never a tenable one once president Musharraf began his campaign against Al Qaeda, for the latter has close links to militants fighting in Kashmir.[9] The functional distinction between those terrorists active in Pakistan and those engaged in India has become meaningless with the discovery that the Jaish-e-Mohammed, a major group fighting in Kashmir, was involved in the attempt to assassinate President Musharraf in 2003.[10]

There is another, neglected aspect to the issue. Links have been uncovered between Al Qaeda and nuclear scientists in the region.[11] Given the recent exposure of the proliferation activity that Pakistan's nuclear-scientific community has engaged in, the possibility of weapons material and technology spreading to terrorist groups cannot be ruled out.[12] Should that happen, the risk of an act of nuclear/radiological terrorism would be high. Nuclear bombs of the kind that states want are difficult to make, but crude ones are not beyond the means of terrorist groups. Radiological dispersion devices or "dirty bombs" – which combine conventional explosives and radioactive materials to spread radiation – would not be difficult to produce.[13] Terrorist groups like Al Qaeda could unleash mayhem in either country if they acquired such capability. India and Pakistan thus face a common threat from terrorist groups that might obtain nuclear or radiological weapons. The threat is sufficiently serious to merit active cooperation on their part.

Another possible source of systemic change could be the effect of globalisation on both countries. Globalisation has created powerful incentives for increasing economic openness and for reducing expenditure on conflict. In an increasingly fast-moving and competitive world, investment is the key to growth, and investment will not flow to places where the returns are likely to be uncertain. From this standpoint, neither India nor Pakistan can afford to continue indefinitely on the path of confrontation, which is expensive and discourages investment. Besides, as military security becomes increasingly technology-intensive and costly, economic weakness has a debilitating impact on it. High military spending without economic growth is self-defeating because it impedes growth and contributes to national weakness. Thus, both India and Pakistan have an incentive to curb a confrontation that is damaging to both of them. However, as of now, that incentive may be offset by the incentives that some politically powerful groups in the two countries have for sustaining the conflict.

State-Level Factors

A powerful source of hostility between India and Pakistan is the problem of national identity. Both countries have experienced insecurity and turbulence in the post-independence period. Pakistan has lost its eastern half, while India has faced recurrent secessionist movements in Kashmir, Punjab, Nagaland, and elsewhere. The dispute over Kashmir is symbolic of the problem of weak identity. As such, it is the most serious (but not, as noted above, the only) obstacle to a rapprochement. Pakistanis believe that a Muslim-majority state must be theirs, while Indians insist that a Muslim-majority state underscores the idea of a heterogeneous India. Both fear a "domino" effect: the loss of Kashmir might generate unstoppable centrifugal forces.

The intractability of the problem is also due to other factors. A radical break from past policies requires a strong government. Neither India nor Pakistan has that kind of government or seems likely to in the near future. Since the 1990s, Indian politics has been more fragmented than ever before, and all governments have been formed by means of inter-party alliances. Coalition governments are vulnerable to attack from opposition parties, and indeed from their own members, if they attempt anything more than symbolic and marginal concessions. For Pakistan, the situation is equally difficult. Though military-dominated governments may appear to be less vulnerable to populist pressures relating to electoral politics, they too are vulnerable to such pressures. Non-democratic elites are prone to make up for their shaky legitimacy by resorting to populist nationalist appeals. This was the case with General Zia ul Haq, and is so with General Pervez Musharraf.

Both societies are susceptible to right-wing pressures that limit the scope for governments to move sharply away from existing policies. In India, there is considerable pressure from the Hindu right wing, notably the "Sangh Parivar" (the Rashtriya Swayamsevak Sangh and its numerous affiliates, such as the Vishwa Hindu Parishad), to which the Bharatiya Janatha party (BJP) is closely linked. The BJP itself, having set in motion a peace process, has indicated that the Congress will be unable to do likewise because "Hindus will not trust it."[14] In Pakistan, religious extremism is strong, nurtured by a high degree of social and political instability.[15] Such pressures, which governments in both countries can only ignore at their own risk, are likely to remain for some time to come. They reflect uneven processes of social and economic change occurring as part of the twin processes of industrialisation and globalisation in both societies. Additionally, the Army in Pakistan has a strong stake in continuing tensions with India since this justifies its dominant role in national politics. An Indo-Pakistani entente would in all probability allow critics to question this dominance much more than has been the case.

Do economic interests count for much? There is certainly a case for improving India-Pakistan relations on economic grounds. While regular trade is marginal, informal trade – by means of smuggling or through third countries – is valued at about $ 1 to 2 billion.[16] A more liberal bilateral trade regime would certainly enhance trade by lowering costs, but is unlikely to increase trade massively. A peace dividend would almost certainly be large with respect to the flow of gas through Pakistan from Iran and Central Asia. Politics, however, remains the chief obstacle to enhanced economic interaction. Pakistan, yet to give India most-favoured-nation status, is apprehensive of Indian economic domination. India, likewise, is reluctant to agree on a gas pipeline through Pakistan for fear of becoming dependent on the latter. From the Indian standpoint, even if relations with Pakistan were to improve dramatically, the risk of terrorist disruption of gas supplies would still be problematic.

Individual-Level Factors:

While international and national factors are important, actual policy decisions are usually made by specific individuals, in many cases by a specific individual. Thus, while individuals are subject to systemic and state-level constraints, they are arguably "the cutting edge of world politics."[17] Such a position is unexceptionable, since it would not otherwise be possible to regard men and women as purposive creatures. Leadership often plays a determining role in shaping policy. Some leaders may be able to transcend major constraints, others may not. If they can, their personal preferences and their personalities and perceptions are important. No analysis of the Cold War, for instance, can ignore the profound impact of a single individual, Mikhail Gorbachev, in bringing about a revolution in US-Soviet relations. Is there a possibility of a South Asian Gorbachev grasping the nettle with both hands and radically transforming India-Pakistan relations?

A leader able to alter the course of entrenched national policy is a rare phenomenon. Leaders can bring transformation only when there is a substantial policy window, i.e., when social conditions are conducive to change or if there is a major crisis. Gorbachev was able to change the course of Soviet (and world) history only because the Soviet Union was ripe for it. The key question is whether there is such a policy window in South Asia. From the Indian standpoint, the pressure is not very strong: the economy is expanding faster than ever, and military expenditure does not consume a very large proportion of revenues. Moreover, ever since Kargil, Indian leaders have had low confidence in Musharraf, who is held in large part responsible for that traumatic event. Nevertheless, reflecting a personal penchant for compromise in problem-solving, former Prime Minister Vajpayee showed a keen interest in mending fences with Pakistan, first in inviting President Musharraf to Agra in 2001, and then, following the long confrontation in 2001-02, once again offering an olive branch to Pakistan in 2003.

The return of the Congress Party to power following the 2004 elections creates an element of uncertainty about the role of Indian leadership in fashioning the course of India-Pakistan relations. It is unlikely that the new leadership will be in a position to attempt a great leap forward. Prime minister Manmohan Singh of the Congress-led coalition that took power in 2004 has pledged to sustain the movement toward improved relations with Pakistan. But he is a leader without a domestic political base of his own, so his ability to make major compromises is very limited. Given the history of opposition to her leadership on the ground of her "foreignness," – not only from the BJP, but also from Nationalist Congress party leader Sharad Pawar, now a cabinet minister in the Singh government – Congress president Sonia Gandhi is likely to be extremely cautious as well.

On the face of it, the challenge is less serious for President Musharraf. Yet, it is not at all clear whether the potential gains from a drastic turn in India-Pakistan relations outweigh its potential domestic fallout. The Army and right-wing opinion together form a substantial obstacle. The key question is whether he (or his successor) has the inclination and the political will to look beyond the unrealistic prospect of a resolution to the Kashmir problem and to seek instead a more incremental approach to the lessening of India-Pakistan tensions. The picture is not yet clear in this respect. Ironically, American political and material support allows him a fallback option. Deferring the resolution of the Kashmir dispute will require taking a significant political risk. To encourage this to happen, Indian leaders will have to make such a policy shift domestically marketable for President Musharraf by providing a substantial inducement. Neither side appears likely to have the gumption at this point, though a more favourable context might allow this to happen some time in the future.

Assessing the Prospects for India-Pakistan Relations

The discussion above shows that there are few factors that evoke optimism about the future of India-Pakistan relations. At the systemic level, the rise of a common terrorist threat is by far the most powerful inducement to cooperation. Unlike other favourable factors, such as nuclearization and globalization, it presents a restricted time frame for an appropriate response. Unfortunately, this is offset by the lack of similar incentive for change at the state level, where the effect of most factors is negative rather than positive. That leaves a very small policy window for a leader to exploit. The critical question is whether leaders on either side have the individual capacity to cut the Gordian knot of India-Pakistan relations. To date, there are few indications that provide a basis for optimism. Barring the occurrence of a serious crisis, there does not at present appear to be much scope for a sweeping transformation of India-Pakistan relations. Over time, as the need for change becomes more pressing, and as obstacles to change come to be viewed more critically on both sides, increasing dissonance between the policy environment and existing practice may serve to bring about a "Kuhnian revolution" and a reordering of preferences and policies.

What are the alternatives? There are three: (i) carry on as before, with occasional lurches into crisis; (ii) marginally improve relations but continue with mutual tensions, bickering, and arms racing interspersed with periodic successes in cooperation; and (iii) move decisively toward a partial positive sum game. The last is obviously the most desirable from an impartial point of view. The example of the India-China relationship is illustrative of its benefits. Despite their unresolved border dispute, a history of war and occasional border confrontations, and tensions over the China-Pakistan nexus, this relationship has developed into a relatively warm one over the past two decades. Trade has grown significantly, border tensions between the two forces have been sorted out through negotiations (1986-87, 2003), and border talks have been held on a regular basis. However, the then foreign minister Natwar Singh's suggestion in May 2004 that this model might be emulated by India and Pakistan has been rejected by the latter.[18] This leaves the first two options available, though the third is still possible if conditions improve. If the lessons of their respective failures have been learned by Indian and Pakistani leaders, the inadequacy of the first option to satisfy their interests should rule it out. That leaves the second option as the most likely for the moment, with the possibility of the third still alive, depending on leadership initiatives on both sides. Some room for hope comes from a wider, comparative perspective that compares India's relationships with other states in South Asia.

India and Other SAARC States

In keeping with the realist outlook characteristic of international politics, the power differential between India and its neighbours generates considerable insecurity among the latter.[19] The weak tend to take recourse to typical strategies against the strong. These are: (i) a tendency to minimise relations with the stronger power (which tends to keep trade and cultural relations low); and (ii) a preference for offsetting weakness by inviting external involvement (balance of power games of alliance formation, and the internationalization of disputes). Thus, all South Asian states except Bhutan and Nepal (both of which can access the sea only through India) have attempted till recently to avoid extensive economic relations with India. Several have sought to balance Indian power by drawing closer to extra-regional powers, e.g., Nepal has cultivated China and Sri Lanka has attempted the same with China and the United States. Bangladesh has tried a variation on this by calling for Nepal's involvement in its dispute with India over river waters. Sri Lanka has in the past tried to internationalise the problem of Tamil repatriation by bringing in the United Nations and the Non-Aligned Movement. SAARC itself is often viewed as a small-power response to a great-power neighbour. From the systemic perspective, such strategies are characteristic of weak states attempting to counter a hegemonic power.[20] At the state level, in most cases, vulnerable elites in unstable national polities have found it expedient to try and keep the regional hegemon at arm's length or to demonise it in order to try and consolidate domestic political support. Finally, at the individual level, leaders have not displayed a capacity to undertake significant shifts in policy. Most regional leaders have operated under pressure from opposition groups and have thus found it difficult to transcend the exigencies of domestic politics by developing close relations with the hegemonic power. There is an important exception, which will be discussed shortly.

On its part, India has also tended to display a classic pattern of great power behaviour vis-à-vis its neighbours. It has broadly followed a strategy of preserving the structural status quo by encouraging closer economic and cultural relations with its neighbours and at the same time by resisting outside involvement in the region. And it has insisted on bilateral negotiations over all its disputes with neighbouring countries. Accordingly, it has preferred to view SAARC as a forum for economic and cultural relations, but not for the resolution of political disputes. From time to time, India has pressurised its neighbours, for instance by compelling Sri Lanka to allow Indian intervention in the Tamil problem (1987), and by minimising Nepal's access to Indian ports (1989). It has intervened militarily to spur the creation of Bangladesh (1971), to foil an attempted coup in the Maldives (1988, though this was at the invitation of that country's government), and to protect its interests in Sri Lanka (1987). At the sub-systemic levels of analysis, Indian elites and leaders have shown little interest in softening this pattern. An exception was the United Front government's short-lived Gujral Doctrine (named after Inder Gujral, who was foreign minister under prime minister Deve Gowda, and later premier himself), a brief and inconclusive attempt to do this during the 1990s.

This brief overview of India's relations with its neighbours illustrates an important political reality. Power politics is a primary shaper of inter-state relations. Even if there is no major territorial dispute of the India-Pakistan kind, relationships remain uneasy, sometimes tense. India-Bangladesh relations are a classic example, with relations bedevilled by disagreements over river waters, migration, and cross-border movements of secessionist groups. This tells us something important: that resolution of the Kashmir dispute is not likely to result virtually automatically in the transformation of India-Pakistan relations and the onset of a high degree of bilateral and regional security cooperation. Some combination of systemic and state-level factors will have to create a policy window that a decision-making body or individual will be willing and able to exploit in order to chart a new course in regional security relations. How feasible is this?

Lest this be taken as an entirely pessimistic treatise, the example of Sri Lanka presents room for optimism. Till the early 1990s, Sri Lanka's relationship with India was by and large in conformity with the pattern described above. However, the election of a new president, Chandrika Kumaratunga, in 1994 marked the beginning of a major change in India-Sri Lanka relations. Acknowledging that for geographical and economic reasons and "everything else" India is "the one country that would be justifiably interested in Sri Lanka," Kumaratunga has asserted that "India should play a role proactively" in her country's peace process.[21] India, having burned its fingers in attempting fruitlessly to subdue with military force the secessionist Liberation Tigers of Tamil Eelam (LTTE), has begun low-profile security assistance to the new government. Economic relations expanded rapidly under Kumaratunga's assumption of the presidency. A bilateral Free Trade Agreement was signed in 1998 and took effect in March 2000. Though the accord established only partial free trade, trade shot up. Within a year, Sri Lankan exports to India rose by 138 per cent, and Indian exports to Sri Lanka by 39 per cent. Sri Lanka's import/export ratio improved from 8.6:1 to 4.9: 1, and its import coverage ratio, which measures the extent to which export proceeds cover disbursements on imports, rose significantly from 11.6 per cent in 2001 to 20.23 per cent in 2002.[22]

The vexed issue of Tamils of Indian origin was effectively resolved with the Sri Lankan government's decision in July 2003 to grant citizenship to 168,141 Tamils. In August 2003, Sri Lankan prime minister Ranil Wickremesinghe proposed a bridge between the two countries as a "win-win development that could change the economic map of the region."[23] In October 2003, the two states agreed to begin talks on a Comprehensive Economic Partnership Agreement (CEPA). The two countries also agreed in principle on a defence cooperation agreement. G. L. Peiris, spokesperson for the Sri Lankan cabinet, declared that the CEPA would "diminish the borders between the two countries and put in place a borderless economy."[24]

What brought about the change? It is plain that a change in leadership perception was crucial. An opinion piece by late foreign minister Lakshman Kadirgamar in December 2003 is indicative of the rethinking that took place.[25] Kadirgamar lays down the basis of his country's policy: (i) recognition that security is not military alone, but has a vital economic component; (ii) acknowledgement of interdependence, specifically regional interdependence, in a globalising world; and (iii) acceptance of India's pre-eminent role and "responsibility" in the fostering of regional peace. All these, it must be noted, relate to systemic factors, and yet are at heart a matter of perception. The overall effect of the change in perception is that instead of playing the old balancing game, Sri Lanka has shifted to a bandwagoning approach, which seeks to draw advantage from a closer relationship with a strong neighbour.[26] Such is the case with Canada and Mexico vis-à-vis the United States. Indeed, the same may be said to be the case with respect to India and the United States. A key aspect is the coincidence of important interests. Apart from the gains derived from trade, both Sri Lanka and India have a common security interest in a negotiated end to the Lankan civil war. A common interest of a similar type will enhance the prospects for wider regional cooperation. It is not enough to argue, as some do, that South Asia's states need to work harder at economic cooperation. A security motive, or at least the absence of security problems hindering cooperation, is necessary.

Conclusion

The possibility of extensive South Asian cooperation hinges on the future of the India-Pakistan relationship. This paper has shown that the scope for a transformation of this relationship is limited, though not absent. Barring a severe crisis, such as a nuclear conflict, the scope for positive change would seem to rest on the Kuhnian model of accumulated dissonance, which could provide a policy window for decision makers. Globalisation and terrorism have already produced that dissonance to a significant degree. The key security issue that could bind rather than separate them is the threat from terrorism. The threat is already there. The question is whether it could be the driver of cooperative politics. On the regional scale, the same issue could have a unifying effect. Most states in South Asia face a terrorist threat. The porosity of borders ensures that the phenomenon is not confined to specific states, but spills over from one state to another. To the extent that specific states attempt to use terrorists as instruments for their strategic objectives, the possibility of cooperation is seriously constrained. But the fact remains that radical groups are hard to control beyond a point and have a way of biting the hand that feeds them. Their very existence provides a policy window for security cooperation between India and Pakistan, and among the states of South Asia as a whole. Ironically, the absence of such cooperation makes it difficult to tackle the roots of violent extremism since it hinders economic exchange and growth. Whether national decision makers will be able to recognise this and build a framework of cooperation is the central question. The emergence of a South Asian security community is a long way away. A beginning could be made by cooperating against terrorism.

References

1. Zaglul Haider, "Crises of Regional Cooperation in South Asia," *Security Dialogue*, Vol. 32, no.4, 2001, pp. 423-437.
2. Jakob Gustavsson, "How Should We Study Foreign Policy Change?" *Cooperation and Conflict*, Vol. 34, no.1, 1999, pp. 73-95.
3. Arnold Wolfers, *Discord and Collaboration: Essays on International Politics*, Baltimore, MD: Johns Hopkins Press, 1962, pp. 3-24.
4. Kenneth N. Waltz, *Man, the State and War: A Theoretical Analysis*, New York: Columbia University Press, 1959, esp. pp.1-15.
5. Robert Jervis, *Perception and Misperception in International Politics*, Princeton, NJ: Princeton University Press, 1976, pp.12-31.
6. J. David Singer, "The Level-of-Analysis Problem in International Relations," in Klaus Knorr and Sidney Verba (eds.), *The International System: Theoretical Essays*, Princeton, NJ: Princeton University Press, 1961, p. 90.
7. Thomas S. Kuhn, *The Structure of Scientific Revolutions*, Chicago and London: University of Chicago Press, 1970.
8. Kenneth N. Waltz, *Theory of International Politics*, Lexington, MA: Addison-Wesley, 1979.
9. Rohan Gunaratna, *Inside Al Qaeda: Global Network of Terror*, New York: Columbia University Press, 2002, pp. 208-209.
10. "Musharraf Plot Suspect Arrested," *BBC News*, 19 May 2004 <http://news.bbc.co.uk/2/hi/south_asia/3728937.stm>.
11. "Pakistan Holds Nuclear Scientists," *BBC News*, 25 October 2001 <http://news.bbc.co.uk/1/hi/world/south_asia/1619252.stm>.

12. On Pakistani proliferation, see Leonard Weiss, "Pakistan: It's Deja Vu All over Again," *Bulletin of the Atomic Scientists*, Vol. 60, no. 3, May/June 2004, pp. 52-59.
13. Rajesh M. Basrur and Hasan-Askari Rizvi, "Nuclear Terrorism and South Asia," Occasional Paper, no. 25, Sandia National Laboratories, Albuquerque, NM Cooperative Monitoring Center, February 2003.
14. Siddharth Varadarajan, "BJP May Play the Spoiler in Foreign Affairs," *Times of India*, 15 May 2004.
15. S. V. R. Nasr, "The Rise of Sunni Militancy in Pakistan: The Changing Role of Islamism and the Ulema in Society and Politics," *Modern Asian Studies*, Vol. 34, no.1, January 2000, pp. 139-180.
16. Kavita Sangani and Teresita Schaffer, "India-Pakistan Trade: Creating Constituencies for Peace," *South Asia Monitor*, no.56, 3 March 2003.
17. Robert A. Isaak, *Individuals and World Politics*, North Scituate, MA: Duxbury Press, 1975, p. xi.
18. "Sino-Indian Model Not Applicable to Indo-Pak Relations: Pak," *Hindustan Times*, 30 May 2004.
19. For a more detailed analysis, see Rajesh M. Basrur, *India's External Relations: A Theoretical Analysis*, New Delhi: Commonwealth Publishers, 2000, ch. 3.
20. For a discussion of balancing strategies in South Asia, see Sridhar K. Khatri, "Foreign Policy and Security Perceptions of South Asian Nations," in Sridhar K. Khatri (ed.), *Regional Security in South Asia*, Kathmandu: Centre for Nepal and Asian Studies, Tribhuvan University, 1987, pp. 201-213.
21. Amit Baruah, " 'India Should Play A Proactive Role,' " *Hindu*, 12 April 2003.
22. Joint Study Group on India-Sri Lanka, *Comprehensive Economic Partnership Agreement*, October 2003, p. 13.
23. Jayaraj Sivan, "A Bridge too Misunderstood," *Indian Express*, 1 September 2003. However, opposition from the Indian state of Tamil Nadu appears to have stalled the proposal.
24. V. S. Sambandan, "Pacts with India Not Pre-emptive: Peiris," *Hindu*, 24 October 2003.

25. Lakshman Kadirgamar, "Securing South Asia," *Hindustan Times*, 15 December 2003.
26. On bandwagoning, see Randall L. Schweller, "Bandwagoning for Profit: Bringing the Revisionist State Back In," *International Security*, Vol. 19, no.1, Summer 1994, pp. 72-107.

SECTION-III

SOUTH ASIA: NON TRADITIONAL SECURITY ISSUES

6

Non-Traditional Threats to South Asian Security

V. R. Raghavan

The region's long history, its civilization record, its religions and languages are a great inheritance. All states and their citizens are proud of that record. The present is however different. Is there a single dynamic that encapsulates South Asia? The issues that drive all policies and practices are two. The first is that of conflict. Our region is marked by wide spread, never ending and violent conflict. The conflicts in the region of non-military or non-traditional threats to security. The other dynamic is that of endemic poverty. Large segments of the populations live at levels of poverty where the existential concern of most citizens is not about the next pay check but of the next meal. The combination of poverty and insecurity is the central challenge of South Asia.

If security is, as it should be, the well being of the citizen, there is in South Asia pervasive insecurity. Over the last few years leading newspapers and journals in India have conducted polls before elections. These concerned public perceptions and aspirations. In each one of them national security figured as the least amongst the citizens' concern. This not because the citizen does not care for the subject. He in fact feels that India is militarily secure. There is not going to be a military Invasion. He is confident of his country's territorial security. His insecurity stems from non-military causes like deprivation, economic deprivation and uncertainties, health and education, corruption and political instability. In other words we are one billion insecure Indians living very secure borders.

In South Asia, India is the only country that shares common borders and boundaries (land and maritime) with all the member states. Therefore, the linkages with India are very strong at the societal, community, economic and other levels. India cannot really make a significant mark without South Asia; nor can South Asia do so without a strong relationship with India. In view of this, attempts to curtail the functioning of SAARC, either through bilateral disputes or discouraging trade and other activities, creates serious impediments in the development of South Asia and the region. The former external affairs minister, Yashwant Sinha's views on the subject provide a quantum leap forward on the future vision of South Asia. He avers,

"South Asia is an integral part of our life, and naturally, a secure, peaceful and prosperous South Asia is important for our future. In political, economic and technological terms, India has made impressive strides. Driven by economic reforms, enterprise and an explosion of aspirations of a growing young population. India's economic growth has been on a high trajectory and will likely exceed 7% this year. Yet we recognise that our own progress will be faster and more secure, when our region is bound together in peaceful co-operation, not divided by conflict and confrontation. India's size is an asset that can be leveraged for the benefit of all of India's smaller neighbours. The myth that, because of the asymmetries in our economies, the smaller countries do not benefit from closer economic integration within South Asia must be discarded. India has no desire but to be able to build economic relations aimed at mutual benefit. Beyond economic development, a spirit of friendship and cooperation can create an atmosphere that will help us address other challenges that bedevil our region: political disputes, terrorism, drug trafficking, trafficking in persons, environmental degradation, illegal migration, sharing of resources and regional imbalances in economic development." [1]

Non-Traditional Threats to South Asian Security

One can list a number of factors, which lead to insecurity. However, when examined closely, they can be grouped under five components. These non-traditional threats to security they lend themselves to being grouped into a few broad groups. They are also not exclusive to any one country of South Asia. These are shared by all states and in fact transcend their territorial boundaries. Therefore they can only be tackled by regional cooperation and collaboration. From this perspective security can be viewed as comprising of five components or dimensions of security. They are the economic, environmental, societal, political and military components.

Economic Security

The traditional argument in this field was between the political structure of anarchy and the economic structure of the market forces. However, the economic security dilemma has in fact been one of relative economic growth as a determinant of state power. Certainly in South Asia, the major dilemma currently is of coping with the impact of globalisation on one hand, and of ensuring the economic security of the poor. Economic activity always triggers survival issues in other sectors. Even economic success can lead to security crisis in some parts of the societal sector. The security of economic resources and supply, fears of economic losers in the global markets, the security dimensions of drugs and weapons linkages etc, form part of both economics of security and security of economics.

The two most cited reasons for investors' lack of interest in South Asia are the political turbulence of the region, and its, primitive infrastructure. What South Asia needs is an economic strategy that will insulate its economic development from its politics. Most of the efforts of the member countries in SAARC have been directed towards creating a South Asian Free Trade Area (SAFTA). It has been assumed that a free trade area along the lines of ASEAN, would offer a large market for potential investors, and increase the attractiveness of the area as a whole to foreign investors. In reality however, movement towards SAPTA has been very slow and most of the tariff concessions have been offered unilaterally by India. South Asia could in fact enhance economic security through joint development of economic infrastructure of the region to make it a more attractive destination for foreign direct investment.[2]

Societal Security

Societal security is closely related to but quite clearly distinct from political and military security. The boundaries of the state and society are not always coterminous in South Asia. The notion of societal identity of large self-sustaining segments of society and the smaller groups and ethnic segments, have serious security dimensions. South Asian states have been affected by this both on the intra-state and inter-state thresholds. The issues of migrations, social and ethnic cleansing, economic competition amongst societal groups and of societal conflicts are important to the societal security of the countries of South Asia. "The impact of global communication in the larger backdrop of globalisation, has significantly altered traditional cultures and the sense of community in the region. This has bred social tensions of huge proportions, resulting in conflict in some instances. The resultant cultural atavism may be the source of great political violence. Every country in South Asia has experienced the rise of a regressive band of cultural politics in an age when traditional institutions and ways of life are threatened by social and economic change. The growth of fundamentalism, not least, majority fundamentalism, aimed at imaginary threats from minority groups, has been ubiquitous."[3] Importantly, therefore, societal security in South Asia should be about the sustainability, within acceptable conditions for evolution, of traditional patterns of language, culture, associations, religious and national identity as well as customs.

Environmental Security

The relationship between national security issues and environmental issues may not seem readily apparent, and indeed security experts have often viewed national security as a concept separate from other disciplines such as economics, ecology or development. However, in the new era of global security, environmental and national security issues are inextricably linked and environmental security is seen as an important aspect of the comprehensive security discourse. Scarcity interacts with such factors as the character of the economic system, levels of education, ethnic cleavages, class divisions, technological and factors, varying according to context, determine if environmental scarcity will produce harmful intermediate social effects, such as poverty and migrations. Contextual factors also influence the ultimate potential for instability or violence in a society, infrastructural capacity and the legitimacy of the political regime.

Some describe this sector as the ultimate security. Certainly for a state like the Maldives a change in environment e.g. rises in global temperatures would mean the extinction of the state itself. Global warming has had the effect of rising sea levels, which in turn directly impacts upon the existence of islands. Such an impact hinders the livelihoods of people residing in these areas, often resulting in a group of people known as *environmental refugees.* The extent of environmental degradation in the mangroves of the Sunderban Delta has been accentuated over time, forcing states and the international community to take cognizance of the plight of these refugees and formulate adaptation mechanisms.

On the other hand, soil erosion, forest cover depletion and loss of agricultural land has led to migration of populations across borders in South Asia. This has heightened security risks and brought about responses from state players on the military dimension. What are essentially human security issues have thus become securitised. There are two agendas, which drive environmental security sector. The scientific agenda is part of the scientific and non-governmental set of activities. The second is the political agenda, which forms part of the governmental and inter-governmental domain. They often overlap in public debates but the security aspect or the sector is always dealt with by the state as its preserve. It is also dealt without regard to the impact of a securitised response on other sectors of security. The issues involved in the environmental sector are numerous, e.g.; ecosystem disruption, energy problems, population issues, food-related problems, economic issues of unsustainable modes of production and civil strife related to environmental issues. The fallout of each of these sub-themes is felt in the security response that the state generates, through its power to determine which interest group to support.

Military Security

The significant change in military security today lies in the arena of asymmetric warfare. Threats of armed attacks against the state and its citizens are more likely to from non-state actors. The other word for this threat is international terrorism. This new phenomena, also called the fourth generation warfare, requires greater cooperation between the security establishments of the region's states. The shift from adversarial to collaborative military effort in the face of the new threat requires a new vision and initiative.

Political Security

Threats from the political -ideological factors, security against supra national integration, threats to international society and law and order from fundamental forces, form part of this sector. They need to be examined in their local, regional and global security dimensions. Is there a possibility in South Asia of such threats getting out of hand and becoming a security risk of high order? Can regional mobilisation take place against the threats of a state's destabilisation through political subversion? The role of the military in affording or denying political security to the people is also an area that deserves to be explored. There is also the question of states and nations. There people who call themselves nations, e.g. the Chechens who want a state of their own. The Tamils in Sri Lanka are in a similar category. There are other examples in South Asia and some of them within Andhra Pradesh (India). On the other hand there are states who have not been able to become nations. The question of the state making and nationalities within states is an important dimension of South Asian dynamic.

Conclusion

In the final analysis, security in South Asia should be viewed through a new perspective where "the key argument is that ultimately state security is for individual security. In the end, the state is the provider of security for its citizens; it is a means to security, and its security cannot be the end of security."[4] The Indian former prime minister Vajpayee, in his speech in Islamabad, rightly pointed out that "We have to change South Asia's image and standing in the world. We must make the bold transition from mistrust to trust, from discord to concord and from tension to peace. ...We have the potential, talent and resources to make South Asia an economic powerhouse of the world. We only need the necessary political will to make this happen. This is the agenda which we leaders of SAARC should strive to advance in the coming years."[5]

These shared components of security require the states of South Asian region to cooperate. Author believes that a new perception of security, which places a premium on human security, on the comprehensive nature of security, and on non-traditional threats to security will help in reconstructing South Asia.

References

1. "After the SAARC Summit: Vision for South Asia", speech by Yashwant Sinha, external affairs minister of India at Woodrow Wilson Centre, Washington D.C., 20 January 2004.
2. Prem Shankar Jha, "Economic Dimensions of South Asian Security", in *Comprehensive Security: Perspective from India's Regional",* New Delhi: Delhi Policy Group, 2001.
3. Rajesh M. Basrur, "Human Security: The State and Democracy in a Globalising World", in *Comprehensive Security, ibid.*
4. *Ibid.*
5. Prime minister Atal Behari Vajpayee's statement at the 12th SAARC Summit on 3 January 2004, see http://meaindia.nic.in/speech/2004/04ss01.html.

7

Energy Security Scenario in South Asia

Anant V Naik

Energy Cooperation in the South Asian region is slowly transforming from concept to reality fuelled by the need, practicability, security aspects and for sustaining development in the region, albeit in fits and surges and on case to case basis.

There are various examples of regional cooperation like the ASEAN, BIMSTEC and SAARC in the Asian region working towards economic cooperation. Another example of note is of the European Union. The underlining objective of these cooperations is promoting socio-economic development and creating an enabling environment for mutually beneficial ties in various fields between the member companies. The initial phase in most of the cases was the most difficult one to start with.

For all that is of concern and matter, there is a strong linkage between energy and economy. A critical input to the economic development is assured, adequate and available supply of energy, which further emphasizes the need for regional cooperation, particularly in the South Asian context, which contains 1.3 billion people –more than one-fifth of the world's population – and is experiencing rapid energy demand growth.

The region is endowed with untapped energy resources but their development, efficient distribution and utilization will require cooperation and trade/exchange amongst the countries in this region, thus improving access to energy thereby contributing to economic growth by way of balancing the regional demand and supply of various energy sources.

The paper attempts to correlate the various facts, findings and views expressed at different forums and of studies on the South Asian region and broadly outlining the facets of energy cooperation within the region.

Overview

Overall, South Asia is in a period of transition as it strives to implement effective economic, political, social and legal structures to support sustained growth.

The South Asian region namely, Bangladesh, Bhutan, India, the Maldives, Nepal, Pakistan, and Sri Lanka has a large population (more than one-fifth of the world total) which continues to grow rapidly. At the same time, despite rapid economic growth during the 1990s, the region has among the lowest per capita incomes in the world. For the year 2005, as per Asian Development Bank (ADB) estimates the growth rate in Gross Domestic Product (GDP) would be 7.6 per cent for India, 5.8 per cent for Pakistan, about 5.5 per cent for Sri Lanka, six per cent for Bangladesh, Bhutan around eight per cent, Nepal five per cent and near about 5.5 per cent for the Maldives.

The South Asian countries would need capital and energy to propel this economic growth and improve the quality of life in an environmentally responsible manner. Energy is the basic building block for socio-economic development. Future economic growth crucially depends on the long-term adequate availability of energy from sources that are accessible, socially acceptable and environmental friendly.

There is a need to focus on and promote the concept of an integrated South Asia energy market by establishing a networking mechanism through which public and private sector stakeholders can influence regional energy policy, consumption pattern and sectoral reform throughout South Asia. The integration of the energy markets would also provide energy security to a large extent.

It is required to build a model to facilitate viable energy projects and other aspects, which could include :

- creating comprehensive energy database and analysis on energy production, consumption, export, import, prices, demand forecasting and elasticity values for the development of regional energy market;
- establishing uniform energy codes, technical specifications and standards for all the countries in this region for smooth regional energy trade and
- public awareness program regarding the benefits of regional energy cooperation and cross border sales of electricity, oil and natural gas.

Energy Overview

The major issue facing South Asian nations today is rapidly rising energy demand with increasingly inadequate energy supplies. Most of South Asia is grappling with energy shortfalls and it is realized by almost all the governments that improving the supply of energy in general and electricity in particular has to be on priority.

South Asia has seen rapid increases in energy consumption in recent years. The Energy Information Administration (EIA) estimates of South Asia's primary energy consumption 'commercial' show an increase of nearly fifty nine per cent between 1991 and 2001. For the year 2001, South Asia accounted for approximately 3.8 per cent of world commercial energy consumption, up from 2.8 per cent in 1991. Despite rapid growth in energy demand, South Asia continues to average 443 kg of Oil Equivalent which is amongst the lowest per capita energy consumption in the world – the world average being 1692 Kg of Oil Equivalent. At the same time in terms of energy consumption per unit of GDP it is one of the highest.

Discounting 'non-commercial' sources of energy South Asia's commercial energy mix in 2001 was forty three per cent Coal, thirty six per cent Petroleum, thirteen per cent Natural Gas, seven per cent Hydroelectricity, two per cent Nuclear and 0.1% "Other" (Table 1). Within the region there are significant variations. India relied more on coal (about 51%) though in recent years natural gas has been growing in importance as a source of energy especially for use in power generation, fertilizer and petrochemical production. While Bangladesh's energy mix is dominated by Natural Gas (67%), Sri Lanka and the Maldives are dependent more or less solely on petroleum (83% and 100% respectively). Pakistan's energy mix is seen diversified among petroleum (43%), natural gas (41%), and hydroelectricity (12%) and Nepal and Bhutan have the highest shares of hydroelectric power in their energy consumption mix.

For this, the countries of South Asia are looking towards diversifying traditional energy supply sources, expanding the use of indigenous energy resources, promoting additional foreign investment for energy infrastructure development, improving energy efficiency, reforming and privatizing energy sectors, and promoting and expanding regional energy trade and investment.

Another important implication of rising energy demand in South Asia is its impact on the region's level of carbon emissions. As of 2001, the South Asian region accounted for 4.5% of global carbon emissions. However, with the demand for coal in India projected to increase rapidly in the coming years and the recent introduction of coal into the fuel mix of other countries, there is likelihood of a significant increase in regional emissions in the future. Further understanding of the Climate Change and its implications for South Asia is discussed later in the paper without going into the specifics.

Rapidly growing power demand coupled with inadequate power supplies is a challenge throughout the region. Electricity shortages have acted as constraint on economic growth. Many countries in the region are looking at private sector investment, both domestic and foreign, to increase power generation capacity in the coming years. Operation of the Utilities and the models adopted which give revenues covering the costs of supply will largely influence the amount and mode of investments to come in.

The South Asian countries also depend on biomass fuels in a major way. But with the growing levels of per capita energy consumption, other sources of energy will have to be exploited and this requires coordinated action by all the member countries.

Table 1

Energy Consumption and Carbon Dioxide Emissions in South Asian Countries, 2001

	Commercial Energy Consumption [1]							*Carbon Dioxide Emissions* [3] *(Million metric tons of carbon)*
	Total (Quadrillion Btu)	*Petroleum*	*Natural Gas*	*Coal*	*Nuclear*	*Hydro electric*	*Other* [2]	
Bangladesh	0.51	29%	67%	2%	0%	2%	0%	8.1
Bhutan	0.01	26%	0%	18%	0%	56%	0%	0.07
India	12.80	34%	6%	51%	2%	6%	0.1%	251.3
Maldives	0.007	100%	0%	0%	0%	0%	0%	0.1
Nepal	0.06	57%	0%	18%	0%	27%	0%	0.9
Pakistan	1.87	43%	41%	5%	1%	11%	0%	29.1
Sri Lanka	0.19	83%	0%	0%	0%	17%	0%	3.1
Total	15.45	36%	13%	43%	2%	7%	0.1%	292.7

1. *Note: Does NOT include such "non-commercial" energy sources as animal waste, wood, and other biomass, which account for more than half of South Asia's total final energy consumption.*
2. *Other includes consumption of wind electric power for India and net imports of electricity for India and Nepal. Other does NOT include biomass or other "noncommercial" sources of energy.*
3. *Includes carbon dioxide emissions from the consumption of petroleum, natural gas, and coal, and from the flaring of natural gas. Tons of carbon can be converted to tons of carbon dioxide gas by multiplying by 3.667.*

Note: Percentages may not add to 100% because of independent rounding.

Source: Energy Information Administration, International Energy Database, August 2003.

For instance, the hydroelectricity potential can be fully utilized if an integrated market is developed for the region. Similarly, with the recent gas discoveries and its usage growing in number of applications, providing access to larger populace is an alternate and viable means. However, gas pipelines although economical require transit through more than one country to take advantage of the economies of scale.

The cooperation amongst the south Asian countries for optimal exploitation and utilization of available resources can lead to the overall development of the region. For countries like Nepal and Bhutan, regional energy cooperation is quite beneficial, as their domestic demand is limited while the production potential enormous.

Geographically, all the countries barring Sri Lanka and the Maldives are on land mass, making it all the more convenient for having cross country pipelines and power grids. The region has the requisite technical capabilities and manpower required to establish such grids when required.

Economically - India at the hub of the region could serve as the main market with its huge energy demand and act as a transient market exchange for other countries of the region.

Such a network of electricity grid and pipelines will increase energy security in the region, reduce cost of generation and fuel transportation, increase grid efficiency and help in the more efficient harnessing of energy resources.

Potential

While transforming the concept of regional energy cooperation into reality, it has to be realized that all the countries have different available resources, they are not equal in size and are at varying stages of economic development.

However, an integrated approach does provide a scope for mutual benefits to all the countries in the region. A look at the resource potential gives an idea of the possibilities available.

Growing demand for transportation fuels and increased industrial power demand has been the major factor behind the growth in South Asian oil consumption in recent years. South Asia has reserves of about 5.8 billion barrels of oil, around 0.5% of the world supply, where as the energy mix pattern shows the importance of crude / petroleum for the regional countries and how much they rely on imports. In the coming years too, the need and dependency on oil imports will remain high.

As per International Energy Agency (IEA), the developing regions will account for 29 mb/d of the 45-mb/d increase in global oil demand between 2000 and 2030. In particular, oil demand in India will more than double, to 5.6 mb/d. A significant increase can be expected in the region too.

The Middle East has been and is expected to remain the primary source of South Asian oil imports though countries of the region have started looking for other alternate sources or diversifying the sourcing options.

At present, South Asia consumes all the natural gas produced domestically. Natural gas is seen as playing an important part in the power fuel basket plus as a means of diversifying away from expensive oil imports, substituting petrol and diesel by CNG/ LPG and greater domestic usage through new technology home appliances.

At the end of 2002 (Table 2), South Asia's proven natural gas reserves were estimated at 63.9 trillion cubic feet (Tcf) with potential of further large resources though not proven. India and Pakistan have roughly equal reserves of 27 Tcf, while the only other South Asian country with reserves, Bangladesh contains approximately 11 Tcf and is estimated to have much larger undiscovered reserves. If these estimates prove to be correct, Bangladesh could become a major gas producer as well as supplier in future mainly to the vast Indian market.

As per the long-term projections of increasing gas demand for South Asia, the region will require significant increases in production and imports. Gas imports would also require construction of infrastructure, either cross-border pipelines or liquefied natural gas (LNG) facilities and domestic gas pipeline infrastructure, which otherwise would limit the usage of gas both within the countries and in the region.

Table 2

Energy Supply Indicators -- South Asian Countries								
	Fossil Fuel Proved Reserves			Fossil Fuel Production				
	Crude Oil, 1/1/03 (Million barrels)	Dry Natural Gas, 1/1/03 (Trillion cubic feet)	Coal, 2003 (Billion short tons)	Petroleum, 2001[1] (Thousand barrels per day)	Dry Natural Gas, 2001 (Trillion cubic feet)	Coal, 2000 (Million short tons)	Electric Generating Capacity, 2001 (Million kilowatts)	Crude Oil Refining Capacity, 1/1/03 (Thousand barrels per day)
Bangladesh	57	10.6	0	4	0.35	0	3.6	33
Bhutan	0	0	0	0	0	0	0.43	0
India	5,367	26.9	93	736	0.80	356.6	111.8	2,135
Maldives	0	0	0	0	0	0	0.25	0
Nepal	0	0	0	0	0	0.01	0.39	0
Pakistan	310	26.4	2.4	64	0.83	4.2	17.7	234
Sri Lanka	0	0	0	0	0	0	1.6	48
Total	5,734	63.9	95.4	804	1.98	350.9	135.8	2,450

1. *Includes crude oil, natural gas plant liquids, other liquids, and refinery processing gain.*

Sources: Crude Oil and Natural Gas Reserves: PennWell Publishing Co., Oil & Gas Journal, 12/23/02. Crude Oil Refining Capacity: PennWell Publishing Co., Oil & Gas Journal, 12/23/02. All Other Data: Energy Information Administration, International Energy Database, August 2003.

South Asia's coal reserves amount to approximately 9% of the world total and while coal accounts for 43% of South Asia's energy consumption, nearly all is produced and consumed by India. The coal reserves of India could serve as base load for power generation in the region.

The South Asian region continues to rely heavily on biomass for residential energy consumption particularly, in rural areas. For instance, Woodfuel is the only important indigenous source of energy for the residential sector in the Maldives, although LPG is now being increasingly used. As per IEA, biomass accounted for about 80% of residential energy consumption in 2000. Given that biomass is primarily used for cooking and heating, the availability of electricity access, used primarily for lighting, is not expected to have a significant affect on biomass use in the future. The IEA projects that biomass use will still account for seventy per cent of residential energy consumption in 2030.

Electricity demand in most of the countries in the region is currently outstripping supply and the region as a whole is characterized by chronic electricity shortages. The main reasons being low plant load factor and generating capacity, poor quality coal, transmission loss and theft. Meeting future electricity demand promises to pose a major challenge for South Asia and as mentioned earlier a regional grid with various supply options could go a long way in tackling this issue.

Scope

The region is endowed with abundant sources of energy like water, forests, coal and gas. The mountainous terrains of India, Bhutan, Pakistan and Nepal have large hydropower potential. Although limited exchange of electricity already occurs between Nepal, Bhutan and India, multilateral cooperation to develop and exchange energy resources will have far-reaching economic and security benefits.

Bangladesh has abundant reserves of gas and can trade in gas with India, which has a huge consumption demand. An extension could be supply of Myanmar Gas to India through Bangladesh giving it revenues as transit charges.

More hydropower export from Bhutan and Nepal to India, Pakistan and Bangladesh could be there with increasing energy demand in these countries.

India is rich in coal reserves and has a well-developed coal industry, which can be used to meet the base load demand for power in the region. This would make gas free for meeting the peak load demands in Pakistan and Bangladesh, working to the mutual advantage of all three countries. Pakistan's increased power generating capacity makes it possible to supply over 3000 MW power to India as well.

Sri Lanka can optimize power supply through a common power grid owing to its links with South India. Similarly, a common grid could lower the transportation costs for supplying natural gas by pipelines and Pakistan could serve as the gateway for supplying natural gas from Iran and Central Asia and as mentioned earlier Bangladesh to the North Eastern parts of India extending to Northern India.

Increasingly the petroleum product cooperation or market is already taking place in the region. India's oil companies have a presence in Sri Lanka. Talks are underway for trade arrangements with Bangladesh, Myanmar and Pakistan. In case of Pakistan the two way proposed trade with India (Gas from/through and Product to) serves as a further security assurance. It could be applicable for other countries in the region and this would ensure greater trust and acceptability.

Addressing the issue of energy through non conventional sources is another major aspect, which needs to be looked into. As is known most of the region has population in the rural areas, many of which may not have easy access to the conventional modes of energy or electricity to be more precise. The problem of lack of access to electricity in rural areas has serious ramifications. First, it limits the productivity of economic activities for a majority of rural households. Second, it forces the use of energy in its least convenient forms e.g. charcoal, crop residues, cow dung and usually in ways that are damaging to both human health and environment. Third, it encourages the pace of migration from rural areas to urban areas and has led to problems like urban congestion.

The region is abundant with renewable energy sources like wind, sun, biomass etc, which could be used for sustaining the rural energy needs in a more efficient manner. The limitations of technology, funding and trained manpower required are slowly being resolved and an integrated approach in the region can work towards promoting the usage and addressing the need for providing energy to the rural masses. These stand-alone self-sustaining units could compliment the national grids and share the load.

Improving the use of renewable energy resources has the advantage of minimal negative environmental impacts as well. There are success stories of rural energy supply, usage of renewable energy sources in terms of technology and innovation for e.g. in Sri Lanka, India and Bangladesh. These need to be shared, further developed and complimented.

For countries like Myanmar, Sri Lanka and the Andaman Nicobar Islands of India, the Ocean Thermal Energy Conversion (OTEC) is an energy technology that may prove of immense potential in the long term or far future. Briefly, OTEC system uses the ocean's natural thermal gradient to produce a significant amount of power, with little impact on the environment. The oceans thus have the potential to help us produce electric power. The details are not spelt here, as it will need proper expert evaluation and understanding for the region, however, is being flagged as a potential source and area of cooperation between the regional countries.

Efficient use of available resources has become important to meet the regional energy requirements. Country specific energy efficient systems and norms have been developed by few in the region. Efforts in this area on facilitating the transfer of knowledge, experience and best practices should be made throughout the region.

Regional Energy Development and Clean Development Mechanism

The dominant source of global CO_2 emissions is from the energy sector accounting to nearly half of the global warming in the past and likely to happen in future. Energy production and use is the single largest anthropogenic source of Green House Gases (GHGs). Energy from fossil fuels consumed for industrial, commercial, residential, transportation, and other purposes result in large emissions of CO_2. A small amount of Methane emissions also takes place from coal mining and the venting of natural gas.

From the global perspective, climate change is of concern for Asia because although the industrialized nations have so far been largely responsible for the present build-up of GHG in the atmosphere, Asia is now likely to be an increasing contributor to worldwide anthropogenic GHG emissions as its energy consumption goes up in line with estimated / required economic development. At the same time there is a debate as to why developing countries of the region should be held responsible at their development stage for a problem, which has largely been a result of the activities of the West.

South Asia, being a region of huge population, poverty a major concern, with capacity and resource constraints, will be additionally stressed due to climate change in this region. More than 50-70% of the total population of this region live in villages and eradication of poverty, improved quality of life and creating sustainable livelihoods would be the foremost priority for the region without impacting the environment.

The Clean Development Mechanism (CDM) of the Kyoto Protocol can provide an opportunity to further catalyse the development process in this region. There is a need to understand impacts and vulnerability of climate change in this region and integrating these into the country's response strategies.

Capacity building, training, taking up feasibility study on CDM, knowledge building, information generation and institutional strengthening both at the government level and in the business sector are few of the areas that need to be targeted.

A Regional Power Grid which enables hydro-power available in some of the South Asian countries such as Nepal and Bhutan to be shared with other countries in South Asia could help in bringing down the carbon content of the grid in each of these countries.

CDM has the potential to bring about significant benefits to developing countries by way of carbon credits etc. Therefore, there is a need to promote CDM projects, leading to the emergence of new opportunities for small-scale CDM projects that can be bundled together, even across national boundaries in the South Asian region.

Bangladesh, India, Pakistan, Maldives, Nepal, Bhutan and Sri Lanka are party to the United Nations Framework Convention on Climate Change and it needs to be explored whether the countries of South Asia can tackle the carbon emissions together and benefit from the CDM.

Conclusion

As is in most of the regional groupings, the need for having a common understood goal, target and plan is a must, which has to be driven in an integrated manner with trust and commitment. Strong Political will and economic considerations are paramount for the success of this concept.

While arguments could be made that local domestic utilization of available resources and self sufficiency in energy management is the most desirable situation the same may not be possible in view of the large increase in energy demand envisaged. Further, for few countries in the region, the potential benefits arising out of energy markets may be restricted due to the limitations of the domestic economy.

Another concern expressed is with regard to the entry of multinationals and corporate leading to decrease in sovereign control and security implications. These could effectively be addressed by strategic planning. The multinationals and corporate are required to infuse investments and newer technologies and to some extent bring in greater competition, better utilization and efficiency and would like to see reasonable returns.

A characteristic of the South Asian region is the rural and poor population. The idea is to ensure that energy cooperation and arising economic benefits help in poverty alleviation and overall betterment of the lives of the people living in this region. This calls for an integrated approach of rural development, where overall development of a village is targeted with affordable energy supply as the core activity and several other supporting / subsidiary activities.

The aim of regional cooperation is also to address a variety of issues such as human development, technology access and environmental sustainability together with the main objective of energy accessibility.

Creating and using the available forums like SAARC, Chambers of Commerce, Industry bodies like CII, Institutes like SAREC apart from the government would be helpful in having an industry-institute-government dialogue to better understand and promote the concept.

Number of bodies like the USAID, UNDP and a host of NGOs are working towards the development of the region. Experts, academicians and environmentalists would be all the more involved if the real gains and plans are clearly spelt out. The issues concerning manpower training, development of design and technologies, institutional mechanisms could be worked out through them.

Concerns that need attention in the regional energy cooperation are many. These include providing reliable, affordable and equitable service, curbing the detrimental effects of global warming, sustainable development, formulating an energy policy and improving public awareness and giving the region an inherent energy security.

Looking at the above aspects, individual countries in this region need to adopt certain measures to create an environment for cross border energy cooperation. The guidelines could include:

- Accelerating reform and restructuring of energy sector after taking into consideration the structure and condition of the economy and political institutions of the respective countries;
- A number of major barriers and prejudices need to be overcome, which require firm commitments and bold decisions from each government in the region;
- Creating enabling environment to allow and encourage private sector participation;

- Establishment of market determined prices for energy. It is critical if financing is to be made available to maintain facilities, establish new capacity in the energy sector;
- Market determined energy pricing would significantly restructure the energy consumption basket towards a clean and efficient energy mix;
- In the reform process, the issue of dealing with marginal consumers, who really do not have the ability to afford energy at its economic cost, should not be overlooked. However, no investor would be willing to take over the burden of such consumers without any compensation guarantee from government. In this regard, it is extremely important to identify the consumers, who really need the support. It is also required to put in place proper mechanisms to support subsidies if unavoidable;
- Strengthening of standard-setting organisations in the region, operation and harmonisation of standards;
- Joint R&D, consultancy and HRD activities and sharing of mutual experiences;
- Stable fuel policy based solely on economic rationale;
- Integrated aligned reforms in all segments of the energy chain i.e Power, Coal, Hydrocarbons and Renewables;
- Legally enforceable transportation and trade agreements;
- Proper groundwork like asset valuation, demand forecasting, consumer profile before energy companies are allowed to operate. The contract between the government and private developers must be mutually honoured and
- Well-established institutional framework consisting of regulatory agencies, the rules and regulations of the sector and policy guidelines.

Emphasis should also be given on the environmental impact assessment for all energy forms.

8

Maritime Issues in South Asia

A. Subramanyam Raju

India has maritime borders with all unlike any other country in South Asia. Sri Lanka has maritime boundary with India and Maldives, whereas Pakistan and Bangladesh have borders with only India. Sri Lanka and India delimited their maritime boundary by signing two agreements in 1974 and 1976. India has come to an understanding with Pakistan and Bangladesh on some of the maritime issues. However, it signed no bilateral agreement with either Bangladesh or Pakistan to settle its boundary.

The paper focuses on examining India's maritime relations with Sri Lanka on maritime boundary, problems of fishermen, threat from sea tigers and construction of a bridge between India and Sri Lanka; maritime boundary dispute and the problems of the fishermen of India and Pakistan; and maritime dispute between India and Bangladesh. Finally the paper discusses joint initiatives towards regional maritime security management in the sea.

1. India and Sri Lanka

The island state of Sri Lanka barely thirty kilometers away from India's southern coastal tip. The maritime boundary of India and Sri Lanka is divided at through three different points in different seas: the Bay of Bengal in the north, the Palk Straits in the middle and the Gulf of Mannar in the South. The maximum distance between these two countries in the Palk Straits is about 45 km and the minimum distance is around 16 km between Dhanushkodi on the Indian side and Thalaimannar on the Sri Lankan coast. They do not have Exclusive Economic Zone (EEZ) in the area. They have rights over 12 to 22 km of water. Crossing that area means crossing the international boundary line rather than the EEZ. The coast of both the countries is larger in the Bay of Bengal and in the Gulf of Mannar. The Palk Straits is shallow waters and its depth is not beyond fifty meters. at any point. In the south the bay is narrower and the Adam's bridge which connects Dhanushkodi and Thalaimannar acts as a barrier to the Gulf of Mannar.

(a) Maritime boundary

India and Sri Lanka signed bilateral agreements on the Boundary in Historic Waters in June 1974 and on the maritime boundary in the Gulf of Mannar and the Bay of Bengal in March 1976. They also signed a Supplementary Agreement in November 1976 on the extension of the maritime boundary between the two countries in the Gulf of Mannar from position 13m to the Trijunction point between India, Sri Lanka and Maldives (point T). Both the countries settled the dispute over the Kachchativu island by 1976 which was there between the two since the British rule.

Kachchativu Island

The British had used Kachchativu island since 1920 as a naval gunnery practice range. The island is one mile long, 300 yards broad and has an area of 285.2 acres. It is a barren, uninhabited place and without drinking water. It is to be noted that the fishermen of India and Sri Lanka had built a catholic church here dedicated to St.Anthony, considered as the guardian of the fishermen. The fishermen and pilgrims of both the countries used to visit the church in March every year for a religious festival, in the belief that St.Anthony would protect them from turbulent seas and inclement weather. People of both countries from northern Sri Lanka and Tamil Nadu used to share their culture and ideas. Historically, the fishermen communities of both countries have similarities. They speak Tamil and continued to have relations for centuries. There was free movement of people before independence and it continued till 1974. After the 1974 and 1976 agreements and the eruption of civil war in Sri Lanka in 1983 the situation changed entirely and the relationship between the people of the two countries underwent a transformation.

After independence, Sri Lanka claimed right over the island. In 1965, it planned to use the island for aerial practice and firing. It requested India not to allow its planes to fly over the area. The Indian government, however, did have some doubts regarding the Zamindari rights over the island. In his speech in the Rajya Sabha in September 1960, Jawahar Lal Nehru, prime minister of India said: "There was a claim on one of the old principal Zamindaris and it was part of the Zamindari. The Zamindari has gone now and I do not know where the matter stands."[1] In the Rajya Sabha, to a question, he replied: " The island is 18 miles east of Pamban. Where Pamban is I do not know." [2] Later prime minister Indira Gandhi said that since both countries had cordial relations, it was not wise to raise voice over the island. She felt that the island was a "sheer rock with no strategic significance."[3] She did not even bother to consult the Tamil Nadu government regarding the island. In 1974 India and Sri Lanka signed an agreement which ensured the sovereign right of Sri Lanka over the disputed island of Kachchativu.

The 1974 agreement

The 1974 agreement has two clauses, which protect a few activities of the Indian fishermen. Article 5 maintains that, "Subject to the foregoing, the Indian fishermen and pilgrims will enjoy access to visit Kachchativu as *hitherto* and will not be required by Sri Lanka to obtain travel documents or Visas for these purposes." Article 6 of the agreement states that, "The vessels of Sri Lanka and India will enjoy each other's Waters such rights as they have enjoyed therein."

The two articles talked only about island's access to fishermen and rights of both the country vessels. Neither Article 5 nor 6 specifically talk about the fishermen's rights near the Island.

However, during the discussions in the Lok Sabha, Swaran Singh, the then minister for external affairs, maintained that the fishing rights of the Indian fishermen were protected and he cited the 1921 agreement, according to which "the Western side of the fishery line was the exclusive fishery right of the Indian citizens and to the east of that was the right of Sri Lanka fishermen. But in spite of that division, the fishermen generally were free to fish even round about Kachchativu and they also used the Kachchativu Island for drying their nets...." On the question of fishermen's rights, Singh continued, "although Sri Lanka's claim to sovereignty over Kachchativu has been recognized, the traditional rights of Indian fishermen and pilgrims to visit the Island remain unaffected".[4] From this statement, one can understand that India believed that the Indian fishermen have rights to fish around the island.

According to the agreement, the Indian fishermen and pilgrims would continue to enjoy their traditional rights. However, the Sri Lankan government did not subscribe to the Indian government's view. It argued that the agreement did not give any fishing rights but only the rights to dry their fishing nets, to rest and the pilgrims' right to visit the island for religious purposes. The nets would become wet only when fishermen fish in and around the Island. However, now the fishermen are using nylon nets and they do not need to dry their nets. The agreement was drafted in such a way that it can lead to ambiguity.

Sri Lanka maintains that the island belonged to it for centuries. There was a meeting between the officials of Madras Presidency and Ceylone on 24 October 1921 to discuss on the demarcation of the Palk Straits and the Gulf of Mannar. The Ceylonese official, Horsburgh proposed that the delimitation should "follow the median line, subject to an incursion beyond that line so as to include the islet of Kachchativu and three miles to the westward."[5] But due to no clear instructions from the British Indian government, the delegation could not proceed further. They only made it a point that the island was within the Zamindari of Ramnad. At a later date Sri Lanka claimed that the Indian government acknowledged Ceylone's claim over the island. Dinesh Singh, the then minister of state for external affairs, during the discussion on the issue in the Rajya Sabha in May 1956, said that there was a meeting in 1921, in which there was the representative from the government of Madras and they had agreed that while the Zamindari rights of the Raja of Ramnad would continue, the island belonged to Ceylone.[6] It is to be noted here that the views expressed by B.P.Peiris, the then Secretary to the Cabinet of Ceylone, did not consider the island as a part of Sri Lanka:

I remember coming across the problem when I was an Assistant Legal Draftsman. I had to deal with a file for the purpose of verifying some of the boundaries of the northern district. In the process of revising the draft proclamation, I had to trace the history of the boundary back over many years. I remember coming across a proclamation issued, probably in the time of Queen Victoria, in which the Island of Kachchativu is excluded from the northern district as it belonged to the Raja of Ramnad.[7]

Further, a researcher from Sri Lanka, in her thesis mentioned that the demarcation of the island was based on the agreement rather than on the equidistance principle.[8]

The 1976 Agreement

India and Sri Lanka had another agreement on the boundary in the Bay of Bengal and the Gulf of Mannar in 1976. Unlike the earlier agreement this one did not deal with any disputed island. However, it deprived fishing rights for India in the Palk Straits. In an exchange of letters between them in March 1976, the Indian foreign secretary wrote to his Sri Lankan counter part stating that "The fishing vessels and fishermen of India shall not engage in fishing in the historic waters, the territorial sea and the exclusive economic zone of Sri Lanka nor shall the fishing vessels and fishermen of Sri Lanka engage in fishing in the historic waters, territorial sea and the exclusive economic zone of India, without the express permission of Sri Lanka or India, as the case may be..."[9]

Y.B. Chavan, the then minister of external affairs, stated in the Parliament: "Consequent to the signing of the Agreement, there was also an Exchange of Letters...This Exchange of Letters also constitutes an Agreement between the two countries...Both countries have agreed that after the determination of the maritime boundary, fishing vessels and fishermen of one country shall not engage in fishing in the waters of the other..."[10]

While demarcating the maritime boundary with Sri Lanka, India tried to have a trade-off between Kachchativu and the Palk Straits. This resulted in the sacrificing of the fishermen's fishing rights in both the areas. S.P.Jagota, the then secretary, Legal and Treaties Division, said that the boundary line was "adjusted in the Palk Bay in relation to the settlement on the question of the Island of Kachchativu."[11] In the name of good neighbourly relations, India concluded these agreements with Sri Lanka. This can be seen in the annual reports of the ministry of external affairs: "The recent agreement with Sri Lanka on the division of historic waters in the Palk Bay, which has also settled the issue of Kachchativu amicably, is an indication of India's earnestness in evolving a policy of friendship and mutual cooperation with her neighbours."[12]

However, there was opposition to the transfer of ownership of the island to Sri Lanka in the Parliament. Atal Bihari Vajpayee, the then member of Parliament of the Jana Sangh, criticized the Indian government for surrendering its rights by handing over the Kachchativu island. He said that the ceding of the island as another "bhoodan" (donation of land) and "an assault on India's territorial integrity."[13] Mookiah Thevar, All India Forward Bloc leader, felt that the mistake made by Nehru in handing over of Aksai Chin to China had been repeated by his daughter.[14] The issue continued to provoke political leaders in Tamil Nadu for decades. Former chief minister of Tamil Nadu, Jayalalitha maintained that the unfortunate decision in the name of good-neighbourly relations led to the killing of fishermen.[15]

The fact is that the Indian fishermen will not easily give up their livelihood as they have been enjoying that for centuries. In an interview, V. Suryanarayan, an academician, told the author that "the demarcation was not done on the median line (equidistance) on Kachchativu Island". He said that "without historical evidence, 1974 and 1976 agreements were made by both the countries". He felt that the "Indian government should have taken the wishes of Tamil fishermen into consideration".[16] He argued that "It would be foolish to attempt the creation of a 'Berlin wall' in the Palk Straits, for the simple reason that the links between the two regions cannot be severed. They are like 'Siamese Twins', what afflicts one affects the other."[17] The island is very important for Indian fishermen. They used to put up huts and stay there for a week for fishing activities.

However, Indian fishermen are being not allowed to go near the island by the Sri Lankan navy. The Sri Lankan government argues that the island was used for illegal activities and hence it has been preventing the entry of foreign elements on Kachchativu. The Indian government never raised its voice against the Sri Lankan move. The government in New Delhi could not take the problems of the fishermen of Tamil Nadu into consideration in its policy towards Sri Lanka. It adopted a sort of accommodative attitude towards the neighbour.

The fishermen in Rameswaram and Pamban told the author in an interview that they were not bothered about who controlled the island, but were insistent upon the restoration of their old rights to fish around the island.[18] For them, the boundary did not matter, but livelihood was important. In the following section, an attempt is made to examine the problems of coastal fishermen of India and Sri Lanka.

(b) Fishermen Problem

The Indian fishermen have no alternative other than enter the neighbours' waters for fishing as their survival depends on fishing in Sri Lankan waters. Similarly Sri Lankan fishermen cross their boundary and enter Indian and Maldives waters for fishing. Since the distance between Rameswaram and Taliamnnar is about 12 km, it would not be possible to restrict the fishermen crossing into neighbour's waters.

Prawns are available in abundance in the Palk Straits and particularly in the Sri Lankan waters. Indian fishermen cross their waters to catch prawns in the neighbouring waters. In spite of the restrictions imposed by the Indian navy, the Indian fishermen enter the neighbours' waters for fishing. They argue that they do not have any other alternative than this as their survival depends on fishing in Sri Lankan waters.[19]

During the civil war, the Sri Lankan navy was not able to distinguish between the fishing boats and boats involved in the nefarious activities. The Sri Lankan navy, instead of identifying the boats engaged in illegal activities, treated all boats activities as threat to its security and used to fire at them resulting in killing of innocent fishermen. The navy personnel followed a policy of shooting first and questioning later. This is against the UNCLOS-III Art 73, which forbids the imprisonment of fishermen who are found poaching.[20] The Sri Lankan navy personnel argued that they suspected the sailors as being LTTE forces and they couldn't go closer to them for identification because the LTTE cadres may attack their personnel. However, the number of incidents has decreased since 1998.[21] This is because of the Indian navy's persuasion not to kill the people without identifying the fishermen. Sri Lankan navy was never strict in restricting the Indian fishing vessels and that vessels which were captured were not for fisheries violations but due to situation created by the civil war.

Some of the Indian coast guard personnel told the author that the Sri Lankan navy often handed over the fishermen who strayed into Sri Lankan waters to the Indian navy. They said that the Sri Lankan navy was cooperating and the fault lay on the Indian side. When the author asked why they could not prevent the illegal fishing, they replied that they were being instructed not to punish the fishermen who were entering neighbouring waters and they could only give suggestions to them. They suggested that instead of poaching in Sri Lankan waters, the government should encourage the fishermen to fish in and around the Andaman & Nicobar islands, where fish is in abundance.[22]

In 2003, a few fishermen of Tuticorin were arrested by the Sri Lankan navy and put in jail. The author interviewed the families of the affected. During the interview, the wives of the arrested fishermen said that their whole family was dependent on fishing activities: they did not have any other source of income, and since women could not fish, they had to depend solely on their husbands. One woman said, "How can we run our family without earning money? My husband is the only one who is earning and if he does not go for fishing, we will starve to death." Further, she claimed that no one, including the owner of the boat, helped them when their men were arrested. When the owner was asked for an explanation over the issue, his reaction was: "How could I help them when I myself was not able to run my own family?" He said that he invested lakhs of rupees on his boat, and when it was confiscated, he did not have money to get it released.

On the Indian side, the authorities are also arresting the Sri Lankan people who enter Indian waters. Once the fishermen are caught and brought before the authority it is a long procedure to release them. Both the central and state governments are involved in decision-making process: there are different ministries/ departments, i.e. ministry of home affairs, ministry of external affairs, ministry of agriculture and state government departments. Unlike Sri Lanka, in India the prosecution procedure takes longer time.

Foreign fishing vessels that are involved in illegal activities are asked to pay penalty, which is beyond the capacity of almost all the fishermen. In a few cases, courts ordered payment of a fine of Rs. 1,00,000. Apart from the penalty, they may undergo on imprisonment for about six months. The Maritime Zone of India Act of 1981 (MZI) provides for imprisonment not exceeding 3 years, or with fine not exceeding Rs. 15,00,000, or with both if the foreign vessels are found in any area within the territorial waters of India or punishable with fine not exceeding Rs. 10,00,000.[23] This is against UNCLOS-III Art 73, which forbids the imprisonment of fishermen who are found poaching.

The MZI grants punishment to the owner or skipper, not the crew, of any foreign fishing vessel found fishing illegally in Indian waters and the boat and its contents can be confiscated. Till 1999, the government of India did not prosecute foreign fishermen but released them. However, later the problem became complicated when the ministry of agriculture took over matters related to MZI offences.[24]

It is noteworthy to mention here that NGOs are playing a significant role in promoting the welfare of the fishing community in India and Sri Lanka. For instance, Alliance For Release of Innocent Fishermen (ARIF) is sincerely working for the release of fishermen from India and Sri Lanka. The people who are working for release of the fishermen of both countries told the author that they provide information to the affected families about the whereabouts of their kin. They also meet and talk to the authorities of both countries to release the fishermen. The affected fishermen in Tuticorin told the author that only ARIF was concerned about their welfare and they were being informed by ARIF about their kin's whereabouts.

Similarly, in Sri Lanka, there are a number of organizations that are involved in securing the release of arrested Indian fishermen. NGOs, trade unions, fishermen's organizations in Sri Lanka are working for their release. These organizations are more effective. Though the NGOs, in India, are not that influential and effective in securing the release of Sri Lankan fishermen, but they are playing a significant role. The staff of ARIF told the author that the government often gets help from them in dealing with fishermen's issues. In the following section an attempt is made to examine how the sea tigers pose threat to Indian fishermen.

(c) Threat from Sea Tigers

Ever since the civil war broke out in Sri Lanka (1983), the maritime zone between India and Sri Lanka became very turbulent affecting the interests of Indian and Sri Lankan fishermen. Apart from the disturbances caused by the illegal movement of the Tamil groups, there began frequent incidents of smuggling of illicit weapons, drugs, pirate activities and assault on security forces by the sea tigers, belonging to the LTTE. The northern coast of Sri Lanka, Velveltiturai and Mannar district served as the centers for the smuggling activity. On the Indian side, Tuticorn, Pattukotiai, Rameswaram, Tiruchendur, Nagapatnam have figured as the smuggling bases.

The LTTE has always depended mainly on sea-lanes for its war material and for items of civilian use. In the past these items were smuggled form South India (Tamil Nadu). The LTTE has its own navy, considered to be a match for the Sri Lankan navy. The LTTE cadres are controlling some of the areas in the northern part of Sri Lanka. They desire to extend their supremacy over the vital sea-lanes.

Tamil Nadu was considered as a base for their activities. Some of the Indian Tamils are believed to be the sympathizers of the LTTE. However, when the Sri Lankan naval authorities arrest, prosecute, and sometimes even shoot the fishermen from Tamil Nadu, the LTTE has never shown any sympathy towards them. The LTTE group also has become a threat to the Indian fishermen. In the interviews conducted by the author in different places in Ramnathpuram district during 29-30 Novemebr 2003, fishermen narrated their woes saying that they were being more severely punished by the LTTE rather than by the Sri Lankan navy. It is to be noted that the Sri Lankan government has lifted the restrictions on Sri Lankan fishermen fishing in its waters. The Sri Lankan fishermen (who are mostly Sri Lankan Tamils) oppose the Indian fishermen (who are Indian Tamils) fishing in their waters. There are reports that the fishermen groups from Sri Lanka also involved in the attack against Indian fishermen who acted as the 'front organizations' of the LTTE.[25] It is reported that the Indian fishermen were over powered by the Sri Lankan fishermen. Such incidents against the Indian fishermen have increased in recent times.

There is another dimension to the problem. The LTTE is demanding that the Sri Lankan government grant them the status of a de facto navy. For it, access to the sea is very important to link with its overseas network.[26] Recently under the Interim Self-Governing Authority (ISGA), the LTTE asked for the control over the marine and offshore resources of the adjacent seas (of the northeast) and the "power to regulate access thereto."[27] If this proposal is accepted then it would become serious problem to India. Then India should deal with the LTTE (non state actor) along with the Sri Lankan government for the release of the fishermen.

Both the countries can improve their relation through constructing a bridge between India and Sri Lanka and through a bridge they can tackle the tigers' activities. Following section discusses the prospects for constructing a bridge between them.

(d) Land Bridge

Sri Lanka proposed a land bridge between Rameswaram in Tamilnadu and Talaimannar in Sri Lanka. Through this, road and rail link would be developed which would offer huge economic benefits to both sides on the Palk Straits.[28] This can be one of the steps promoting cooperation between the two countries.

This bridge would facilitate improving trade between the two countries and enhance the capacity of the Trincomalee port in addition to that of Colombo port. The Bureau of Investigation of Sri Lanka prepared a detailed study for the proposed bridge and estimated the construction cost as $880 million. It was reported that the depth of water does not exceed seven meters at any point. The study proposed a six-lane combination of bridges, causeways and rail track. Since, the distance between Mannar and Dhanushkodi is about 22 km, it is difficult to construct a single bridge.[29] There should be structures, which have a combination of bridges, trestles and causeways. [30]

The bridge could become a connecting link between the national highways in south India and those in Sri Lanka. It would facilitate a continuous road and ferry link from Madurai to Trincomalee for cargo and passengers. Major cities of southern India can be connected to Madurai through road and rail linkages.[31]

However, the Tamil Nadu government opposed the construction of a land bridge. The then Chief Minister of Tamil Nadu, Jayalalitha argued that the matter must be viewed not only from economic point of view but from the angle of the security of Tamil Nadu and India.[32] She felt that the LTTE brought the "gun culture and worse still, the horror of suicide bombing" into the peaceful state of Tamil Nadu.[33] She argued that though peace talks were being held between the LTTE and the Sri Lankan government, "the LTTE had always found some pretext to revert to its patented brand of ugly terrorism after a quiet phase of peace negotiations."[34] Hence she felt that the proposed bridge would be premature and unwise.

The Tamil Nadu government's apprehensions about the security of Tamil Nadu may be unfounded. It is not difficult to prevent the activities of the LTTE and their crossing into India through a land bridge compared to crossing on sea. Both countries had agreed at government level to construct a bridge between them. However, this proposal has yet to materialize.

2. India and Pakistan

Pakistan shares border with Iran on the west, Afghanistan on the northwest, China on the northeast, the Arabian Sea on the south and India on the east. It shares more border with India. Pakistan and India agreed on some of the issues related to maritime boundary. They are: arbitration of the Sir Creek boundary dispute between 1965-1968; the Indo-Pakistan Western Boundary case Tribunal's Award in February 1968 delimited a line of 403 km that was later demarcated by joint survey teams. Another agreement between the two countries was on Advance Notice of Military Exercises, Maneuvers and Troops Movements signed in April 1991 which provides for giving advance notices on exercises, maneuvers and troops movements to prevent any crisis.[35]

(a) Maritime boundary

Two issues involve in the dispute between India and Pakistan – the delimitation of the boundary along the Sir Creek and the demarcation of the maritime boundary in the Arabian Sea. The Rann of Kutch is located between the Sind province of Pakistan and the Gujarat state of India. It is neither enough to navigate nor enough to farm. It has two distinct formations i.e. Great Rann and the Little Rann. The Great Rann has 18,000 sq.km. and lies almost within Gujarat and extends 256 kms. From west to east the width is between 40 and 100 km. The Little Rann stretches from east to west for about 110 km. and has about 500 sq.km. In the north, the Rann lies in Sind, a province of Pakistan and its south and east are the Kutch and Kathlawar regions of the Gujarat state of India. The Rann submerges in water four to five feet deep during May to October and the rest of the year It becomes a salty desert. Sir Creek is a 100 km. long estuary in the marshes of the Rann of Kutch which lies on the border between Gujarat and Sind. It is a fluctuating tidal channel and not a flowing creek. Till 1954, the border around the Sir Creek between India and Pakistan had been opened. Later it became a contentious issue between them. Pakistan insists demarcating the Creek boundary as a precondition for delimiting the maritime boundary. It demands drawing a line on the basis of the principle of equity, whereas India wants to draw a line along the middle of the Creek. Both the countries are yet to resolve the problem. It is believed that the Creek has sub-sea oil and gas deposits.

The Sir Creek dispute stems from maps drawn in 1914 and 1927. They draw different boundaries along the 100 km length of Creek. The 1914 map depicts the boundary on the east bank of the Creek. The later map portrays the boundary along the mid point of the Creek. India argues that there was no dispute in this sector, whereas Pakistan argues that it is a disputed area. India maintains that there was a dispute between the two sides on the Kutch-Sind border i.e. between the Sir Creek and Khori Creek. But this dispute was settled in 1913. However, Pakistan argues that the entire Creek is on its eastern bank and represented in 1914 map belonging to it. Pakistan claims about one-third of the Great Rann, about 3,500 sq.km. and argues that it was under the control of Sind. India opposes Pakistan's view and maintains that the entire Rann of Kutch is a part of the Kutch region of Gujarat. The Kutch acceded to India in 1947 and in 1950 it became the part of the then state of Bombay and later it became part of the state of Gujarat in 1960.

After the war between India and Pakistan in 1965, both the countries had signed an agreement on 30 June 1965 for a cease-fire and status quo in the Kutch. Article 3 (i) of the agreement declared:

In the event of no agreement between the Ministers of the two Governments on the determination of the border being reached within two months of the cease-fire, the two Governments shall...have recourse to the Tribunal referred to in (ii) below for determination of the border in the light of their respective claims and evidence produced before it, and the decision of the Tribunal shall be final and binding on both parties.[36]

The agreement provided a tribunal for determination of the border. The tribunal announced its verdict on 19 February 1968 and awarded approximately 900 sq.km in the northern part of the Rann to Pakistan and the rest to India. Pakistan was given the areas of south of Rahim-ki-Bazar i.e. Pirol Valo Kun, Dhar Banni and Chhad Bet and the two deep inlets on either side of Nagar

Parker promontory. The tribunal verdict was based on three grounds: a.) the intensive Sind activity; b.) these areas were totally surrounded by Pakistani territory; c.) the paramount consideration of promoting peace and stability in the region.[37] India was not happy with the verdict. If India agrees to Pakistan's claim or vice versa either country could lose or gain only about 250 sq miles of ocean and ocean floor.[38]

India and Pakistan had six rounds of talks during 1969-1998 but could not come to an agreement. Under the Lahore Declaration of 1998, both agreed to "conclude an agreement on prevention of incidents at sea in order to ensure safety of navigation by naval vessels, and aircraft belonging to the two sides."[39] In other words, both the countries realized the importance of maritime cooperation. During 1997-1999, the naval forces of both the countries had negotiations to promote cooperation between them. Both the countries face similar problems on sea. They should realize that there are far more serious threats to their national security. These two countries can keep the dispute aside and undertake joint initiatives to share benefits.

Due to undefined boundary between India and Pakistan, the fishermen of both the countries, who stray into each other's waters, are facing problems. The following section discusses the fishermen problems.

(b) Fishermen Problem

Indian and Pakistani fishermen are being arrested/ killed by authorities of the other side. Indian fishermen are suspected collaborating with Research & Analysis Wing, while Pakistani fishermen are suspected to be the agents of Inter-Service Intelligence. The fishermen of both the countries are often arrested for crossing borders and they are becoming victims of undefined boundaries. They are being treated as prisoners of war. The arrests of fishermen started from early 1987.

Due to commercialization, thousands of fishermen have been displaced from their livelihood through the destruction of the Indus Delta. Many of them left with no option but to migrate to other places. Gujarat has the largest coastal area in India and has a rich heritage of live corals and coral islands in the Gulf of Kutch.

The coral reefs[40] play an important role in marine life. But they are being dredged out due to various reasons. For instance, sand dumes and mudflats are being removed and that led to damage of marine life.

Till date the fishermen of each nation have not been arrested on the ground that they were carrying arms and ammunitions on board. There is no clear policy regarding the release of the arrested fishermen. There are incidents where the fishermen were being arrested and kept in jails for years together on both sides. For instance, 180 Pakistani fishermen were kept in jail in India for more than five years and similarly 193 Indian fishermen were kept in jail in Pakistan by 1997. Their release always depends on the state of relations between the two countries. Often the fishermen are released in equal numbers on both sides. The arrested fishermen on both sides are suffering during their stay in jail. There is no proper sanitation facilities, lack of privacy and keep many of them in a crowded place.[41] The fishermen mistake is to cross over into the neighbour's waters for their livelihood. They are socially and economically poor. Since both the states are not able to come to an agreement on demarcating their sea borders, it is better both the nations adopt a humanistic and sympathetic approach towards the fishermen who are crossing into each other's waters. Karamat Ali, Director, Pakistan Institute of Labour Education and Research (PILER) rightly pointed out that "It is a criminal negligence on the part of both the countries. There should be a demarcation according to UN Sea Conventions."[42]

The South Asian Labour Forum (SALF), trade unions and labour support groups of both India and Pakistan have been pressurizing their respective governments to release the arrested fishermen. Muhammad Ali Shah, President of the Pakistan Fisher Folk for UN has said that "Fishermen should not be made the victims of enmities and boundary disputes between two countries. Nowhere in the world such a practice is in place. This is the tragedy of this region where fishermen are treated like prisoners of war." [43]

Fortunately a breakthrough has been made by India and Pakistan to agree on a bilateral code of conduct minimizing the inter boundary cross over by the fishermen. Over the last two years, as part of the on going peace process the maritime dispute mechanism has been consciously incorporated into the negotiations agenda. There is evidence of both the countries adopting a benign and human approach in treating the maritime trespassers. Nevertheless, positive bilateral initiatives need to be concretized into long term plans to put an end to arrest the fishermen, who cross each other's waters. Both the countries should establish Maritime Risk Reduction Centres which could provide a ground to solve the fishermen problems if they were caught during poaching into each other's waters. Both the countries are in favour of creating a buffer zone, extending five nautical miles into each other's maritime boundary.[44] The Indian vice-chief of the naval staff, Sureesh Mehta said that "Talks are progressing very well and in the interest of both sides, we are at the culmination stage and the final bit should be clinched in this round of talks. The coast guard has the full backing of the navy in whatever steps it is planning to take." He further said that "The boundary is notional and no markers are possible on the high seas. Unable to afford costly direction finding equipment, fishermen stray into the maritime zone of the other country, where they are arrested. At the time of arrest, they cannot understand the gravity of their crime."[45] Also both the sides are in favour of setting up a hotline between the two sides. If buffer zone is set up and hotline installed, the problems of the fishermen, who cross into neighbour's waters would be reduced.

3. India and Bangladesh

Bangladesh is bordered on the west, north, and east by a 2,400-kilometer land frontier with India and on the southeast by a land and water frontier (193 kilometers) with Myanmar (Burma). After Bangladesh got independence from Pakistan in 1971, it signed agreements with India: a comprehensive new boundary agreement, 1974; the Indo-Bangladesh Land Boundary Agreement, 1974 (but it has yet to be ratified); the Indo-Bangladesh Water Sharing Treaty, 1996; India lifts nontariff barriers, 1998; a Joint Indo-Bangladesh Chamber of Commerce has been established. However, both the countries have differences over the issue of demarcating territorial waters.

(a) Maritime boundary

India and Bangladesh have dispute on two issues i.e. demarcation of maritime boundary and sovereignty over a small island.

Through the 1974 and 1982 agreements between India and Bangladesh, the former gave lease in perpetuity over Tin Bigha land to the latter and the former has acquired sovereignty over the area. India's right to access through the corridor remain intact. However, both the countries are yet to demarcate their maritime boundary over the small island called New Moore or Purbasha in India and South Talpatty in Bangladesh. It is situated 2 nautical miles off the coast of India and 5 nautical miles off the coast of Bangladesh. This small island emerged in 1970 after the wake of acute volcanic activity in the area. It was appeared on a satellite picture in 1975.

India wants to draw the equidistant or median line, whereas Bangladesh favours the application of the equitable principle. Both countries have taken a rigid stand over the island. This area is considered to be rich in oil. India claims the island on the ground that the flow of the Haribhanga river is to the east of the island, and the island lies on the natural prolongation of Indian territory. Whereas Bangladesh argues that the river flows to the west of the island and it would be not possible to separate the natural prolongation of Indian territory. Both the countries are very particular about the island because of natural resources in the Ganges–Brahmaputra delta of the Bay of Bengal. If sovereignty of India over the island were recognised, it would get an additional 16,000 sq. metres of continental shelf and if Bangladesh's sovereignty over the island were recognised, it would get a lesser area compared to India. There were many meetings held between India and Bangladesh on the maritime dispute since 1974, but to no avail.

Unlike the clashes between the fishermen of India-Pakistan and Indo-Sri Lanka, the clashes between India and Bangladesh are very minimal.

It is important to know that India, Pakistan and Bangladesh can claim their respective continental shelves only after demarcating their boundaries under (UNCLOS)-III. The process has to be completed by 2009. Until then, none of the countries can explore and exploit the resources in their EEZ or in their continental shelf.

4. Conclusion

The littoral states of South Asia have been facing more or less similar problems on sea such as: terrorism, piracy, drugs, narcotics trade, illegal trade etc. Since, these problems cannot be tackled by any single country, all the South Asian countries have to cooperate with each other. By resolving them they can create a better future for their people through mutual understanding and cooperation.

Settling the maritime boundaries are essential because demarcation of sea boundary is not just a political issue, it has human dimension as well. Unless the countries settle their disputes over the maritime boundary, they cannot work collectively to tackle the problems facing by them. The littoral states of the region have to have a holistic view to resolve their maritime borders.

It is important that the governments of coastal states should consider that the fishermen problems are to be understood on humanitarian grounds. As fishing is one of the key sources of livelihood and employment, the fishermen go in search of fish wherever they are available. In their pursuit, hardly they respect the maritime boundaries. As it is the case everywhere, so is the case with the fishermen of South Asia. They cross maritime boundary and enter the neighbours waters. Sometimes, the fishermen unwillingly and unknowingly cross into other's territory because of engine failures, no clear demarcation, of tidal currents, cyclone and lack of navigational aids.

There has to be a networking among the fishermen of South Asian countries to bring them on a platform where they can discuss their problems and share their experiences and their ideas. The coastal states of South Asia have to think in terms of encoding a common maritime conduct and regional maritime law. So that most of the problems of the fishermen can be addressed without much delay in case they enter each other's waters. This can also protect the rights of fishermen and promote their welfare and security.

However, this problem will remain as long as political will for long-term solutions is lacking. The South Asian countries have to realize that they have to shift from the security of the borders to the security of the people.

There is a greater need to enhance mutual cooperation on maritime security. Such cooperation may include measures such as joint naval patrolling, controlling of smuggling and pirate activities and strengthening communication networks. Through cooperation the South Asian countries can improve shipbuilding and weather forecasting. The Indian satellites monitor the dynamics of clouds over the Indian Ocean region and the Indian Meteorological Department uses meteorological data from these satellites for operational weather forecasting.[46] Hence, India can share its data and analysis with other South Asian countries. They have to jointly work to develop early warning systems to avoid problems on the sea such as floods, tsunami etc. Apart from such measures, there is a greater potential for enhancing and institutionalizing economic cooperation in the exploration and exploitation of sea resources in the Indian Ocean waters.

References

1. *Rajya Sabha Debates,* New Delhi: Parliament Secretariat, 1 September 1960, cols.3049-3050.
2. *Ibid*, col.3050.
3. *Hindustan Times,* 2 March 1968, cited in V.Suryanarayan, *Kachchativu and the Problems of Indian Fishermen in the Palk Bay Region*, Madras: T.R.Publications,1994, p.17.
4. *Lok Sabha Debates*, New Delhi: Parliament Secretariat, 23 July 1974, cols. 200–201.
5. Cited in Suryanarayan, n.3, p.11.
6. *Rajya Sabha,* 17 May 1956, cols.1683-1684.
7. See W.T.Jayasinghe, *Kachchativu and the Maritime Boundary of Sri Lanka*, Colombo: A Stamford Lake Publications, 2003, p.41.
8. "This delimitation was based on agreement rather than on the equidistance principle, as the primary purpose was to settle the dispute over the Kachchativu Island, which states the parties had agreed to hand over to Sri Lanka. Hence, the boundary line was

drawn so as to pass just one mile West of the Island of Kachchativu; in order that the Island would fall within the maritime boundaries of Sri Lanka", Anne Nirmala Vijayalakshmi Chandrahasan, *The Application to Sri Lanka of the Emerging New Regime of the Law of the Sea, in Relation to the Delimitation of Sri Lanka's Maritime Bpundaries and Jurisdiction over Sea Zone, and Areas of the Seabed,* unpublished Ph.D thesis, Colombo: University of Colombo, 1983, pp.58-59, cited in Suryanarayan, n.3, p.25.

9. Cited in V.Vevekanandan, "Crossing Maritime Borders: The Problem and Solution in the Indo-Sri Lankan Context", in K.G.Kumar (ed), *Forging Unity: Coastal Communities and the Indian Ocean's Future,* Chennai: International Collective in Support of Fishworkers, 2003, p.79.
10. Cited in *ibid.*
11. See V.Suryanarayan, "Fishing and Troubled Waters", *The Hindu*, 3 October 2003, p.10.
12. Cited in *Annual Report of the Ministry of External Affairs, 1974-1975,* New Delhi: Ministry of External Affairs, 1975, p.24.
13. T.S.Subramanian, "Raking Up Kachchativu: A War-Cry from Jayalalitha", *Frontline,* 21 Septemebr-11 October 1991, p.50.
14. *Ibid.*
15. "Drop India–Sri Lanka Bridge Project", *The Hindu*, 25 July 2003, p. 6.
16. Author's interview with V. Suryanarayan, Hyderabad, 5 Jul 2003.
17. Suryanarayan, n. 3, p. 4
18 Author's interview with the fishermen of Rameswaram, 29–30 Nov 2003; and Pamban, 1–2 Dec 2003.
19. In his filed study, the author met the affected fishermen's families in Tuticorin and Rameswaram districts.
20. UNCLOS-III Part-V, Article73, under Enforcement of laws and regulations of the coastal State, "Arrested vessels and their crews shall be promptly released upon the posting of reasonable bond or other security."
21. See A.Subramanyam Raju and S.Keethaponcalan, *Maritime Cooperation between India and Sri Lanka*, New Delhi: Manohar Publishers, 2006, p.33.

22. Author's interaction with the navy personnel in a seminar on *Maritime Security: Emerging Trends*, Department of Defence and Strategic Studies, University of Madras, 18 December 2005.
23. [The] Maritime Zones of India (Regulations of Fishing by Foreign Vessels), Act, 1981 (Act No. 42 of 1981), Chapter IV, no. 10.
24. Vivekanandan, n. 9, p. 86.
25. "Navy Coast Guard to Step Up Vigil", *The Hindu*, 8 March 2003, p.6.
26. V. S. Sambandan, "The LTTE's Blueprint", *Frontline*,vol. 20, no. 23, 21 November 2003, p. 14.
27. *Ibid.*
28. Ranil Wickemesinghe, "Making Our People Rich", *The Hindu*, 25 August 2004, p.10.
29. The longest bridge constructed is the 1.6 km long Storbel in Denmark. See Arjuna Mahendram & Rajive Casie Chitty, "Hanuman's Bridge: Facilitating Trade and Investment between Sri Lanka and Southern India", *South Asian Survey*, vol.7, no.1, January-June 2000, p.26.
30. Following places have structures: lake Ponchartain (38.4 km) Louisian, USA; Chesapeake Bay Bridge Tunnel (28.3 km), Virginia, USA; King Fahd Causeway (25 km), Bahrain, KSA; Sunshine Skyway (24.5 km), Florida, USA. See *ibid.*
31. *Ibid*, p.31.
32. See n.15.
33. *Ibid.*
34. *Ibid.*
35. For details see Commander Rajesh Pendharkar, *The Lahore Declaration and Beyond: Maritime Confidence-Building Measures in South Asia*, Occasional paper no.51, Washington D.C: The Henry L Stimson Centre, February 2003.
36. R.P.Anand, "The Kutch Award", *India Quarterly*, Vol. 24, no.3, July-September 1968, p.186.
37. The Indian nominee opposed the verdict and gave reasons for opposition. For details see Alok Kumar Gupta, "Other Territorial Disputes with Pakistan: Rann of Kutch and Sir Creek", in P.Sahadevan (ed), *Conflict and Peacemaking in South Asia*, New Delhi: Lancers Books, 2001, pp.272-295.

38. K.Raja Menon (retd.), "Maritime Confidence Building in South Asia", in J.R.Jummola (ed), *Maritime Confidence Building in Regions of Tension,* Report n.21, Washington D.C: The Henry L.Stimson, 1996, p.78.
39. *Ibid.*
40. Coral Reef is the feeding and breeding ground for various marine organizations. It acts as carbon sink by absorbing carbon-di-oxide and converts it into calcium carbonate. It protects the seashore from tidal erosion. It provides people with living sea walls against tides, storm surges and hurricanes.
41. For the fishermen experience in jail, see ,Cited in Charu Gupta & Mukul Sharma, "Blurred Borders: Coastal Conflicts between India and Pakistan", *Economic & Political Weekly*, 3 July 2004, vol.39, no.27, pp. 3010-3013.
42. Cited in *ibid,* pp.3005-3012.
43. Cited in *ibid*, p.3012.
44. Sandeep Dikshit, "Fishermen: India-Pakistan deal in sight", *The Hindu*, 30 November 2004, cited in www.thehindu.com/2004/12/01/stories/2004120105431200.htm.
45. *Ibid.*
46. Gaurav Rajen, *Cooperative Environmental Monitoring in the Coastal Regions of India and Pakistan,* see http://www.cmc.sandia.gov/links/cmc-papers/sand-98-0505-11/sand-98-0505-11.html

SECTION-IV

ECONOMIC COOPERATION: SEARCH FOR NEW SYNERGIES

9

The Process of Integration in the SAARC Region

V.R. Panchmukhi

The SAARC process began with great expectations. It is true that the initiatives launched in the early part of the SAARC process did not measure well in relation to these expectations and visionary perspectives. There were also many detractors of the SAARC process right from the beginning. These detractors, both from within the region and from outside the region had been arguing that SAARC is a nonstarter and that it will soon vanquish into history. But it is gratifying to note that there were also strong believers in the SAARC process and it is they who have kept the SAARC spirit alive and growing.

Some of us very sincerely believe that SAARC has made steady progress, though at a slow pace. We should recall that in the beginning, economic areas of cooperation were not brought under the SAARC framework. Thanks to the initiatives of Mahbub-Ul-Huq, the then commerce minister of Pakistan, the area of trade cooperation was brought into the framework of cooperation, in addition to the erstwhile sectors, such as, culture, sports, roads, etc, which were already included in the SAARC framework, right from the beginning. In fact, it was at this time that the SAARC Secretariat took the right kind of initiatives in launching a programme of fostering studies, in the different institutions in the SAARC region, on the scope, content and strategies pertaining to economic cooperation. We should recognize that India had played, at this stage, a leadership role by providing analytical and practical inputs into the task of identifying the potential areas of cooperation and the strategies required to realize the benefits of economic cooperation in the region. For instance, the Indian research institution, viz. Research and Information System for the Nonaligned and Other Developing Countries, (RIS), played a role in conducting the relevant studies and also in organizing expert group meetings and preparing synthesis reports for the SAARC Secretariat. The outcome of these initiatives was the preparation of the study, which came to be known as the TMS study (Trade, Manufactures and Services Study) in the SAARC Secretariat. In fact, this study became the basis for many practical actions and policy initiatives, launched in the subsequent periods, at the level of the member countries, for fostering cooperation in the economic areas. Thus, beginning from a situation of aversion to the inclusion of economic areas in the agenda of cooperation, the SAARC process struck a new path for effective economic integration, with a view to fulfilling visionary goals laid down in the SAARC Charter.

The process of economic integration in the SAARC region seems to have derived its guidelines from the textbooks on economic integration. It was conceived that the first phase should be one of Preferential Trading Arrangement (PTA), to be soon followed by the scheme of Free Trade Area (FTA). It was envisioned that FTA should be followed by the approach of Customs Union and then by that of Economic Union. In author's view, this focus on the approach of trade liberalization alone, without looking into the other supporting programmes, that are required to enhance trade capabilities in the trade partner countries, is one of the factors responsible for slow progress in the pace of economic cooperation in the region. The SAARC member countries have 'wasted' lot of their time in the arduous exercise of negotiating the scope, depth and profile of trade liberalization, without examining the critical issue as to how the additional trading opportunities created by the policies of trade-liberalization could be exploited by facilitating additional investment flows, encouraging technology transfers and by strengthening human resource development in the region.

In the absence of an integrated approach to the process of economic cooperation and with overemphasis on the agenda of mere trade liberalization, many other critical issues such as, benefits from trade and distribution of the benefits of trade liberalization have now come to the foreground. We are aware that the theme of 'benefits from trade' occupies an important place in the literature on trade. However, in practice, in the context of trade liberalization, it is not just enough to recognize that there are many positive effects of trading in the trade partner countries. The trade partner countries would like to assess the incremental benefits of cooperation, that accrue to them and also to weigh the costs of non-cooperation as against the benefits of cooperation. Further, why should a country agree to reduce its trade barriers and liberalize its trade flows, if this action implies that its trade-partner country benefits relatively more than itself? It should also be noted that in the context of the assessment of the distribution of benefits, the conceptual issues as to what constitutes 'benefits' and as to how one calculates the extent of their distribution assume special significance. The time frame considered for such an assessment would also be of special importance.

Unfortunately, this important theme of identifying the benefits of trade liberalization and the methodology of quantifying the extent of their sharing among the trade partner countries in the region, have not received adequate attention from the research community of the region. In the absence of comprehensive studies on this subject, the debate on the distribution of benefits of trade liberalization has become highly politicized and has therefore become a contentious issue in the whole process of cooperation in the region.

We find that the relatively smaller trade partners have started arguing that it is the relatively larger members, like India and Pakistan, who benefit more than the others. Increasing volume of trade deficit with India has become a contentious issue. It is puzzling to find that those very countries, which were initially enthusiastic about trade liberalization in the region are now holding back the process of liberalization on the ground that trade liberalization is not benefiting them, as much as it does the relatively larger countries. This type of assessment of the benefits is not correct.

Take for instance, the issue of increased trade deficit with India. Incremental imports from India are of three types. Firstly, they consist of essential consumer goods and basic needs of the people of the importing country. Secondly, they are intermediate goods and capital goods that are of great use in fostering rapid development in the importing country. Thirdly, they consist of such goods that may have some negative impact on the local industries and economic activities of the importing country. It is obvious that the first two categories of effects should be counted as positive benefits and it is only the last part, which is often insignificant, should cause worry to the policy makers of the deficit countries.

Further, as stated earlier, the real approach for taking advantage of trade liberalization lies in focusing on those production and service activities that would expand the trade-capability, in particular, export capability of the deficit countries. In the absence of proper research studies and reflections on these dimensions of the process of trade liberalization, highly politicized negative comments have been damaging the process of trade liberalization itself. It is high time that this tendency is checked by the adoption of some holistic approach to the task of economic integration in the region.

We should bring production harmonization as a complement to the process of trade liberalization. The RIS study on Trade, Manufactures and Services, proposed that there should be a SAARC Development Fund for facilitating the conduct of feasibility studies on trade-creating joint ventures in the region. It should be recalled that in the early 1990's, a unique institutional framework called "SAARC Fund for Regional Projects" was established with participation of the development financial institutions of the member countries. The main objective of this Fund was to facilitate the conduct of techno-economic feasibility studies for trade-creating joint ventures in the region. Unfortunately, this institutional innovation has not yielded the desired results since it was not backed up by adequate information flows and suitable policy support.

Often, we measure the advantages of the schemes of trade liberalization, such as, SAPTA or SAFTA, in terms of the increment in intra-regional trade. Such an approach is not proper. In fact, many times, schemes of region-specific liberalization would attract investments from outside the region and this would end up in expanding trade capabilities for exports to third country markets outside the region. The fact that the intra-regional trade within the SAARC region is small and that it is not expanding fast in the recent past, should not worry us much, as long as there are indications to the effect that trade liberalization is resulting in the expansion of overall trade capabilities of the member countries.

Many times, it is observed that many schemes launched in the SAARC region have not yielded the desired results. The SAARC programmes of cooperation have not focused on what one may call as people centric approach. Many critical people centric issues, such as, eradication of poverty, creation of additional employment opportunities, providing better access to education and health facilities, improving access to safe drinking water and empowerment of women and backward communities ought to receive hitherto greater attention and practical action with a view to fostering effective people's participation in the programme of cooperation in the region. To put it differently, the recently proclaimed, United Nations Millennium Development Goals, (MDG's), should become one of the main agenda of cooperation in the region. By making the tasks of realizing the MDG targets by 2015, as the joint responsibility of the SAARC region, the main goals of fostering people's welfare, as enshrined in the SAARC Charter, would be fulfilled and the extent of people's participation in the SAARC process would also be increased.

The SAARC process has often been hijacked by some grandiose pronouncements of vision, without spelling out a practical and feasible road map for realizing this vision. The pronouncement that we should set up a South Asian Economic Union with a common currency and uniform fiscal regime, belongs to this category. Formation of an Economic Community in the region, on the lines of European Economic Community, may be a desirable goal for a distant future. However, to give the impression that it is a feasible goal in the next few years would mean putting ourselves on an illusory path. We are aware as to how the process of economic integration in the European Region has passed through many critical phases, beginning from modest sectoral integration programmes, such as coal and steel. Even to day, the programme of common currency has not been implemented in all parts of EU. Moreover, the programme of fiscal harmonization is also facing many practical and conceptual difficulties. We should spell out only those schemes that are feasible in the short span of the next five to ten years. Declaring South Asian region as a Common Economic Area, for facilitating hitherto more streamlined investment flows, technology flows and information flows within the region would be a feasible proposition. Further, initiatives for establishing suitable institutional framework for participation of the private sector and the NGO's in the programmes of cooperation, should also receive priority attention.

The SAARC process of cooperation should adopt a framework of specific sectoral schemes of cooperation. Some of the specific sectoral schemes of cooperation, that would place the pace of cooperation in the region on an hitherto faster track:

The first specific sectoral programme of cooperation should be, mentioned earlier, in the field of UN Millennium Development Goals. Of course, there are many sub-sectors and sub-targets, within the broad framework of MDG's. These are concerned with the goals, such as, poverty eradication, access to safe drinking water, empowerment, curtailment of specific diseases, challenges of sustainable development and south-south cooperation. SAARC secretariat should take the initiative of setting up task forces, involving the governments of the member countries as also the private sector and the NGO's, on each of the MDG's. Since there are some possibilities of mobilizing special resources for the purposes of MDG's, the SAARC level initiatives would be great benefit to the region as also for the individual countries.

Second would be South Asian Programme for constructing a South Asian Textile Sector. The SAARC member countries should evolve their policy coordination in such a way that the SAARC region should have its own multinational in the textiles sector and evolve a South Asian Brand in textiles. Why not India- its private sector, phase out some of its textile products with a view to facilitating Bangladesh, Nepal and other countries to step-in into the 'vacated' lines of activities? India could move on to the higher levels of products in the ladder of the production curve and/or move on to higher levels of technology. This is what is advocated in what is known as the 'flying geese model' of restructuring at the international level. Such a restructuring of production can be 'engineered' even in a market driven paradigm of development and trade, provided the private sector and the policy makers are made aware of the advantages of schemes of restructuring at the national and international levels. Of course, detailed techno-economic studies are required for fostering such new structures of production and trade and some innovative policy initiatives are also called for.

Third sectoral programme of cooperation is concerned with the agricultural and the rural sectors. In recent periods, even the enthusiasts of reform programmes have realized that agriculture has been neglected for a long time, in the process of development and structural changes. So we must go back to the strategy of focusing on agriculture and the rural sectors, if the welfare of the large masses of people in the region has to be improved. There is a large volume of literature that spells out the relative strengths and weaknesses of the individual countries in the different dimensions of the agricultural and rural sectors and it is possible to work out an integrated programme of cooperation in the tasks of development of the agricultural and rural sectors.

The fourth sector is the IT sector, wherein some member countries, in particular, India has acquired significant comparative advantages and skills. We are aware that leading Indian companies, such as Infosys and Wipro have already launched many outreach activities for the benefit of other countries. There is lot of scope for expanding these initiatives with a view to evolving the South Asian region as a strong IT region in the world.

Fifth point is slightly different from the other sectoral suggestions given earlier. The South Asian intellectuals should pool their intellectual resources for launching a new debate on some analytical questions of current relevance. These questions may be wide ranging in nature. What constitutes of development? What is the 'optimum' degree of globalization in a given stage of development? Similarly, what is the 'optimum' degree of liberalization in a given stage of development? When should a country open up its capital market and adopt full or partial capital account convertibility? How to 'forecast' the impending situations of economic and financial crisis? How to realize development without compromising on 'Values' of the society? These are only some of the illustrative questions that deserve attention at the analytical and policy levels.

We may observe that in the recent years, focus has been on the goals of realizing higher and higher growth rates. Would growth alone imply 'development'? We may recall that during the periods of the late fifties and early sixties, we used to make a clear distinction between growth and development. We used to recognize that development is some thing more than growth alone. The UNDP report on Human Development, brought out some time in the mid-nineties, had categorically advocated that the developing countries should avoid five types of growth. These five types were categorized as follows: 'Jobless Growth', implying growth that does not create additional job opportunities, 'Ruthless Growth', implying growth that aggravates inequalities, 'Futureless Growth', implying growth that inducts environmental non-sustainability, 'Voiceless Growth', implying a growth profile that does not encourage empowerment and finally 'Rootless Growth', implying growth that ends up in destroying the cultural roots of a society.

South Asian region is rich in the intellectual resources. We should take some initiatives for generating debates on such basic analytical issues, such as the ones stated earlier, and in particular the issues such as the scope and content of development and strategies of development in the emerging new contexts of globalization and market-driven framework of development.

10

Economic Cooperation in South Asia: Challenges and Constraints

Dushni Weerakoon

1. Introduction

As a region, South Asia was fairly late in embracing the concept of regional economic cooperation that gathered fresh momentum in the latter half of the 1980s. It took a decade after the initial establishment of the South Asian Association for Regional Cooperation (SAARC) in 1985 for South Asia to turn its attention to the promotion of trade through a regional agreement. Nevertheless, having accepted the concept of regional economic cooperation, SAARC was quick to set itself an ambitious agenda. The proposal to set up a South Asian Preferential Trade Agreement (SAPTA) was accepted and came into formal operation in December 1995. In 1996, SAARC member countries agreed in principle to go a step further and attempt to enact a South Asian Free Trade Agreement (SAFTA). Despite the apparent commitment to economic cooperation within a regional framework, South Asian countries have, in reality, exhibited a marked reluctance to open their markets to each other. Much of the failure can be attributed to the swings in political relations between India and Pakistan, a seemingly irreversible situation in which SAARC appears to have lost its relevance as a forum through which an economic agenda can be meaningfully realized.

The purpose of this paper is to examine whether regional economic cooperation – constrained as it is by political factors – has a future in South Asia in the context of a rapidly changing global economic environment. The paper is organized as follows. Section I examines the rationale for preferential trade in South Asia and the likely benefits, drawing on existing empirical literature. Section II focuses on the progress of the SAPTA agreement to date and the emerging environment for bilateral FTAs between SAARC countries. Section III examines the complex political-economy forces that underlie the economic agenda under SAARC and assess whether South Asia is ever likely to break free of its political shackles sufficiently to allow substantive progress in economic integration and Section IV concludes.

2. Free Trade in South Asia: The Empirical Evidence

South Asian countries that had fairly open economies in the immediate post-independence period in the 1940s, had become some of the most highly protectionist in the world by the 1970s. Tariff, and even more importantly, NTBs (Non-Tariff Barriers) were extremely high, state interventions in economic activity had become pervasive, attitudes to foreign investments were negative, often hostile, and stringent exchange controls were in place. But this started to change in the late 1970s. In 1977, Sri Lanka initiated a process of policy liberalization and was in turn followed by other countries in the 1980s. However, this was often a rather hesitant liberalization process and was very uneven across countries. It was from the early 1990s, with the start of a major reform process in India that the region as a whole really started to liberalize. By the end of the decade, though important policy barriers to trade and foreign investment remained, enormous progress had been made in the direction of trade liberalization throughout the region. But it should be noted that even by the mid-1990s, in a global comparison of import protection rates, South Asia remained a highly protected region.[1]

In the area of trade policy, comprehensive tariff reforms were implemented, aimed at, among other things, progressive reductions in the level and dispersion of tariffs and quantitative restrictions.

Figure 1

Average Customs Duties and Percentage of Tariff Lines Subject to QRs

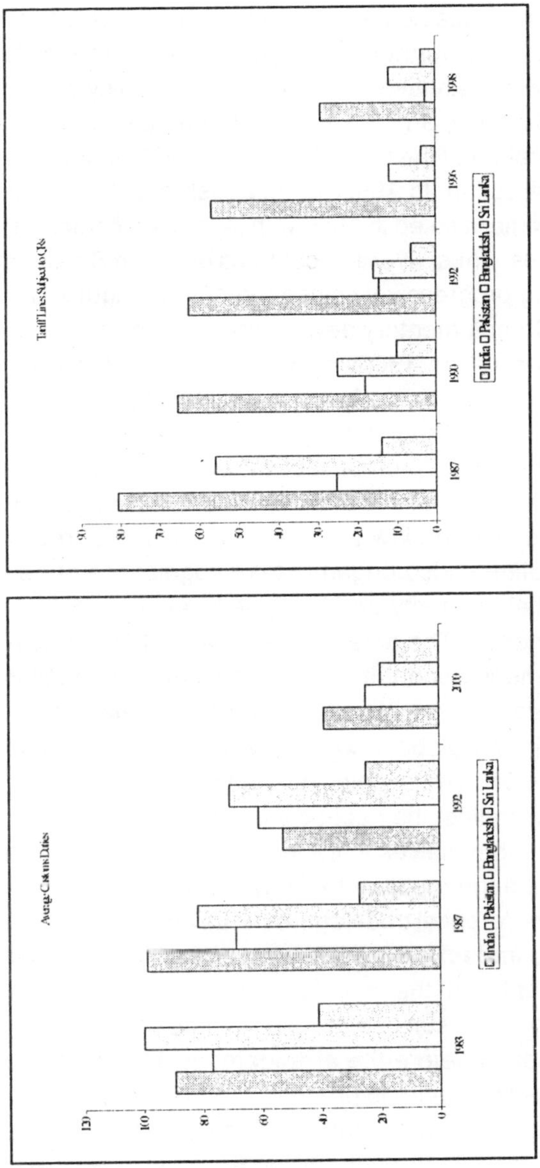

Source: World Bank, 2003.

In July 1991, India began the process of dismantling its highly complex import licensing system, permitting the phase-out of all NTBs on tradeables except those on consumer goods. In 1993, Pakistan took further measures to rationalize its tariff structure after the substantive attempts at trade policy reforms initiated in 1988. Similarly, Sri Lanka also embarked on further tariff cuts and simplification of the tariff structure in 1990 under its 'second-wave' of liberalization. In 1992, Bangladesh accelerated its tariff reform programme initiated in 1986 with significant compression of custom duty rates. Thus, average customs duties in South Asia have been declining progressively since the 1980s (Figure 1).

Complementary developments in the global economy in the latter part of the 1980s and early 1990s also began to exert its influence on the South Asian region. The global economy witnessed an explosion of regional trade agreements (RTAs) from the latter half of the 1980s, prompted by the apparent faltering of negotiations under the multilateral framework of the Uruguay Round. South Asia – although slow to take up the issue of regional economic cooperation – also began to take cognizance of developments in the global economy and hastened to implement its own regional trade agenda. The emergence of new RTAs in North America and Latin America and the expansion of existing ones in Europe and East Asia saw the increasing marginalization of South Asia as a region in the global economy. For South Asian countries, in the absence of an entry point into one or more of these more dynamic regional bodies, the next best option appeared to be to cooperate amongst themselves in the hope that it would generate economic benefits in the medium to longer term.

Preferential trade agreements are judged in economic terms by their impact on trade flows and on the welfare of both the participants and the rest of the world. Arrangements that are 'trade creating' will result in a greater volume of trade as compared with the situation before the arrangement. This comes about through enhanced efficiency in production and lowered prices. On the other hand, arrangements that are 'trade-diverting' will result in a lower volume of trade through raising the level of overall protection and distorting trade and investment patterns.[2]

There have been a number of empirical studies that have looked at the prospects for regional integration in South Asia but their results remain mixed. A 1993 World Bank study concluded that most of the pre-conditions required for a successful trading arrangement were not present in South Asia.[3] These pre-conditions included: high pre-arrangement tariffs; a high level of trade in the region before the arrangement; the existence of complementary rather than competitive trade; and differences in economic structures in countries concerned. The study found that only the first condition was met in the case of South Asia and it concluded that the region would be better off liberalizing trade unilaterally and by joining an already established group. Studies by Srinivasan and Canonero[4] and Srinivasan[5] using the gravity model also suggest that South Asia is better off undertaking unilateral liberalization. However, they also find room for some potential gains from preferential liberalization and argue that smaller countries are likely to gain more than larger countries from regional integration.[6] The results of a study by Pigato[7] suggest that regional liberalization will generate significant welfare gains both for India and the rest of South Asia.[8] However, India's gains are estimated to be much higher under unilateral liberalization than under preferential liberalization. On the other hand, the benefits to the rest of South Asia from preferential liberalization are larger than that from unilateral liberalization. Besides the welfare gains suggested by the simulations, the case for encouraging an intensification of regional cooperation rests on broader considerations. First, the study suggests that it could complement efforts to open up to world competition and make the region a more attractive location for multinational companies and foreign capital. Second, and most important, it is considered a step towards better political relations and peace. It is argued that additional economic benefits from reduced military spending following a settlement of regional disputes could well be substantial. Alternatively, there are others who argued strongly that regional trade integration initiatives in South Asia will yield a net welfare loss and slowdown unilateral liberalization.[9]

While the empirical evidence has remained inconclusive, a notion that deeper regional trade integration can create spillovers that would strengthen ties between member countries has persisted in the minds of South Asian policy makers. This was bolstered by the belief that increased economic integration would carry with it the ability to not only secure new and larger markets for traditional products, but also enable the diversification of domestic economic structures. An integrated market was also viewed as a means of enhancing the ability to take advantage of global investment capital, and manufacturing and services-related technological efficiencies.\

The inability to derive firm conclusion on the economic impact of integration is not unique to South Asia. The debate on the costs and benefits of preferential trade initiatives – whether theoretically or empirically – remains largely unresolved, as does the question of whether a region-wide FTA will benefit small countries more or less than large countries. Theoretically, it can be argued that openness to trade will allow small economies to specialize in a few product sectors/ or services and to derive larger benefits by overcoming the limitations of scale economies due to the small size of their domestic markets.[10] On a priori grounds, there are some yardsticks that have been set out whereby trade creating and thus welfare increasing circumstances are established to estimate potential gains from participating in a preferential trading arrangement.[11] These include:

- the higher the level of the pre-union tariff in the home country;
- the higher the tariff level of the partner country;
- the larger the volume of trade with the partner country;
- the smaller the volume of trade with the rest of the world;
- the closer the relative prices in trade with the partner country are to those prevailing in the rest of the world;
- the larger the economic size of the country's partners in the agreement (where economic size in this instance is represented by GDP and volume of trade);
- the more diversified the economic structure of the country's partners to the arrangement;
- the more the economic structure of the partner/s resembles the rest of the world outside the preferential agreement.

Applying these criteria, the highest levels of average customs duties at the present time are to be found in Bangladesh and to a lesser extent in India. Thus Bangladesh would stand to gain from participation in preferential/free trade integration. By contrast, Sri Lanka has the lowest average tariff and its gains from liberalization of tariffs would be much less. Under the criterion dealing with the pre-union volume of trade, it is a fact that the share of any single South Asian country in the trade of another is quite low (with the exception of Nepal whose total trade with India accounts for over 35 per cent of its total world trade). Nevertheless, the Maldives and Bangladesh also have a fairly high proportion of their total trade with India (Table 1). Maldives, in fact, has a higher share (18.5 per cent) of trade with Sri Lanka. For these countries, participation in FTA would be relatively more beneficial as the proportion of their pre-union trade is much higher.

Table 1: Volume of Trade (2001)

	Share of SAARC trade in total trade of country	*Share of trade with India in total trade of country*
Bangladesh	10.4	9.4
India	3.0	
Maldives	29.7	10.6
Nepal	35.9	35.4
Pakistan	2.9	1.6
Sri Lanka	8.1	6.3

Source: IMF, *Direction of Trade Statistics,* Yearbook 2002.

The larger the partner in a preferential trading arrangement, the higher the potential benefits for other participants. The size of the Indian market is overwhelmingly dominant as compared with any other country in the region. Therefore, according to the criteria on volume of trade and economic size in general, entering into a FTA in which India is participating should be beneficial for the medium-size and smaller economies of the region. In additions, under the criteria dealing with economic diversification and similarity of the partner's economic structure with the rest of the world, the smaller economies stand to gain. India is relatively economically diversified and is a significant producer and exporter of diversified manufactured items. This can serve the smaller countries in their attempt to both diversify their exports and at the same time obtain a variety of consumer and producer goods at the lowest prices possible. An agreement of a small economy with a large one can be economically promising and potentially beneficial to the small country. Outside of trade liberalization under the multilateral trading system of the WTO, a potentially rewarding trade policy option for small and relatively lesser developed economies would be participation in as large (both in number and economic size of participants) and as liberal (from a market access point of view) a preferential trading arrangement as possible. Thus, potential benefits to the smaller economies of South Asia will be critically dependent on how liberal preferential trade will be in reality.

Although trade complementarities in South Asia are limited at present due to similar production structures, the potential for intra-South Asian cooperation in both trade and investment is not entirely absent.[12] There are important structural changes in intra-regional trade that may be important indicators of future trends. Textile, machinery and equipment have become increasingly more important in intra-regional trade and a larger proportion of exports going into the region are now manufactured products, while in the past, it was primary products.[13] This shift into manufactured product trade, associated with the higher level of industrialization of the region, opens up opportunities for scale economies and intra-industry trade to play an increasing role.

3. The Experience of Preferential Trade in South Asia

Although acceleration of economic growth through regional cooperation was incorporated as an objective of the SAARC Charter in 1985, it was not until the late 1980s that South Asian governments made an explicit commitment towards promoting an economic agenda. A Committee for Economic Cooperation (CEC) was set up in 1991 to examine a proposal for a PTA, the framework of which was finalized in 1993. The resultant South Asian Preferential Trade Agreement (SAPTA) provides for the exchange of concessions between members on tariffs, para-tariffs and NTBs.

Table 2: Number of Tariff Lines and Tariff Range Negotiated under SAPTA

Country		*Number of tariff lines*	*Tariff range*[a]		
			SAPTA-1	*SAPTA-2*	*SAPTA-3*
Bangladesh	All	407	10	10	10
	LDCs	144	10	10	10-15
Bhutan	All	109	15	10-15	10
	LDCs	124	10-15	10-15	10-20
India	All	472	10-90	10-50	10-25
	LDCs	2082	50-100	50-100	50
Maldives	All	172	7.5	7.5-10	10
	LDCs	6	7.5	7.5-10	..
Nepal	All	328	7.5-10	7.5-10	5-10
	LDCs	163	10	15	10-15
Pakistan	All	262	10	10-15	10-20
	LDCs	229	15	15	30
Sri Lanka	All	155	10-20	10-20	10
	LDCs	44	15-25	60	10-75
SAARC	All	1095	7.5-90	7.5-50	5-25
	LDCs	2762	7.5-100	7.5-100	10-75

Notes: (a) as a per cent of MFN tariff rate.

Source: Compiled from the Consolidated National Schedule of Concessions of Member States.

Four basic modes of negotiations are provided, namely: (i) product-by-product; (ii) across-the-board; (iii) sectoral; and (iv) direct trade measures.[14]

SAPTA came into formal operation with the ratification of the first round of negotiations on 226 product items in December 1995. A second round of negotiations on a further 1900 product items was completed in 1996 and a third round, encompassing a 2500 product items was concluded in 1998. India has offered the largest number of concessions followed by Bangladesh, Pakistan and Nepal (Table 2).[15] India has also offered the highest margins on tariff concessions, but given that its MFN rates have tended to be higher than those of its partners, this is to be expected.

As the rounds of negotiations proceeded, some concessions were offered in the face of increasing criticism of the limited nature of tariff preferences granted. While the first and second rounds were conducted on the basis of a product-by-product coverage, the third round included chapter-wise negotiations on a very limited basis. In 1998, the rules of origin requirements of fifty per cent (forty per cent for LDC member countries of SAARC) were relaxed to forty per cent (and thirty per cent for LDC member countries). In addition, each country was required to identify existing para-tariff and non-tariff barriers (NTBs) prevailing on items on which concessions had been granted. Nevertheless, such concessions failed to address the larger problems associated with the SAPTA process. These have been well identified in the literature.[16] The most limiting factor has been the actual trade coverage of preferential access granted. In fact, it has been estimated that on average only 8.4 per cent of tariff lines in the case of imports from non-LDC countries (and 6.2 per cent in the case of imports from the LDC countries are covered by the tariff concessions in the three concluded by 1998.[17] In reality, products imported under SAPTA concessions translated to only fifteen per cent of total imports between SAARC member countries.[18]

As would be expected, SAPTA therefore, has had little or no impact in changing the existing trade patterns in South Asia. Intra-SAARC trade which accounted for less than three per cent of trade in South Asia for much of the 1980s increased gradually to over four per cent in the first half of the 1990s primarily on account of the increased trade flows associated with unilateral liberalization efforts across the region (Table 3). There has been no discernible increase with the implementation of SAPTA given the singularly ineffective mode of negotiations.

Table 3: Intra-SAARC Trade

	Intra-SAARC trade (US $ mn)	*World trade of SAARC countries (US $ mn)*	*Share of intra-SAARC trade in world trade of SAARC countries (%)*
1980	1210	37885	3.2
1985	1054	44041	2.4
1990	1584	65041	2.4
1995	4228	104159	4.1
1996	4914	111479	4.4
1997	4390	115961	3.8
1998	6073	121331	5.0
1999	5640	129738	4.4
2000	5884	141978	4.1
2001	6537	139585	4.7

Source: IMF, *Direction of Trade Statistics*, various issues.

Nevertheless, there was a general feeling of optimism as the groundwork was being initiated to consider issues related to the transition to a free trade area. India took the lead under its 'Gujaral Doctrine' to remove NTBs on nearly 2000 products for its South Asian neighbours ahead of its WTO commitments and proposed that implementation of SAFTA should be brought forward to 2001 (from the proposed date of 2005) at the SAARC Heads of State Summit in 1998.[19] Unfortunately, political relations between India and Pakistan were to deteriorate with the election of the more rightwing BJP government, and subsequent nuclear test explosions by both India and Pakistan in 1998. The incursion of Pakistan into India held territory (Kargil) in 1999 and the resultant military standoff, and change of leadership in Pakistan on the heels of a military coup were to further weaken relations between the two countries. As the deterioration in bilateral relations spilled over on to the SAARC process there was an inevitable toll on the SAARC economic agenda, prompting a change of direction which could well be argued to have made the SAPTA/SAFTA process of marginal interest to the region.

The change in direction manifested in the form of bilateral trade agreements between SAARC countries. While India had already granted access to its market on a preferential bilateral basis to Bhutan and Nepal, the defining agreement was to come in the form of the Indo-Lanka Free Trade Agreement (ILFTA) signed in December 1998. Under the ILFTA, India agreed to remove tariffs on 1351 products, immediately upon the coming into force of the treaty.[20] However, both countries agreed to maintain negative lists that will safeguard 'sensitive' domestic industries whereby the FTA would not apply to items placed under such a list. India submitted a negative list of 429 items and agreed to phase out prevailing tariffs on the balance items over a span of three years: fifty per cent reduction of Indian customs duties in the first year; seventy five per cent in the second year; and hundred per cent in the third year.[21] Sri Lanka will, therefore, be able to have duty free access to the Indian market (excluding those items coming under the negative list) three years after the FTA becomes operative.

In return, Sri Lanka submitted a negative list consisting of 1180 items and undertook to grant immediate duty free access to India on 319 items. In addition, a fifty per cent margin of preferencewas offered on a further 889 items, with the preferential reduction raised to seventy, ninety and hundred per cent over a three year period. The duty on the balance items (excluding those that do not fall within Sri Lanka's negative list) are expected to be phased out over an eight year period –thirty five per cent of the existing duty level by the end of the first three of the eight years; seventy per cent of the existing duty level by the end of the sixth year; and hundred per cent removal of duties by the end of the eighth year. Thus, India will have duty free access to the Sri Lankan market for its exports (excluding those items in the negative list) after eight years of the signing of the FTA.

Table 4: Applicability of FTA to Indo-Sri Lanka Traded Commodities

	Sri Lanka's Concessions		*India's Concessions*	
	No.	%	No.	%
Negative	623	21.4	50	13.1
0 %	3	0.1	68	17.9
50%	598	20.6	218	57.4
25%	-	-	44	11.6
Other	1683	57.9	-	-
Total	2907	100.0	380	100.0

Source: Compiled from Sri Lanka Customs Database.

The ILFTA is by no means a free trade agreement in the conventional definition, which assumes that tariffs will be eliminated with respect to 'substantially all trade'. Estimates of those items retained under negative lists suggest that items placed on Sri Lanka's negative list accounted for over twenty per cent of India's total exports to Sri Lanka at the time the agreement came into force, and the Indian negative list accounted for over thirteen per cent of Sri Lanka's total exports to India (Table 4). Nonetheless, the agreement was certainly a step forward in comparison to market access granted under the SAPTA process.[22] This is clearly evident from the data in Table 5 which lists the number of concessions granted to Sri Lanka by India under SAPTA and the ILFTA applicable to goods actually traded between the two countries. Under SAPTA concessions offered by India to non-LDC member states (484 items), only 30 items were of actual trade interest to Sri Lanka. By contrast, the total number of traded goods on which immediate zero tariff reduction and 50 per cent concessional reductions offered to Sri Lanka under the ILFTA amount to over 280 items.

While the idea of 'fast-track' liberalization – allowing those countries willing to proceed at a quicker pace of liberalization the means to do so while others join the process at a slower pace – has been discussed for some time, the actual outcome has been that SAARC countries are increasingly engaging in bilateral agreements outside of the regional framework altogether. Pakistan

Table 5: Concessions on Traded Products to Sri Lanka by India under SAPTA and ILFTA

HS Code Chapters		*Composition of SL exports to India*	*No. of concessions granted under SAPTA*	*No. of concessions granted under ILFTA[a]*
01-05	Live animals, animal products	2.2		2
06-14	Vegetable products	38.8	6	20
15	Animal or vegetable fats and oils	7.3		3
16-24	Prepared foodstuffs	0.8	4	28
25-27	Mineral products	0.2	2	3
28-38	Chemical products	1.0	6	36
39-40	Plastics & rubber	11.3	4	10
41-43	Leather products	0.2		4
44-46	Wood products	0.1	3	7
47-49	Paper products	9.6	2	21
50-63	Textile articles	10.9		
64-67	Footwear	0.2	1	4
68-70	Stone, plaster, cement	1.0		11
71	Pearls	0.3		4
72-83	Base metal	14.0	1	37
84-85	Machinery & mechanical goods	1.7		58
86-89	Transport equipment	0.0	1	9
90-92	Optical, photographic equip.	0.1		10
93	Arms & ammunition	0.0		
94-96	Misc. manufactured articles	0.2		19
97-99	Works of art	0.0		
Total	Total	100.0	30	286

Notes: (a) Concessions on items offered immediate zero duty and fifty per cent tariff reduction only.

Source: Compiled from Sri Lanka Customs Database

in turn proposed FTA with Sri Lanka, the Framework Agreement of which was signed in July 2002. In addition, both India and Sri Lanka have indicated interest in extending FTAs to Bangladesh in the near future. Given the diversity of SAARC countries, bilateral FTAs are likely to differ significantly from one another in terms of its coverage, rules and regulation, depth of tariff reductions, etc. This will not only create serious problems for SAARC in managing its external trade relationship, but also add to the cost of doing business, as investors and traders will have to deal with differences in scope and speed of tariff reduction and rules and regulations.

The fragmentation of the regional negotiations into bilateral deals holds serious implications for the proposed transition to a free trade area. It is implicitly a recognition that the SAARC process has failed to deliver on the economic front. The emergence of bilateral deals brings into question the rationale for continued engagement in the SAARC economic process for some of its members. In the case of Sri Lanka, for example, it has little economic benefits to gain having already assured itself of access to key partners in South Asia through bilateral deals. The only way that SAARC can regain its relevance and initiative as a forum to drive the economic integration process in South Asia is if the SAFTA treaty goes beyond the current bilateral agreements in freeing trade between member states. The key question then is whether the political-economy relationships that govern negotiations are likely to permit such a scenario to unfold.

4. The Political-economy Relations in South Asia: Is there a Role for SAFTA

The underlying political-economy relations that have governed SAARC were evident even at its inception. As succinctly outlined by Maas,[23] the initial negotiations on membership pointed to the pervasive influence of geo-politics in the region. In defining which set of countries constitute 'South Asia', the status of Afghanistan was to dominate the discussion. Prior to the Soviet invasion of Afghanistan in 1979, it was largely perceived as a part of the South Asian region given its strategic importance as a gateway to the Indian subcontinent from Central Asia. Following the Soviet invasion (and the Iranian Revolution), Afghanistan came to be regarded more as a part of South West Asia, while Pakistan came to the forefront as an anti-communist 'frontline' state. According to Maas,[24] India was therefore keen to include Afghanistan in SAARC as one means of diluting Pakistan's strategic importance. While the final decision was to exclude Afghanistan, it nevertheless is an indicator of the often combative political relations that was to govern the SAARC process (In the recent summit in Dhaka, the member states of SAARC have agreed to include Afghanistan as a member).

Despite the almost immediate skepticism, SAARC was launched on the premise that traditional conflicts in South Asia had lost much of their edge and the region was increasingly subject to new sources of conflict, which could be contained more effectively through bilateral and multilateral modes of cooperation. The new conflicts were argued to originate from three sources: involvement in each other's domestic conflicts; transfer of arms and weapons to the region from outside; and possibility of a nuclear arms race between India and Pakistan.[25] To some extent they were seen as persisting from the lack of conflict control mechanisms in the region and here, the emergence of SAARC as a formal regional forum was seen in a positive light. In addition, it was also maintained that the ethnic diaspora across between India and its neighbours created a natural progression to build support for regionalism by supporting the emergence of a common South Asian identity. However, it can be rightly argued that when ethnic groups draw support across national boundaries, the optimistic assumption that old conflicts have waned is not entirely true.

In reality, the influence of the old sources of conflict was fairly obvious from the early SAARC process as member countries decided to exclude 'contentious bilateral issues' from the agenda. It was seen as a pragmatic answer to complex issues in South Asia given the host of bilateral problems that existed – primarily between Pakistan and India, but also between India and its smaller neighbours including Nepal, Bangladesh and Sri Lanka. It could well be argued, however, that the region lost a vital opportunity to permit a role for SAARC as a mediator in regional conflicts. As a result, the ebb and flow of bilateral relations, particularly between India and Pakistan, have had an undue influence in dictating the course of SAARC's economic agenda.

It is not surprising that some political economists have drawn what seems to be an inevitable conclusion that the most likely scenario for South Asia is that it will remain locked in an unstable situation.[26] The argument put forward is that in light of the Indo-centric nature of the region, any change will require that India adopts a more accommodating stance.[27] However, it is rightly argued that India may regard accommodation as unnecessary given that it considers itself powerful enough to cope with any tension in the subcontinent, where such reluctance in turn will then serve to strengthen anti-Indian hawks in Pakistan. Moreover, given the economic predominance of India in the region, any meaningful effort towards regional trade integration will require active Indian participation. However, such an integration of economies that has India as the dominant member may be perceived as a threat to blur Pakistan's political and strategic identity and thus may never be fully acceptable. It is difficult, therefore, to oppose the view that South Asia may never benefit from a true spirit of regionalism.

In this political-economy backdrop, the question of whether South Asian countries will commit to regional free trade that will require considerable commitment to open access to their markets than shown in the past is questionable. SAFTA will generate a sense of genuine interest only if it goes well beyond the current bilateral agreements. Not only will it have to offer more liberal terms, but the timing of its implementation is also likely to be critical. In the context of successive postponement of SAARC summits, negotiations on a draft treaty could not begin until 2002 and could only be signed at the Islamabad summit of 2004. While it is a step forward, SAFTA is to be fully implemented by 2013 for the non-LDC member states (and 2016 for LDC members), well after existing bilateral FTAs are expected to be fully implemented in 2008.[28] In addition, such a long phase-out of tariffs will also offer little by way of preferential gains given that most of the South Asian countries are in any event engaged in the process of reducing tariffs and other barriers on a unilateral basis. SAARC countries may also be tempted to negotiate key traded commodities on to their respective negative lists provided for under the SAFTA treaty. However, this is likely to defeat the ultimate purpose of an FTA guaranteeing free trade in the region.

As SAFTA negotiations proceed, it also appears increasingly to be out of step with strategic trade policy alternatives that are cropping in the face of a rapidly changing global economic environment. India and Sri Lanka have begun negotiations to go further from the framework agreement of the ILFTA towards a broad Economic Partnership Agreement. This is intended to take economic cooperation beyond trade in goods alone to include moves to increase market access to each other on a preferential basis in areas of investment and services. In turn, both India and Sri Lanka have begun to seek similar agreements with Singapore, while bilateral FTAs are also being pursued with more advanced economies. Such bilateral deals are also being complemented through engagement in other regional blocs to strengthen links with more advanced Southeast Asian economic through the Bangkok Agreement and the BIMSTEC (Bangladesh, India, Myanmar, Sri Lanka, Thailand Economic Cooperation) Agreement. India and Pakistan have also gained observer status at the ASEAN in pursuit of their strategic trade policies with East Asian economies. These new developments are likely to shape not only trade policies but also are seen as means by which a country's broad reform agenda can be tied in to facilitate more market oriented reforms. The mere fact of attempting to negotiate with more advanced economies can help to galvanize the domestic reform process, particularly as they begin to go beyond trade in goods and come to include trade in services and investment. These initiatives are supported by emerging new evidence that appears to suggest that unlike the trade diverting effects of preferential trade agreements, the so called 'third wave' of PTAs which cover non trade provisions — particularly those related to investment and services – offer more optimistic findings in terms of real economic gains.[29]

5. Conclusion

Although SAARC was slow to embrace the concept of economic cooperation, having done so, it moved swiftly thereafter to set itself an ambitious agenda. It could well be argued that the initial schedule of moving South Asia towards a free trade area within a span of five years or so was too ambitious. It also had the unfortunate effect of raising expectations and of irrevocably tying the perceived success or failure of SAARC firmly to the achievements on the economic front. With hindsight, given the long history of political tension in the region, it appears that SAARC leaders were perhaps naïve in their belief that political differences could be set aside to allow headway on the economic front. Progress on economic cooperation has long been viewed as one the means of building confidence through binding of South Asian economic interests. But the experience of SAPTA negotiations indicate not only the lack of commitment of SAARC countries to open their markets to each other but also that economic cooperation is doomed to achieve little in the absence of political goodwill amongst member countries. The introduction of bilateral free trade agreements among SAARC countries is likely to lead to further fragmentation of a common South Asian goal towards regional integration.

The question then remains whether economic cooperation within the framework of a regional arrangement in South Asia has any future. The first step that has to be taken is to acknowledge the limitations of past performance. In turn, it should lead to a healthy debate of whether deeper economic integration is desired by all member countries. If SAARC countries are to go forward without loss of credibility, mere rhetoric on commitment to freer regional trade will not suffice. It will have to be matched at the negotiating table by a willingness to commit to a clearly delineated agenda and an undertaking to insulate the economic agenda as far as possible from regional politics. Recent experience has not been promising and leaves little room optimism. As the momentum in trade policy negotiations moves away from SAARC, the consequences for the organization itself could be grave. There would then be little political impetus to make it more effective even in the future.

References

1 R. Blackhurst, A. Enders, and J.F. Francois, "The Uruguay Round and Market Access: Opportunities and Challenges for Developing

Countries", in W. Martin, and L.A.Winters (eds.), *The Uruguay Round and the Developing Countries*, Cambridge: Cambridge University Press, 1996.

2 See J.Viner, *The Customs Union Issue*, New York: Carnegie Endowment for International Peace, 1950.

3 J. De Melo, A. Panagariya and D. Rodrik, *The New Regionalism: A Country Perspective*, Washington, D.C :World Bank, 1993.

4 T.N.Srinivasan, and G. Canonero, "Liberalisation of Trade Among Neighbours: Two Illustrative Models and Simulations", South Asia Discussion Paper Series, Supplement II to IDP No. 142, 1993.

5 T.N.Srinivasan, *Regional Trading Arrangements and Beyond: Exploring Some Options for South Asia - Theory, Empirics and Policy*, Report No:142, Washington: World Bank, 1994.

6 While the gravity model has a number of advantages in analyzing intra-regional trade, particularly for preferential trade agreements, it also has many limitations. It does not take into consideration the possible impact of the terms of trade associated with trade creation. Hence, the simulated results based on a gravity model are generally biased upwards. The estimates also give the results in a static framework and the extent of intra-regional trade will possibly increase further if the estimation is carried out in a dynamic framework, incorporating the effects of factors like terms of trade, scale economies, technology spill-overs, investment flows, etc.

7. M. Pigato, C. Farah, K. Itakura, K. Jun, W. Martin, K. Murrell and T.G. Srinivasan, *South Asia's Integration into the World Economy*, Washington, D.C.: World Bank, 1997.

8. The study employs the Global Trade Policy Analysis Project delete model which takes into account the production structure of each region of the world, bilateral trade between regions, and major global trade distortions.

9. A. Panagariya, "Trade Liberalization in South Asia: Recent Liberalization and Future Agenda", *The World Economy*, vol. 22, no. 3, 1999.

10. For example, it has been estimated that small economies will benefit from gains from trade under the proposed Free Trade Agreement of the Americas (see World Bank, 1995).

11. See M. Michaely, "Trade-Preferential Agreements in Latin America", Policy Research Working Paper, World Bank, Washington, D.C., 1996.
12. For a study of trade and investment links between India and Nepal, see I.N.Mukherji, "India's Trade and investment Linkages with Nepal: Some Reflections", South *Asian Survey,* vol.5, no.2, 1998, and for a study of trade and investment linkages between India and Sri Lanka, see I.N.Mukherji , "Indo-Sri Lanka Trade and Investment Linkages: With Special Reference to SAPTA and Free Trade Agreement", *South Asia Economic Journal*, vol. 1, no. 1, 2000. For a more detailed assessment of potential trade-investment nexus in South Asia, see S. Jayasuriya and D. Weerakoon, "Foreign Direct Investment and Economic Integration in the SAARC Region" in T.N. Srinivasan (ed.) *Trade, Finance and Investment in South Asia*, New Delhi: Social Sciences Press, 2001.
13. D. Weerakoon, "Indo-Sri Lanka Free Trade Agreement: How Free is it?", *Economic and Political Weekly,* vol. 36, no.8, 2001.
14. 'Product-by-product' means negotiating at HS 6-digit tariff line. 'Across-the-board' means a uniform reduction applying to all products under negotiations. 'Sectoral basis' means negotiations on tariff, para-tariff and NTBs, as well as other trade promotion or cooperation measures for specified products or groups of products closely related in end use or in production. 'Direct trade measures' means negotiations to promote trade through buyback arrangements, state trading operations, government procurement, etc.
15. The LDC member states within SAARC have also been offered a larger share of such concessions *vis-à-vis* the non-LDC states. Thus, some concessions have been offered only to LDC states. The LDC members of SAPTA have also been offered higher tariff preferences than the non-LDC members.
16. Weerakoon, n.13, I.N.Mukherji,n.12.
17. See *World Bank,* 2003.
18. I.N Mukherji, "Charting a Free Trade Area in South Asia: Instruments and Modalities", a paper presented at the Second Conference of the South Asia Network of Economic Research Institutes (SANEI), Kathmandu, 26-29 August 2000.

19. The 'Gujaral Doctrine' by India was essentially based on the principle of offering concessions to its smaller neighbours on a non-reciprocal basis.
20. The products were to be named within 60 days of the signing of the agreement. However, the exchange of lists was delayed until March 2000 due to various reasons, including some opposition by both Indian and Sri Lankan interest groups.
21. With the exception of concessions on textile items in Chapters 51-56, 58-60 and 63 where the margin of preference will be restricted to twenty five per cent.
22. The ILFTA also has more relaxed rules of origin requirement *vis-à-vis* SAPTA, allowing products having a domestic value addition of thirty five per cent to qualify for preferential market access. In addition, those Sri Lankan exports having a minimum ten per cent content of inputs originating from India will qualify for preferential market access under a reduced total domestic value addition of twenty five per cent.
23. C.D. Maass, "South Asia: Drawn Between Cooperation and Conflict" in E. Gonsalves and N. Jetley (eds.), *The Dynamics of South Asia: Regional Cooperation and SAARC*, New Delhi: Sage Publications, 1999.
24. *Ibid.*
25. *Ibid.*
26. *Ibid.*
27. India accounts for seventy four per cent of the region's total population, seventy six per cent of its GNP and sixty four per cent of its export trade.
28. The ILFTA become fully operational by 2008 while the proposed FTA between Pakistan and Sri Lanka is also set to follow a similar time frame for implementation.
29. R.P. Adams, J. Gali Dee and G. McGuire, *The Trade and Investment Effects of Preferential Trading Arrangements: Old and New Evidence*, Productivity Commission Staff Working Paper, Canberra, May 2003.

11

Envisioning A South Asian Union: Challenges

J. Laxminarasimha Rao

The twentieth century witnessed the emergence of a number of regional organizations and blocks. A few of these are created for military purposes and most are established for economic purposes. The last decade of the earlier century provided for greater impetus for regional cooperation across the world. As global tensions and rivalries being relaxed with the end of the cold war, greater incentives for regionalism flourished. The situation also brought economic prosperity and creation and distribution of wealth to the centrestage of inter-state relations. Search for new markets, formation of new trading blocks are the dominant themes of economic discourse beyond geographical boundaries. To a large extent, issues of economic cooperation have taken precedence over strategic and political considerations. In fact, strategic issues are constructed from the economic angle. Under the influence of global changes, the regional organizations either tried to transform or tried to activate and expand by bringing a few structural changes. Thus EEC transformed into EU and expanded with new members across the Europe, APEC is created across the regions and ASEAN incorporated the Indo-China states. Economic compulsions are driving the members of a regional grouping to have simultaneous membership in other groupings defying the logic of a region.

The changing global situation and the emerging challenges influenced the countries of South Asia to move in the direction of regional cooperation. But it is a late starter in the direction of regional integration. For a long time the region remained untouched by the wave of regionalism that swept different sub-regions including Africa and Latin America and Asia. Only in the early years of 1980s, initiative for regional cooperation in South Asia was taken and by the middle of the decade it assumed institutionalized form. By this time the countries of South Asia realized that regional integration provides the best opportunity to member states to cope with the regional and global challenges. By joining together, the member countries are in a better position to acquire better leverage for dealing with the global system of finance, money and trade.

II

South Asia consisting seven countries – Bangladesh, Bhutan, India, Maldives, Nepal, Pakistan and Sri Lanka – is having one fifth of world population but only 3.4 percent of world trade and less than 2 percent of world output.[2] The region is placed between the ASEAN group in the East, the GCC group in the West and China in the North. It is the most asymmetric region in term of demography, geography and economic development. There are variations in political institutions and huge gap in threat perceptions.[3] Only with India all other countries share common borders. The region is a Indo-Centric one. Most of the countries of the region view India with suspicion and perceive threats from it. Further there are border disputes between India and others. These conditions to a great extent determine the bilateral and regional relations in South Asia. Despite asymmetries, border disputes and political rivalries, South Asian countries came together and formed a regional organization in the middle of the 1980s. The initiative came from one of the smaller countries of the region having second largest population. The working paper was drafted by the country, which took the initiative, and various rounds of discussions were held over it in the region. Finally SAARC had emerged in 1985 to promote regional cooperation and integration in South Asia.

The SAARC charter, adopted by the Heads of State on 8 December 1985, contains peace, freedom, social justice, economic prosperity as objectives to be achieved by mutual understanding, good neighbourly relations and meaningful cooperation. It also provides a framework within the spirit of friendship, trust and understanding. Intra-state relations and regional cooperation is based on the respect for principle of sovereign equality, territorial equality, political independence, non-interference in internal affairs of others. The charter, though aims at welfare of the people of the region, economic growth in member countries and self-reliance, there are no clear indications how these can be achieved. Articles 6 and 7 emphasize on activities of the Technical Committees and Action Committees, but the meeting of these Committees turned out to be ritualistic and bogged down into political controversy.

Until a decade ago economic cooperation did not figure in the agenda. The concept of regional economic cooperation was viewed with skepticism. The distrust and intra-regional rivalry directly influenced the gradual evolution of the South Asian regionalism. From its very inception, the functioning of the SAARC is crippled by unanimity of decision and exclusion of bilateral and contentious issues from its ambit. Thus initially agreed areas of cooperation did not include the vital areas of trade, investment, joint ventures, industrial cooperation, and harmonization of fiscal, monetary and social policies. It is these areas that constitute the building blocks of integration and sustaining it. Thus South Asia failed to usher the economic dynamism of the rest of Asia. The average growth rate for South Asia was only 4.6 per cent against 8.8 per cent in Southeast Asia in the last quarter of the twentieth century. On the trade front other Asian countries increased their share of world trade by about eighteen per cent between 1970s and 1990s whereas South Asia's share declined by twenty five per cent.[4] This situation arose as there lacks a framework for assessing the SAARC in terms trade creation and growth of intra-regional trade prior to the creation of the South Asian Preferential Trade Areas (SAPTA).

Generally it is the political questions that dominate every aspect of relations among the SAARC countries. The crucial political question is the extent of commitment on the part of the member countries. It seems that all the members are not enthusiastic supporters of regional cooperation and integration but the reluctant partners. As a result the driving force is missing. Economic cooperation requires a driving force as an element of voluntarism, an opportunity of gain and a risk of loss in meeting the obligation. The binding force is that none of the countries are members of any other regional bloc. Similarly commitment is weak due to lack of unity. Hardly there has been an occasion that all the SAARC countries have spoken in one voice.

The SAARC summits are affected by structural limitations. There is no institution where bilateral and contentious issues can be discussed. In fact, SAARC organization bars discussion of such issues though they have been influencing the SAARC process and evolution. Had open regionalism is practiced the separatists conflicts such as Kashmir crisis, Northeast India problem, Tamil issue in Sri Lanka, Nepalese problem in Bhutan, tribals' question in Bangladesh could be addressed.

Major hurdles for economic cooperation in the South Asian region are political divisions, rivalry and conflicts. The forces of demand and supply, comparative cost advantages and human capital do not govern trade, investment and macro-economic policies in the region. Thus the increasing pace of globalization of trade, capital and investment are the major challenges for the region though they equally provide new opportunities. The member states of the SAARC do not take a similar stand in international fora and speak in different voices. They, too, refuse to accord the status that is normally given to others to fulfill international obligations. For instance, at the ministerial meeting of the WTO in December 1996 they did not adopt a similar stand. Some opposed trade and labour issues being linked while others did not oppose because child labour is not an issue in some countries.[5] At the regional level, Pakistan has been regulating its trade with India by denying MFN (Most Favoured Nations) status for political reasons. It argues that its production base would be destroyed by the Indian competition.[6] The argument is not tenable as Islamabad's protectionism is exclusively directed to imports from India. This policy indicates that security concerns dominate over trade. But such actions and policies are increasingly becoming unsustainable in the framework of the WTO and globalization.

Further, the SAARC as an institution advocates collective economic benefits. This connotes that acting together for common ends is cooperation. But it is less than integration. There is no merging of identity, the institution only facilitates interaction. Thus SAARC articulates the broad objectives of the organization and excludes contentious issues.

III

Despite mutual distrust, competition, rivalry and acrimonious debates about the issues, the South Asian states initiated steps to promote greater understanding, economic cooperation and harmonious integration. Major countries of the region opted for liberalization policies as part of structural adjustment programme either at the behest of the World Bank or due to fulfill obligations under the WTO regime. Whatever may be the reason, these countries started looking at the world from a new angle. They took steps to integrate their economies with the world economy. Under this they opened their economies for competition, efficiency and standardization. Further they promoted trade, investment and reduced tariffs and adopted measures to reduce non-tariff barriers for promotion of trade. These means resulted in the South Asian countries moving in the direction of according MFN status to each other in the region and adopting Preferential Trade Area and Free Trade Area at a latter stage.

It is viewed by scholars that under a preferential trade arrangement, members of a regional group grant preferences or concessions for both tariff and non-tariff restrictions on imports. This would lead to an increase in imports and promote mutual trade and thus contributing to the economic development of the members in a region. The assumption of a preferential arrangement is that goods and services produced by members are in demand among the other members of the region and tariff and non-tariff barriers are the impediments to trade. Following on these lines, the sixth SAARC summit held in Colombo started discussions on Preferential Trade Arrangement in 1991 by establishing Inter-Governmental Group (IGG) to suggest measures for trade liberalization in South Asia.

The IGG met twice to draft SAPTA agreement. The framework agreement on SAPTA was signed at the seventh SAARC summit held in Dhaka in April 1993. The eighth SAARC summit held in New Delhi in May 1995 formally approved the SAPTA. During the negotiations, the SAARC study on Trade, Manufacturers and Services had recommended in its report that as a first step all the countries in the region should accord to each other atleast MFN status[7] Thereafter, the member countries could follow a product by product approach for extending tariff concessions on products of mutual trade interest.[8] The report was seriously examined and considered by the IGG while drafting the SAPTA agreement. The initial negotiations revolved around tariff preferences on a product-by-product basis and the least developed countries such as Bangladesh, Nepal, Bhutan and Maldives are to get special consideration and treatment.

During the first round of negotiations – SAPTA-I- a total of 226 products were offered concessions by member states. Of these, India offered tariff concessions on the largest number of products i.e., 106, Pakistan on thirty five products, Sri Lanka on thirty one products; Maldives on seventeen products, Nepal on fourteen products, Bangladesh on eleven products and Bhutan on seventeen products. India, on an average offered fifty per cent cuts (with a minimum of ten per cent on some products) and others on an average agreed ten per cent cuts.[9] The agreement laid down safeguard conditions under which a member state can temporarily suspend preferences on account of surge in imports from any member state, which causes injury to the domestic producers or causes balance of payments.[10] It also provided for voluntary exist to any member state.

The total value of trade during the first round increased to six per cent of intra-regional trade in 1993. India offered concessions equivalent to $ 12.1 million while it received concessions worth $ 40 million.[11] The figures though small, member states lost $ 4.5 million customs revenue. The benefits made the South Asian states to move forward for greater economic cooperation and integration by launching the second round of negotiations at the SAARC commerce ministers meeting in January 1996. The IGG met in Colombo in March, in Islamabad in September, in New Delhi in October and in Kathmandu in November 1996. The round was completed and came into force in March 1997 and known as SAPTA – II

The SAPTA – II covered wider exchange of concessions and extensive range of goods. All the countries offered concessions on as many as 2013 products. Of these, India has offered tariff concessions on 902 commodities, of which 390 offered to all and 512 are offered to least developed countries of the region. The range of duty concessions offered by India varied from ten per cent to fifty per cent. In return India received concession on 474 products. Pakistan offered concessions on 363 products; Sri Lanka on ninety five commodities; Bangladesh offered an elaborate list comprising 226 items; Bhutan on forty seven; Nepal list covered as many as 233 commodities; the Maldives offer included only five items.[12] Another feature of the SAPTA-II is that it has listed all-important Non-Tariff Barriers (NTBs) with particular reference to Quantitive Restrictions (QRs).

The SAPTA agreement is modest step to promote greater economic integration among the South Asian countries. It provides a framework to encourage intra-SAARC trade enabling the member states to accord discriminatory treatment in favour of products manufactured in the region. Its instruments include exchange of tariff concessions on a preferential basis and direct trade measures such medium and long term contracts containing import and supply commitment in respect of specific products, buy-back arrangement, state trading operations (Article 4). The agreement also provides for a number of approaches to trade negotiations such as product-by-product basis, across the board tariff reductions, sectoral agreements and also reducing para-tariffs related to border charges and fees, other than tariffs on foreign trade transactions and non-tariff barriers (Article 5) for promoting intra- SAARC trade.[13] The agreement also consists rules envisaging step by step liberalization of South Asian Trade and periodic rounds of negotiations for extending concessions.

SAPTA, inspite of its laudable principles, could not shift changes in intra-regional trade that it is supposed to do. There are many reasons: (a) the commodities covered by it have too low to make any major impact on the regions total import; (b) the commodities offered for tariff concessions were also low if a comparison is made to the total imports of the respective countries. For instance, India imports around 6,600 commodities from different parts of the world, of which only 324 originate from the SAARC countries.[14] As of the tariff concessions, out of the 106 commodities offered for India, it imported hardly twenty three items during 1993-94; while Bangladesh offered concessions for twelve items, it imported only six from India in 1992-93; Nepal offered concessions for eleven items, it imported only three; Sri Lanka offered concessions for thirty one items but imported only seventeen items from India in 1993-94. One of the major countries in South Asia, Pakistan has not extended MFN status to India, though it identified 578 items as eligible for imports from India, of which it imported thirteen products.[15] Further, the least developed and smaller countries seek a withdrawal of all import restrictions by India on their imports. Bangladesh requested India to remove all tariffs and non-tariff barriers on its exports to obtain access to the huge Indian market. On the contrary, Sri Lanka over the years pressed India for a fast-track approach to bilateral trade to enable both move towards a free trade area in a short span of time.[16] India and Sri Lanka signed a Free Trade Agreement in December1998. Bangladesh's and Sri Lanka's requests are based on that the present incremental concessions under SAPTA only benefit commodities of these countries whose production base is narrow thus limiting the benefits. A trade regime providing unrestricted access to the Indian market for all goods from these countries would enable investors from the region and from global to invest in these countries. Such a development would transform the economies of these countries. It also creates new growth centers providing an opportunity for more people to benefit from the South Asian integration.

Establishment of SAPTA is considered the first step towards a Free Trade Area (FTA) and then to an Economic Union. In early stages of their evolution, the EU and the ASEAN introduced preferential trading arrangement particularly product-by-product preferential tariffs. The rationale of Preferential Trading Arrangement is based on the theory that 'the second best' where discriminatory Regional Trading Arrangements such as a common market with zero internal tariffs and a common external tariffs on non-members are best steps towards the "first step" of non-discriminatory free trade at global level.[17] From the EU experience, it becomes clear that a region can become dynamic with the increase in output, income and employment, and improving terms of trade and attracting FDI to Increase a region's competitive exports and with spill-over effects over to non-members through preferential trade arrangement.

In South Asia with the increasing reduction of average tariff levels, streamlining the number of tariff bonds, phasing out of QRs and subsidies, intra-regional trade increases. India's exports increased from $ 487 million in 1990 to $ 1446 million in 1996 accounting from 2.73 per cent to 4.20 per cent. Similarly imports increased from $ 97 million in 1990 to $ 195 million in 1996.[18] The increase varies with the countries. Intra-SAARC trade is a little more than three per cent. Though it is small, it is the reality due to a number of weak trade linkages.

To overcome the weak structural intra-SAARC trade linkages and to move towards further trade liberalization, the South Asian countries launched another step i.e., South Asia Free Trade Area (SAFTA). It is also a move to make economic integration irreversible.

At the twelfth SAARC summit held in Islamabad in 2004, an agreement was signed and the heads of state/governments adopted a declaration, which generated interest and debate. The declaration provides a roadmap for a South Asian Economic Union and the goal of common currency in the region. Para (3) of the Islamabad declaration states: "We reiterate our commitment made at the eleventh SAARC summit at Kathmandu in January 2002 for the creation of a South Asian Economic Union". The then Indian prime minister A.B. Vajpayee envisaged the idea of moving towards an Economic Union and contemplating the vision of having a single currency for the region.

At the summit an agreement was signed to establish SAFTA that comes into effect from 1 January 2006. As per the agreement the countries of the region would have to reduce tariffs between zero to five per cent for the least developed countries. SAFTA ministerial council has been envisaged for the administration and the implementation of the agreement. It suggests a number of measures that the members may adopt including the removal of barriers to the intra-SAARC investment, harmonization of customs facilities, transit facilities for efficient intra-SAARC trade and simplification of procedures for business visas. The agreement also identified the areas of cooperation, which include:[19]

- Energy cooperation;
- Strengthening transportation, transit and communication links across the region.

- Harmonization of standards and simplification of custom procedures;
- Cooperation through joint ventures;
- Setting up of a South Asian Development Bank ;
- Cooperation among Central Banks ;
- Adoption of common positions at multilateral fora.

SAFTA is an attempt to forge economic unity inspite of the asymmetry flowing from India's economic clout. Advantages flow from FTA because geographically contiguous countries can operate as low transaction costs in the background of proximity of markets, availability of infrastructure across the region and more or les similar consumption pattern.

Another important gain is that FTA creates a large market, which enhances investment both from within the region and from outside. In the contemporary period, FTA enables the countries of the region to cope with the challenges of globalization. The member countries may acquire a better leverage while dealing with others in the global system of finance and aid.

In the case of SAFTA, an econometric study through simulation on the basis of different assumptions was conducted by T.N. Srinivasan covering the different rates of cuts in tariffs. The study concludes that unilateral trade liberalization promises substantial gains; if all tariffs on intra-South Asian trade are abolished, total trade increases by between three per cent of GDP of India and fifty nine per cent of GDP of Nepal and in between for the others. A tariff reductions by fifty per cent increases trade between one per cent of GDP for India and nine per cent for Nepal. It says the increases are much larger for Sri Lanka and Bangladesh. South Asia may do better as a group while dealing with the European Union, NAFTA and East Asia.[20] The gains from SAFTA can be further increased by promoting intra-SAARC investment, technology flows and joint research and development projects, joint ventures, removing policy barriers such as modernization of infrastructure, telecommunications, customs clearance facilities and creating necessary institutions, opines Charan Wadhva.

SAFTA, inspite of wishful thinking and excellent projections, suffers from inherent deficiencies, numerous difficulties and uncertainties. One should not forget that the region took a decade time to create SAPTA and a little less than another decade to move to SAFTA. Despite efforts for such a long time, the SAFTA contains no specific provisions for deeper integration except defining the measures to be initiated in very general terms. This provides an opportunity for the members not to make specific commitment towards the goal. Second, the areas identified for cooperation are constituted as part of the declaration rather than part of SAFTA . This provides enough scope for the members to dilute their involvement and commitment. Third, FTA operations may be curtailed unless rules of origin and certain trade facilitation measures such as application of common external tariffs and harmonization of non-tariff barriers against external (outside the region) imports are adopted. Fourth, the asymmetry of the regional economies vis-à-vis the Indian economy places the smaller states in the grip of the danger of the domination of the Indian economic clout. For instance, the signing of the Indo-Sri Lanka Free Trade agreement was received with skepticism in Colombo. Similarly, unless Pakistan is persuaded in opening its economy according MFN status and about the economic advantages of regional economic integration in South Asia, the SAFTA would fail in its objective.

In addition to these, South Asian trade under SAFTA suffers from different impediments. Unless these problems are addressed and done away the move towards an Economic Union and common currency goal would remain simply a dream. The common impediments that are becoming obstacles for South Asian trade are:

Intra-SAARC lower trade

The South Asian intra-regional trade is very small and insignificant. On an average it is less than three per cent of world trade and is about four per cent of region's total trade. Whereas out of the $ 25 trillion global market a year, NAFTA accounts for about $ 7 trillions; the EU accounts for about $ 7.5 trillions; and East Asia accounts for about $ 6 trillions.[21] Before the creation of

SAPTA, SAARC intra-regional trade has declined as a share of world trade from 3.2 per cent in 1980 to three per cent in 1992.[22] This means SAARC regional market could not absorb more products from the region. It also shows that in South Asia the market is small and trade complementarities are limited. In the ASEAN region, intra-regional trade contributes about ten per cent of its world trade because of greater complementarities. Intra-regional trade in South Asia suffers due to disparities in the level of economic development of the countries in the region. Almost all are caught up in the foreign exchange crisis, widening gap in the balance of payments. Further, high cost of production, lack of strong technological base and innovation make the goods uncompetitive in the region.

Since 1990s, SAARC intra-regional trade has increased significantly through imports by all countries from India except Pakistan. The situation improved further for Indian exports with trade liberalization in the region. The principal destination for all countries exports continues to be the European Union and North America. The situation continues to be so because of prevalence of restrictive trade regime in India and others have little to export to India.

Market Barriers

Another impediment that comes in the way of trade in South Asia is market access, which is a function of many factors such as the stage of liberalization, rules of origin and supply capability. Market access is not only determined by tariff reduction but also by non-tariff barriers. SAPTA and SAFTA could address only tariffs issue to some extent but the non-tariff barriers are not on the priority list. Though tariffs are reduced, South Asia is still having high tariffs in the form of auxiliary customs duties or para-tariffs acting as barriers to market access. Para-tariffs are not categorized under basic custom duties, they come in the form of landing charges, port charges, warehouse charges, etc. Under Gujral doctrine India removed NTBs over 2000 products without requesting for reciprocity from other member countries. The NTBs removal will help only if they are applicable to actively traded goods. As this is not the case, it could not take the trade momentum far off in South Asia.

The rules of origin governing preferential trade or free trade has a link to market access. The preferential trade and free trade have to be in a position to prevent "free riders" using preferential tariffs. For instance, a Korean or a Japanese company based in Bangladesh can use tariff concessions under preferential trade or free trade to sell Korean goods in the Indian market. But if the rules of origin say that forty per cent or fifty per cent of products should be from the region to qualify for exports, it discourages the foreign firm located in Bangladesh to enter into the Indian market.[23] This rules of origin act as an impediment in enlarging the trade in the region.

Supply capability can be another issue regarding market access. A small country like Nepal or Bhutan may not be in a position to supply the quantity required by a country like India. To overcome this, such countries have to go through production diversification and broadening manufacturing sector to meet the demand. Nations can promote joint ventures with buy-back arrangements to address the problem, opines Kelegama.[24] This strategy is adopted by India and Bhutan in the hydro-electric power sector.

More Competitive and Less Complimentary Economies

The individual economies of SAARC countries are more competitive and less complimentary. Almost all the countries' production base is narrow and produces more or less same products and competes in the regional and international markets. It is often said that some fifty years ago the economies were more complimentary as different countries were producing different products. At present India, Nepal, Bangladesh and Pakistan produce more or less same variety of textiles and readymade garments and export to Europe and North America. Same is the case with leather goods. Tea is produced by India and Sri Lanka and both compete with each other in the same markets.

The South Asian region constitutes a small market. It means South Asian trade complimentaries are limited. In the ASEAN region, trade complementarities are greater as intra-regional trade forms about sixteen per cent of its world trade. Here, the choices of products are wide and they are competitive in terms of quality and price. Whereas in South Asia, the goods produced on a large scale do not appear to meet the required consumer demand of the importing country. For instance, Pakistan offers a large market for tea exports of Sri Lanka and India. But a large part of Pakistan tea requirement come from outside the SAARC region because CTC tea imported by Pakistan is not available in adequate quantities. Similarly, machinery and manufactured goods produced by India found to be lesser in quality compared to the ones that come from outside the region. These problems can be overcome with the modernization and restructuring of industry in the region. Though the conditions are undergoing change for the last few years in certain sectors, it has to go a long way from the present one in improving mutual trade in the region.

Lack of Transit Facilities and Circular Routes

For a smooth unhindered, trade transport linkages are vital. Since some of the South Asian states and some regions in these countries are land locked providing transit facilities play an important role. While bilateral trade and transit treaties have governed the transit facilities among the SAARC countries, a common regional transit arrangement is yet to be worked out. Inadequate linkages, poor infrastructure along with poor communications network act as impediments in the growth of trade. Circular routes escalate prices of products. It is roughly estimated that all SAARC countries could benefit to the tune of $ 2 billions from providing transit facilities to each other.

Prevalence of many restrictions, complex and cumbersome procedures make all the countries loose much and pay heavy price. Because of unnatural and circuitous routes, Bangladesh and Pakistan are foregoing freight and license charges in foreign exchange and India is incurring huge costs on its exports.

Shipments are also delayed. For instance, it takes forty five days to transport a container from Delhi to Dhaka, if same is permitted through railways it would take just two or three days. The Southern border of Tripura is only seventy five kilometers from Chittagang port of Bangladesh. Since access for Indian goods are not allowed to Chittagang port, goods from Agartala of India have to cover a distance of 1,645 Km to reach Kolkata (Calcutta). If transit facilities are provided by Bangladesh, the distance to the Kolkata port would be reduced to just 350 kms. Similarly if shipments of Assam tea are allowed through Chittagang airport, it is possible to cut the journey by sixty per cent.[25] Bangladesh also imports cotton from Pakistan which takes about forty days as the consignment has to go through Colombo or Singapore. If it is allowed across India, it would reach within four days.[26] The main reason for this sorry state of affairs is political. As long as political will is lacking, not much can be expected. However, the Islamabad declaration recognized the importance of strengthening transport, transit and communication links across South Asia.

Lack of Standards and Poor Information Facilities

The other impediments that come in the way of intra-regional trade are absence of standards and inadequate information about the products available for trade. The standards include port and customs procedures; quarantive regulations – zoo sanitary and physiosanitary; quality control and certification; product specifications in drugs, chemicals and processed food; product ratings; and packaging and labeling etc. Further, there is lack of arbitration laws and procedure for quick dispute settlement.[27]

Availability of information about products to a greater extent promotes trade. But lack of significant information about products is a major obstacle in South Asia. Member countries import many goods they need from outside the region when they are available within South Asia. Information is not pooled and the manufacturers do not conduct proper market surveys and fail to promote their produce. Information flows have problems. Telecommunication system is weak and information flow is slow and congested during business hours. In the case of Pakistan, there is also a penal charge on telephone calls to India.[28] Cargo clearance in India takes twenty two days against Sri Lanka's ten days and Dubai's just five hours.

Absence of Proper Institutions

South Asia does not have necessary institutions to enable it to mature into an effective regional grouping. The present institutional structure headed by the secretary general is devoid of any provision for qualified professional members of staff to deal with complicated and complex problems that are unique to South Asia. It has become a major handicap for the performance of the SAARC. The secretariat has to attend to specialized nature of work, which it is not able to do much justice in the midst of increasing problems and challenges.

An adhoc structure, group of eminent persons established at the ninth SAARC summit articulated a vision transforming SAARC into a free trade area and from there to South Asian economic community. Its report submitted to the tenth SAARC summit was neither discussed nor endorsed but its vision of a roadmap to an economic community has become part of the Islamabad declaration. Approval of such visions without creating proper institutional framework may not take South Asia anywhere.

Adhocism, unilateral decisions and informal actions, sometimes, resulted in accusations and strong reactions from certain quarters against some member states. They are interpreted as actions of domination in the region. In Bangladesh, there is domestic opposition to Dhaka exporting natural gas to India. Similarly, when the Indo-Bangladesh trade turned in favour of New Delhi in 1991-92, the opposition Bangladesh Nationalist party strongly spoke of India's growing dominance in the Bangladesh economy. If proper institutions are in place such misplaced notions and grievances could be dealt without giving scope for the rise of similar apprehensions in other countries.

To overcome the impediments and to stimulate trade in South Asia, there is a need for technological development, improvement in professional skills and management practices, higher investments in Research and Development (R & D) and making greater access to the regional markets in the era of globalization. Removal of tariff and non-tariff barriers can take trade forward but such measures are not enough to stimulate trade to move towards an economic union. Efforts are to be made to translate whatever production complementarities are there into trade complementarities by allowing investments and starting joint ventures, improving transport and communication facilities, maintaining quality controls and harmonization of customs procedures. Efforts are to be made to reduce the prices of local produce by providing inter-state transit facilities across the South Asian region.

Industrial development can focus on export-oriented industries. As textiles, leather, jute, minerals and agricultural products are common to the whole region proper policies and strategies are to be adopted to coordinate production, quality and pricing across the region. There are many investment opportunities in various mineral based industries too. India is the largest producer of aluminum, iron and steel is a major industry. In Nepal magnetite, limestone, lead and zinc exist. In Bhutan, there are opportunities in the fields of gypsum mining, cement manufacturing. In Bangladesh, there are large deposits of natural gas. So complementarities can be increased by widening the industrial base and diversification of products and exports. To do this, foreign capital can be invited across the region. Smaller states would also gain confidence as the benefits become visible.

As the SAARC process is slow, trade liberalization could not bring sufficient changes in the mindset of policy makers of all the South Asian states, some of them adopted different strategies to increase their trade. To overcome asymmetry, opposition from some, indifference to avail and exploit the new opportunities by a few and refusing to recognize oncoming challenges by some others made some of them to take a new course. Increasing pace of liberalization and a strong desire to derive greater benefits from globalization are forcing the states to attain competitive edge and to acquire greater bargaining power. The course adopted by the South Asian states is signing bilateral free trade agreements among some of them and the strategy of triangle and quadrangle growth areas within South Asia and creating free trade areas between South Asia and others / trans-South Asia trade regimes.

India has signed bilateral free trade agreements with Nepal, Bhutan and Sri Lanka. It is also ready to give similar status to Bangladesh. Pakistan also entered into a similar agreement with Sri Lanka. But free trade between India and Pakistan is still a distant dream as many obstacles come in its way. SAFTA has to go a long way. India's regional trade in South Asia is around one per cent of its total foreign trade. Even if one assumes that it is going to increase significantly, it cannot meet the needs of growing Indian economy. It feels disappointed with the way things are moving in SAARC. To meet the growing demands of the economy, India has adopted the strategy of growth triangle with Sri Lanka and Maldives and growth quadrangle with Bangladesh, Bhutan and Nepal.

The strategy of growth triangle[29] is used to mix resources, division of labour to produce different components of products to exploit trade potential, to overcome dominant economic power by forging business links and ethnic compatibility.[30] India, through bilateral agreements wants to use water resources and develop hydro power for the development of Nepal and Bhutan and also itself. It is also aiming to harness the eastern river basin, develop infrastructure and exploit natural resources for mutual benefit. The growth quadrangle aim at bringing together India's north-eastern states with Bangladesh, Bhutan and Nepal to promote hydro co-operation in international river basin consisting of Ganga and Brahmaputra. The cooperation includes power projects, irrigation facilities and strengthening communications between the countries in this particular area.

In the recent past India has been trying to reach out to trans –Asia trade networks such as IOR-ARC, Bangkok agreement and

BIMSTEC.[31] Some of these efforts may aim at redefining and redrawing the map of South Asia to promote greater economic cooperation by taking a cue from EU's and ASEAN's expansion after the cold war. It may also be an idea to project the economic interests of various nations beyond a particular geographic locations particularly a nation of a billion people by adopting an all together different strategy.

IV

The idea of South Asian Union is attractive and becoming popular among scholars, statesmen and intelligentsia. It tilts away from regional conflicts, animosity, distrust and suspicions that dominated the South Asia region for half a century. It also envisions and ensures a new agenda of cooperation in political, economic, social, cultural and technological fields. Dawn of new perception and cooperation pushes the forces of negativism to the background and releases new ideas and forces to take the region to greater scales of prosperity and peace.

Political rivalry, conflict and mutual threat perceptions are not unique to South Asia. Almost all the regions have experienced more or less similar problem. However, total transformation has taken place when some regions could move away from conflict-ridden agenda to association and to community and then to union. This became possible because of unprecedented economic prosperity, cooperation and peace through collective effort.

The idea of South Asian Union is aired for the last few years. The group of eminent persons has envisaged a South Asian Economic Union by 2020 to be achieved in two stages, viz., by creating a FTA by 2010 and a Customs Union by 2015. At the Islamabad summit of the SAARC nations, A.B. Vajpayee, spelt out the idea of the region moving towards an economic union and contemplating the idea of a single currency for the region. Prior to this, the former prime minister of Nepal, Surya Bahadur Thapa suggested that a South Asian community is possible through a partnership of nations. The most important of all is that the Islamabad declaration reiterated SAARC's commitment to move towards a South Asian Economic Union. Most of the statements are general in nature without offering a concrete blueprint how it can be realized. The group of eminent persons, however, suggested concrete steps necessary to move towards a union. They are: cooperation for infrastructure development, particularly transport and energy, trade facilitation measures including harmonization and mutual recognition of standards, creation of a single investment area, monetary union and plans for vertical integration to promote specialization and several structural adjustments.[32] Others include harmonization of macro-economic policies, integration of labour markets, free flow of people, services and capital and a common identity and community feeling.

Then, the question is how the idea of a union is going to be realized and when? At this stage it may seem a difficult proposition but not an impossible task. Because already in the past there prevailed political and economic coherence, administrative unity, exchange of currencies and free movement and travel of people in a geographic entity called Mughal empire and British India. The historical links, shared social, economic and cultural values continue to remain stronger even in the present days.

During the Mughal period, single political authority and administrative set up created an integrated economic unit. Though Aurangazeb's political authority was challenged by Shivaji, there were no currency conversion problems. Mughal currency was freely convertible from Lahore to Dhaka and to Golconda in the Deccan even when Marathas were at war with Mughals. The system survived the disappearance of Mughal empire and was further expanded under the British throughout South Asia.

The British integrated whole of South Asia by a common administrative, educational, judicial and political system. They built rail and road, water, telecommunications and energy networks. The past infrastructure remains intact and can be revived if there is a political will. The past integration provided a sense of identity across South Asia among elite as well as masses. The integrated values and physical infrastructure is recognized more at unofficial level rather than at official level. Thus bulk of interaction and economic activity tend to be unofficial. At official level slowly steps are being initiated to convert the unofficial contacts into formal contacts. Since the process has to go a long way it requires commitment and vision. Then the cooperation among the South Asian countries may lead to the establishment of a South Asian Union.

The economic cooperation has to begin in some sectors which are important and which can transform the conditions in South Asia.

Services

In the contemporary times services have become an important driver of the economies. Rapid developments in technology are resulting in the growth of service sector. Technological innovations in a number of fields are leading to the emergence of new services in a variety of areas. Recent advances in informatics and communication technologies have added a new dimensions to the role of services in the economic growth of countries. The information technology used in the production process has significant impact on the quality and competitiveness of products in market. The efficiency and productivity of the economy is to a great extent determined by new technologies. A lot of employment is being created in the service sector across the border in fields such as transport, communications, banking, insurance, health, data processing, tele-medicine and tourism management. In the West, service sector accounts for sixty per cent to seventy five per cent employment in certain sectors contributing more than fifty per cent of the GDP. In South Asia also service sector accounts for nearly fifty per cent of the GDP of most of the countries. It also figures significantly in the South Asian trade.

Under the WTO, the South Asian countries are demanding for the removal of restrictions for the free movement of people providing services. But they are not willing to do the same in the region. The SAFTA agreement does not include provisions for the liberalization of trade in services. There exist a number of restrictions on the people's movement in the region. Inspite of this, a large number of people cross each other's border either legally or illegally. Therefore, it is better to regulate the traffic by formal means and procedures at the earliest.

South Asia is fast emerging as a hub of service providers. Large numbers of people from within and outside visit the region as tourists, pilgrims, professionals, students, medical care seekers as well as providers. Nepal, Maldives, Sri Lanka and India are the major tourist destinations. India is a major destination point for students, health care seekers and IT professionals. A number of doctors and nurses from India are working in Bangladesh, Nepal, Maldives and Bhutan. Similarly Indian managers and professionals are in service in Nepal and Bhutan. As Indian and Pakistani managers are running textile mills in Bangladesh whilst Bangladeshi cooks and waiters are in Maldivian tourist resorts and Indian cities like Bombay, Kolkata and others. With the improvement in the quality of services, the trade in services would likely to grow across the region.[33]

India is emerging as one of the global players in software technology and IT services. Others have the potential to contribute to the IT market. India can play a role in enhancing the capacity of others in the IT sector in the region.

Tourism is an expanding trade area throughout South Asia. It is one of the largest foreign exchange earning sectors. It is highly labour intensive and can make a significant difference in the economies of Nepal and Bhutan and others. A number of investment opportunities are available in areas such as adventure sports, hotel accommodation, package tour, air links, tourism and travel services. But there exist cumbersome procedures in obtaining visas, foreign exchange restrictions. Further, there is lack of direct flights and lack of information and data about accommodation, tariffs and guided tours that are hardly conducive to business opportunities. Though these problems have been identified a decade and half back, the moves are slow in rectifying them. Once obstacles are removed and promotion measures are encouraged, there is a greater scope for investment, business and trade in the sector. The move also promotes greater understanding among people of the region.

Investment

A move towards economic union should be accompanied by free movement financial flows and investment measures across the region. The SAFTA agreement leaves out liberalization of investment in the region. This is seen as a shortcoming by the scholars because smaller economies such as Sri Lanka, Bangladesh and Nepal can not take the advantage of the market of a billion people. Since these countries are having imbalance trade with India, the flow of capital into their economies would correct the situation. Structural changes are also necessary in the production capacities to transform the comparative advantages of these economies.[34] Thus removal of constraints on the movement of capital is necessary for creating trade-creating investment in the region. Muchkund Dubey opines that since India is the major source of investment, it should take special measures in facilitating free movement of capital at least to the least developing countries in South Asia. He cites the Eminent Persons Group Report, of which he is a member, that India should permit partial convertibility of the rupee on the capital account for the limited purpose of investment.[35]

Since for quite some time India has been taking significant measures to attract foreign investment into the country in the form of increasing foreign equity, automatic approval of FDI in the green industries, it too can adopt measures for removing regulatory constraints on the flow of investment. Similarly, other countries also have to adopt measures that would not affect Indian economy. Mutual confidential measures are necessary to liberalize investment climate in the South Asian region.

Harmonization of Macro-Economic Policies

Any move towards Economic Union involves harmonization of fiscal, monetary and exchange rate policies. Member states would have to have more or less same interest rates, budgetary deficit and inflationary control measures. To achieve this, trade must be freed and South Asia's trade should be much higher than the present one per cent of the global trade. The Institute of Policy Studies (IPS), Colombo, has shown that the intra-regional trade should exceed fifty per cent of the global trade of the member states to opt for an effective programme for monetary cooperation in the region.[36] For this to happen, it is necessary to bring down the tariffs to zero to five per cent and to eliminate all the non-tariff barriers and to phase out the negative list within a time frame. And free flow of capital and labour has to be ensured.[37]

On the goal of having a common currency across South Asia, a study was carried out by the IPS and Regional Information Systems (RIS), New Delhi, examining the consequences arising out of the move towards exchange rate harmonization and common currency. It suggested that a parallel currency rather than a common currency may be put in place, largely to underwrite trade and investment transactions in the region.[38] At the official level little discussion has taken place on the issue so far.

Similarly, no discussions are held on the issue of exchange rate harmonization. Despite this an underground market thrives mediating capital transfers and exchange rate. The system works so efficiently setting its own parallel exchange rate, converting all the regional currencies into dollars and vice-versa, maintaining equilibrium among currencies that is close to official exchange rate.[39]

Given the asymmetry in the economies of the countries in the region, competition among the SAARC countries themselves in the global market, no smaller country can permit its currency be overvalued with respect to the Indian rupees. India is less likely to subordinate its macro-economic policies to suit to the interests of others. In such a situation, Rehman Sobhan advocates that the smaller countries would have to take a lead in setting their macro-economic targets and India should pay attention to the concerns of its neighbours.[40] Such a process may evolve into harmonization of economic policies, which in turn may lead to an economic union in South Asia. However, macro-economic policies at the regional level may have adverse impact on the economies of least developed countries. A variation in exchange rate can nullify trade advantages under free trade area ; government price regulations can affect competitiveness; and variance in interest rates can influence the flow of investment into a few countries. Despite these adverse effects, some degree of harmonization is necessary in order to reach the stage of economic union.

A South Asian Identity

Apart from intensive economic bonds, a region also requires an identity to forge stronger relations across the borders. A regional identity brings together the elite and masses across the region. Political divergences, economic disparities can be minimized in the evolution of a union if a regional identity exists. South Asia as a concept has no historical basis. Entire region – in its history, culture and civilization – is either India or India and its neighbourhood.[41] The cultural unity in the amidst of diversity is India centred. That is why other countries assert their identity and separateness. South Asia as a concept brings others into focus with identities. As an idea representing the whole region, it has to be formulated, shaped and promoted, argues I.P. Khosla.[42]

Inspite of ideational problems, the South Asian region has to be construed as a civilizational or a socio-cultural area because its identity is due to historical and cultural legacy. It also existed as an integrated community[43] prior to the partition of the Indian subcontinent. Culturally all the countries are bound by common threads and share an identity despite plurality of languages, faiths and communities. That is the reason there goes unparalled interactions at the level of civil society in the region. Today Imran Khan, Sachin Tendulkar, Jayasuria, Muralitharan, Amitab Bachan are recognized and adored across South Asia. Similarly the voice of late Mohammad Rafi, Lata Mangeshkar, Runa Laila and late Nusrat Fateh Ali Khan are heard and their appeal transcends national boundaries. A sense of cultural and civilizational unity has sustained an identity inspite of political divisions, threat perceptions and mutual rivalries lending shared concerns across the region.

There is increasing awareness and understanding among the people of South Asia. People desire greater cooperation and resolution of political issues. So that trade increases, they benefit from peace and live without the threat of war or fear of terrorism. The states need to respond to the people desires by demonstrating statesmanship in addressing the regional issues in a framework of open regionalism. For this to happen, South Asia requires visionary leaders. Since such leaders cannot come from vacuum, efforts for cooperation and strengthening political, economic and social relations have to go on. A systematic framework to synchronize and reconcile the interests of all has to be worked out at the civil society level. So that the FTA could evolve into a customs union which would further lead to a common exchange rate policy and eventually to a common currency in South Asia. Finally efforts are to be made towards a union in the region. Till that time negotiations have to go on and efforts are to be made at governmental level and among NGO's, Human Rights Groups, TRACK II and TRACK III levels. Media do can play a positive role in popularizing the efforts towards a union. Here vernacular press can take the issues to the public and mobilize the opinion throughout South Asia.

References

1. Jeffrey A. Frankel, Ernesto Stein and Shang – Jin Wei, *Regional Trading Blocks in the World Economic System*, Washington: Institute for International Economics, 1997, pp.106 and 268-269.

2. See *RCSS Newsletter*, October 2002, *Human Development in South Asia 2001*; *World Development Report 2002* and *Military Balance, 2001-2002*.
3. Naiz A Naik, "SAARC – From Association to Community: Prospects and Problems", *South Asian Survey*, Vol. 6, no.2, July-December 1999, p 334
4. Saman Kelegama,"SAARC – From Association to Community: A Small Country Economic Perspective", *South Asian Survey*, Vol. 6, no.2, July – December 1999, p.261
5. Rehman Sobhan, "Regional Cooperation in South Asia: A Quest for Identity", *South Asian Survey*, Vol. 5, no. 1, January-June 1998, p.10
6. See *SAARC, Report of the Second meeting of coordinators for finalizing the Regional Study on Trade, Manufactures and Services*, SAARC, New Delhi, June 1991, p.87, cited in Saman Kelegama, "SAPTA and its Future", *South Asian survey*, Vol.3, nos. 1-2, January-December 1996, p.155
7. *Ibid.*
8. Charan D. Wadhva, "Assessing SAARC Preferential Trading Arrangement", *South Asian Survey*, Vol.3, nos. 1-2, January-December 1996, p 180
9. *Ibid.,* p.181
10. See T.N. Mukherji, "South Asian Preferential Trade Arrangement : India's Role", *South Asian Survey*, Vol. 6, no.1, January-June 1999, p.26
11. Swapan K. Bhattacharya, "Interface between Trade and Sustainability in South Asia", *South Asian Survey*, Vol.8, no. 1, January-June 2001, pp 47-48.
12. For details see Ayubur R. Bhuyan, "Regional Cooperation in South Asia: Outlook and prospects under SAPTA", *South Asian Survey*, Vol.3, nos. 1-2, January-December 1996, p.199.
13. Rajesh Mehta and Swapan K. Bhattacharya, "SAPTA-I, SAPTA-II and SAFTA: Impact on India's imports", *South Asian Survey*, Vol.4, no.2, July-December 1997, p.260
14. *Ibid.*
15. In fact, India and Sri Lanka signed a FTA in December 1998 creating a free trade area between the two countries. As per the

agreement both the countries agreed to eliminate tariffs on imports on all goods except those included in the negative list in three and eight years respectively. It is generally perceived that both the countries signed the agreement, as the trade liberalization under SAPTA is too slow. Some also consider that it is a move from regional to bilateral trade negotiations.The agreement envisages free trade only in terms of elimination of tariffs on imports. There is no reference to the removal of non-trade barriers such as import controls, quantitative restrictions, licenses, quotas and prohibitions. See J. B. Kelegama, "Indo-Sri Lanka Free Trade Agreement," *South Asian Survey*, Vol.6, no.2, July-December 1999, pp. 283-294.

16. Wadhva, n. 8, p.175
17. Mukherji, n. 10, p. 25
18. Rehman Sobhan,"The Twelfth SAARC Summit: Charting a Road Map for South Asian Cooperation", *South Asian Survey*, Vol.12, no.1, January-June 2005, p. 5
19. Cited in Wadhva, n. 8, pp, 181-182.
20. I.P.Khosla, "SAARC and India : An Overview", *South Asian Survey*, Vol.6, no.1, January-June 1999, p.13.
21. Kelegama, n.6, p. 158.
22. Saman Kelegama, "SAARC – From Association to Community: A Small Country Economic Perspective", *South Asian Survey*, Vol.6, no. 2, July-December 1999, p. 262.
23. *Ibid*, p.264
24. See Muchkund Dubey, "The Twelfth SAARC Summit : Deeper Integration in South Asia", *South Asian Survey,* Vol. 12, no.1, January – June 2005, p.32
25. Rehman Sobhan, "The Twelfth SAARC Summit : Charting a Road Map for South Asian Cooperation", *South Asian Survey*, Vol.12, no. 1, January-December 2005, p.10
26. Kelegama, n. 22, p. 267
27. *Ibid.*, p. 270
28. In the West, states realized benefits through regional groupings, whereas in Asia, states instead of entering into formal agreements between the governments they chose industrial houses for cooperation. In this arrangement three or more nations came

together and took advantage of greater specialization, diverse natural resources and factor endowment.

A Growth triangle require geographical proximity, varying levels of development with different resources and each country should have its own share of export items. In such a case, the size of market is not a constraint and the scope of complementarity is widened as two or three countries are involved. See Arpit Rajain, "Promoting Cooperation Through Growth Triangles and Quadrangles in South Asia", *South Asian Survey*, Vol.6, no. 1, January-December 1999, p.65.

29. SAARC Tripartie Study For the Expansion of Economic Cooperation including sub-regional cooperation and Informal trade. Nepal: Preliminary Study Report, Centre for Research and Analysis (CPRA), Kathmandu, cited in *ibid*, p.74.
30. BIMSTEC is a sub-regional grouping consisting countries of South Asia and Southeast Asia such as Bangladesh - India – Myanmar – Sri Lanka and Thailand to promote Economic Cooperation to exploit synergies in their capabilities and resource endowments for development. BIMSTEC decided to establish a free trade area in the Bay of Bengal region. It identified the sectors including trade and investment, technology, transport and communications, energy, tourism and fisheries. See *Future Directions of BIMSTEC: Towards a Bay of Bengal Economic Community*, New Delhi: Research and Information System for the Non-Aligned and other Developing Countries (RIS), 2004.
31. Cited in Kalyan Raipuria, "SAARC in the New Millennium: Need for financial vision", *South Asian Survey*, Vol. 8, no. 1, January – June 2001, p. 29
32. For details see *ibid.*, pp 15-16
33. Cited in Sobhan, n.18, p-8 and Dubey, n.25, p.28
34. Cited in Dubey, n.24, pp 29-28.
35. *Ibid*, p.30
36. *Ibid.*
37. Cited in Sobhan, n.18, p.13
38. *Ibid.*
39. *Ibid.*, p.14
40. I.P. Khosla, "Constructing The South Asian Community", *South Asian Survey*, Vol.6, no.2, July-December 1999, p.189

41. *Ibid.*
42. Cited in Sridhar K. Khatri, "The Politics of Becoming A Community: Stages and Prerequisites", *South Asian Survey*, Vol.6, no. 2, July-December 1999, p. 224

12

A South Asian Single Currency

I.P. Khosla

Introduction

The successful launch on 1 January 1999, of a single European currency has generated interest in other regions of the world about the possibility of some form of monetary cooperation leading perhaps to a single regional currency. This was the beginning of the third stage of Economic and Monetary Union in Europe, and it attracted wide attention for two reasons: it marked the irreversibility of eventual full economic integration and it heralded the entry of Europe into the list of economic super-powers.

However, even before this the group of eminent persons constituted by the summit meeting of the South Asian Association for Regional Cooperation (SAARC) held at Male had recommended in 1998 that a South Asian Economic Union be completed by the year 2020, with which "it should be possible to put in place a single monetary system, including a common currency". The statement of the prime minister of India in December 2003 that over the long term South Asia can think in terms of a common currency is also a welcome advance over the rather conservative thinking of the government of India in the past eighteen years about the speed at which South Asian economic cooperation should move forward.

However, this entire subject has to be seen in perspective. Such a proposal is only for the very long term. At the end of such a period there would be advantages in having a single currency for our region, which indeed is one of the logical and necessary steps to economic union. Transaction costs for trade and monetary movement within the region would be eliminated, thus giving a boost to the flow of both goods and capital. The synchronization of inflation and macro-monetary policy, which is a necessary pre-conditions for getting onto the approach path to a single currency, would lead to greater coordination in growth policies and growth rates, and probably a higher growth curve for the entire region. Reserves will be higher for the entire region than for any one country, hence an increase in the international stability of the currency and perhaps even of its ability to withstand hostile speculation, though this will require much faster growth over the entire region.

In the short term, however, the disadvantages of such a step clearly outweigh the advantages.

In the meanwhile we have to learn the lessons of other experiences to ensure that the move towards a single currency in South Asia is successful.

The Euro of today is a good place to learn these lessons. It has been the result of an operation involving: narrow band fluctuations in the respective values of the different currencies, with each currency value to be judged against that of the European Currency Unit; this prepared the next step of fixed exchange rates; harmonization of macro-monetary and trade policy, specially such policies as would affect inflation; and, of course, a single market and full freedom for the flow of currencies within the economies participating in the system. These seem to be the minimum pre-conditions to be met before a single currency can be Introduced.

And this is the place to start looking for the detail of the real benefits this step might offer, compared to the obvious disadvantages.

Although the Euro is the boldest, the largest scale, and arguably the most efficacious such experiment, there have been some earlier attempts, of which some examples may be given for purposes of illustration, and how feasible it might be to have a single currency in South Asia.

Earlier examples

The Latin Monetary Union (LMU) had its origins when France and Belgium linked their currencies in 1832; then Switzerland, Italy and Greece joined in and by 1865 this grouping was formalized in the LMU with a fixed exchange rate between the member countries currencies, each of which was linked to gold. There were problems since there was no provision for the convergence of macro-economic policies, and the central banks of each of the country members remained independent. In fact the LMU, despite these problems, was not dissolved till the eve of the 1914-18 War. But it was not like a modern currency union, since at the time linking a country's currency to gold was considered the norm, as was the positive value of keeping the exchange value with gold more or less fixed.

From 1870 all the major trading countries had linked their currencies to gold in this manner, except India and China, which were linked to silver. The economic reasoning behind this was that a deficit in the balance of payments would lead to reduction in domestic money supply, a contraction in price levels and a consequent increase in exports and decline in imports, which would tend to reverse the deficit, thus restoring equilibrium. There is similarity between this and having a single currency, in that both abjure the use of exchange rates to restore equilibrium. The two assumptions behind this, that the prices of goods and factors of production will adjust to external change and that they will adjust quickly, have been challenged since then; in reality price levels have been found to be 'sticky', in the word used by Roger Dornbusch.[1]

Another example is that of the UK and Ireland. The latter, even after independence from the UK in 1922, continued to follow the monetary policy of the Bank of England. This was advantageous since the Irish economy was tightly bound to that of the UK, which took some ninety seven per cent of its exports and was small compared to the latter. That figure gradually came down to fifty per cent by 1979, when Ireland broke away from the UK and joined the European Monetary System.

Panama, similarly, uses the US dollar. In 1998 Argentinean President Carlos Menem had proposed dollarization as the first step towards a single currency with the US. Officials and business groups in El Salvador and Mexico supported a similar step, and it was even forecast, somewhat unrealistically, that "by 2030 the world will have two major currency zones – one European, the other American"[2], the latter naturally encompassing all the Americas.

The situation is comparable to that which prevails between India on the one hand, and Nepal and Bhutan on the other. With Nepal there is an exchange rate which may be called pegged plus. Indian currency is freely accepted in Nepal, though it is not legal tender. In effect the rate between the Indian and Nepalese currencies continues for long periods to be fixed, though there have been changes (the peg actually allows day to day changes within the limits fixed, as was the case in the European so-called 'snake in the tunnel'). With Bhutan the rate is not pegged but fixed.

There are other examples. The East African Currency Union between Kenya, Uganda and Tanzania, which was started in 1967 and continued for ten years, is one. The three kept their own central banks, there was virtually no coordination of macro-economic policies, and the union could not have lasted long; that it lasted as long as it did was due to the fact that all three currencies, as well as the bulk of their trade, were tied to the UK as the former colonial power, all having achieved independence in the early 1960s.

Six islands of the region formed the East Caribbean Currency Area in 1965. A single central bank managed the currency, though the member countries had separate fiscal policies. This is an example of small economies with very similar structure, but not diversified, finding it advantageous to form a single currency area.

None of the above examples are relevant for South Asia, which has several large economies, one of which is diversified and much larger than any of the others, and which are in many cases not dependent on each other in trade terms. Though even the European Union (EU) is not ideal as an example, it is the one which is worth recounting in some detail for three reasons, apart from the fact that it is the largest example of its kind. First, because the launch of the Euro was preceded by a most thorough going theoretical analysis; second there was extensive empirical ground work, which has established a solid body of economic facts linked to those theories, and which can be of use in any region of the world; third, because the enormous political and economic difficulties in preparing the ground work, in some sense, presage what could happen in South Asia, though our region has even more problems.

Basic parameters

For analytical purpose, it is of advantage to divide the varying regimes that govern changes in the value of one currency against another – fully flexible, controlled float, pegged, fixed, single currency – into two categories: flexible and fixed. Within a region, in the latter case, the currency could be flexible against non-regional currencies. This simplification does not, of course, always adequately reflect the developments in the real world.

The biggest problem in having a single currency area is political. Few countries would be normally willing to give up the sovereign right to design and print their own bank notes, put into circulation as much money as they think right, and have their currency reflected in the exchange rate tables of the world. It has come to mean as essential a part of sovereignty as a flag or a capital city and a constitution. Giving it up appears to be as much of a sacrifice as would be the giving up of those and other central prerogatives of a sovereign state. We may, however, consider this from the economic angle only.

The central economic question in considering the advantages and disadvantages of a single currency arises from the fact that a change in the exchange rate is an important instrument in the hands of government in responding to relative changes in the external economic environment, the so-called exogenous changes. It is no longer possible for a country in a single currency area unilaterally to change its exchange rate as a mechanism for readjusting its international trade and payments position. In a fixed rate system the country could leave the system, but presumably at a price. Thus the benefits of either system must outweigh those offered by the ability to use this mechanism.

This may be illustrated by a well-known example. The macro-economic numbers like national product, price levels and monetary holdings change at different rates in different countries over longer or secular periods. An illustration of the effect of this on foreign exchange is the growth of the US economy between 1880 and 1914; this was phenomenally high compared with the economies of Europe, even including Germany, which itself grew much faster than others did like the UK and France. By 1914, US production of coal, iron, steel, energy, all the inputs for manufacturing, was higher than that of any country in the world. It consumed more energy than the combined consumption of the next five industrialized countries, Germany, the UK, France, Russia and Austria. It produced more motor vehicles than the rest of the world together. In the circumstances its burgeoning production sought and found markets abroad, which generated large foreign exchange surpluses. At one point one third of the world's gold stock was held by the US. In circumstances of flexible exchange rates this would have led to a rise in the price of the dollar until, through reduced exports and increased imports, some equilibrium was restored.

However, during this period the US dollar was tied to gold with a peg that allowed fluctuation between $4.84 and $4.90 for one pound sterling, which in turn was fixed to gold. Thus not only gold but also capital flowed into the US. Quite apart from the war and the subsequent economic crises that occurred in the 1929-1933 period, this was an important reason the gold standard could not have been successfully revived. We see here how 'stickiness' got in the way of the standard economic reasoning for the gold standard. The balance of payments surplus should, even without a change in the dollar value, have eventually led to monetary expansion and a consequent rise in prices; exports should have fallen and imports risen to restore equilibrium. This did not happen because the surplus was in large part mopped up or sterilized by the US monetary authorities; and in part because the expansion in US output was so large compared to its foreign trade (this was around eight per cent of US GDP at the time) that the monetary effects would have been too small, even without sterilization, to change price levels enough. In this case only an exchange rate change would have helped.

It is not possible to carry the comparison between this and the situation in South Asia in the twenty first century too far. It seems, however, to illustrate the problems that might need to be tackled in advance or which may arise from three factors: the size of India's economy, which accounts for seventy five of the GDP of the region, with a higher percentage in manufacturing, which would cover most exports; the growth of the Indian economy which has generally been faster, during the last two decades of the twentieth century, than any other in the region; and its trading position, in which trade accounts for a small part of its GDP but is still dominant, in comparison with the other regional countries, in the South Asian trade of its partners.

To a limited extent in the medium term there will always be sectors and regions in the different member countries of a fixed or single currency area, which are in cyclical or technological decline or upsurge. This creates the same problem as inflationary pricing out or the reverse. Theoretically this can also be solved by factor mobility. Assuming that capital and labour can easily move, a decline in industry and opportunities in one area would be compensated by growth in another; capital and labour would then move to the latter and there would be few adverse effects. In practice labour is willing to take a substantial drop in income before moving, which may not be politically acceptable. Those that are willing to move are the younger and better trained for whom safety nets are not so necessary. In the event it is necessary to have special schemes for fiscal subsidies, incentives for startups, retraining programmes.

Another comparison can be made with the situation within one country, being a single currency area, in case of a relative change, such as a decline in one industry or locality. When liberalization and the expansion of the large-scale sector took place in India in the 1990s there was a contraction in the small-scale sector, leading to considerable hardship for labour and entrepreneurs. It was strongly argued that for allocative efficiency, equitable income distribution and healthy social and economic growth there had to be fiscal measures, support policies so that these sections were not left at the mercy of market forces. If South Asia becomes a single currency area, there will, similarly, have to be sizable fiscal transfers to ensure equitable growth, and it does not seem that the political will for such action is present at the moment.

The above examples derive from the effects of varying growth rates on trade and thence on financial flows.

The second example is even better known, more recent and derives from the immense and global increase in the availability of loose cash under private control in the financial markets of the world. The first effect of this was the collapse of the Bretton Woods world financial *architecture* based on fixed exchange rates and the convertibility of the dollar into gold. When the US decided in August 1971 to snap the link between gold and the dollar, and to float the dollar against other currencies, it was because of diminished confidence in the link which led to heavy buying of gold; that in turn was because the economic fundamentals of the US were unhealthy due to overspending, deficits and inflation. The US held sixty eight of the worlds gold in 1950; by 1974 it was down to twenty seven per cent. It was the fixed exchange rate, which led to the speculative attack on the dollar.

Then there were series of financial crises that erupted in the 1990s due to the fact that speculators decided to target one currency after another. The European crisis of 1992 when Britain and Italy opted out of the Exchange Rate Mechanism, the currency collapses of Mexico (1995), Southeast Asia (1997), Russia (1998), Brazil (1999), were all because the countries concerned tried to keep a fixed or stable exchange rate for their currencies. The speculators thought the economic fundamentals could not support that exchange rate and began the attack. The governments defended the currency, thereby losing a large part of their hard currency holdings and making subsequent recovery that much more difficult. In each case the government had to give in, with grave consequences to the economy. In each case, if the government had floated the currency, the crisis could have been avoided; their currencies would have devalued gradually, with no loss of hard currency; in fact their competitive position in world markets would have improved. So within a fixed currency area there will be those who believe they can ride out a crisis by devaluing, others who do not.

"Fixed exchange rates, being hazardous to a country's economic health, should be avoided."[3]

A single currency is no guarantee that such a speculative attack will not happen, for then that single currency will be attacked. The loose cash available in the financial markets of the world is so large that no currency, including the dollar and the Euro, is safe from such an attack, if speculators decide the economic fundamentals do not support the fixed exchange rate.

Of course a single currency could also be made to float, but then why have one? There is not positive advantage here, only a possible reduction of the disadvantage.

Economic theory: The OCA

Theorizing on fixed exchange rate or single currency areas does not provide convincing positive reasons why any two or more countries should become part of such an area. It does provide the negative correlation: the specified conditions in which such a step would have minimum, or even no adverse effects. The heart of the theory is based on the work of the Canadian economist Robert Mundell, largely done in the early 1960s.[4]

His work covers two aspects: the economic pre-conditions necessary for a single currency, basically what sort of economic relations should exist, in advance, between the different states entering such an arrangement so as to minimize the disadvantages; and the monetary and fiscal policies needed to make the single currency work after it has been introduced.

The first aspect is covered by the better known but less important of his theories: that of optimum currency areas (OCA). In this he goes into the advantages in brief, including lower transaction costs and reduced uncertainty about relative prices, and then deals with the disadvantages in detail, mainly the one already mentioned, that what happens if there are changes in circumstances, often called shocks, which for instance lower demand, hence growth and income in a particular region. He emphasized the importance of labour mobility in offsetting the adverse effects. Later economists went into other factors like capital mobility, regional specialisation and fiscal transfers, but his main point was labour mobility. On this count the Eurozone is not an

OCA, since there is hardly any labour mobility in practice. We do not find labour from the poorer regions of the Eurozone moving into those, which are wealthier. Problems of difference in language and culture, varying educational and job eligibility conditions, mutual non-recognition of educational qualifications, existing social safety nets, mean that, whatever the legal position, actual mobility is absent. When jobs are available, legal and illegal immigrants from outside the Eurozone come to fill them. There is, as is well-known, no actual labour mobility in South Asia except between India and Nepal.

R.I.Mckinnon[5] took the OCA theory forward by suggesting that an open economy is better suited for it, the degree of openness depending on the proportion of external trade to total GDP or total economic activity.

The link between the degree of openness, or propensity to trade, the domestic multiplier (which is inversely related) and exchange rate changes is known. The effects of local fiscal or economic expansion will be felt more on the domestic economy the less open it is, the higher the multiplier, and the more rigid the exchange rate. In reverse exchange rate changes will impact an open economy more than a closed one; so between open economies exchange rate changes are not the best instrument for adjustment.

P.B.Kenen[6] later suggested that entry into a single currency area is more feasible and beneficial if a country has a diversified economy and a diversified range of exports and imports. In such a case the balance of payments is likely to be more stable and there will be less pressure to use exchange rate changes to cope with exogenous changes. Further, any shocks will not be asymmetric in their impact over the single currency region. This of course seems to go against the idea that specialisation is of advantage. If there is to be a lot of trade in a single currency area for growth and maximization of total output, then different regions within it will have to specialize according to their comparative advantage, the condition which is necessary for high mobility of goods within the area. This brings us back to the likelihood of asymmetric shocks, which, it is generally agreed, are not good for a single currency area. As for South Asia, the economies are not, with one doubtful exception, diversified. Even in the case of India, which may be considered the exception, the heavy dependence on just four items – leather, gems, garments and textiles - for virtually the entire export growth in the last decade and a half (more recently joined by IT products) shows that the economy is vulnerable to external shocks; Kenen would not have thought of it as a fit case for an OCA.

The condition under which specialisation would not give rise to this problem is if members of the OCA specialize among themselves, yet succeed each in specializing in a sufficiently large range of goods so as to reduce the asymmetrical effects of shocks. This requires a high level of development, such as is found in Europe but not in South Asia.

High capital mobility is another requirement for an OCA. The argument is that in response to changes within the area the mobility of capital will obviate the need for exchange rate changes. Suppose technical improvements lead to greater profitability of an industry located in one country. Capital from other countries in the OCA will then flow to that country. The money supply will expand, prices and incomes will rise. Over a period of time, with downward pressure on the interest rate, the capital flow will reduce the advantages and will stop. If exchange rates could be changed the adjustment would be that much quicker dampening the impact of the market on growth. The market actually benefits already privileged areas in the region; in other words it accentuates maldistribution within a single currency area. In the EU there has been social tension because prosperous sub-regions like Baden-Wurttenberg in Southwestern Germany, Spanish Catalonia, the French Rhones-Alpes and Northern Italy consistently outpaced others in growth rates. Hence a Council of Regions and Regional Growth Fund had to be set up to reduce disparities. For the success of the Euro, countries like Germany and the Netherlands have to be permanent donors, while those like Ireland and Italy are permanent recipients. In the recent (May 2004) expansion of the EU this has become a major problem. If sufficient funds are not put into the modernization of the ten new and poorer countries, they may not be able to join the single currency early. Seventy billion Euro are being put in the first two years alone, about ten per cent of the combined GDP of the ten.

In South Asia this problem could be even more severe. The disparities being sharper, there will be a stronger temptation to blame poor growth or inequity on a single currency. And fiscal transfers on a large scale are unlikely.

Even discounting the macro-economic effects, it is not agreed among economists that stable or fixed exchange rates promote trade and investment, though the empirical data seem to suggest that this is so, and European policies for several decades have been based on the presumption that it is so. The explanation has to depend on the presumption that financial traders and investors look for high safety and low profits; as we have seen, this is not always the case. Developing countries and emerging markets are particularly vulnerable.

An important way of testing whether a region is suitable as an OCA is by assessing what are likely to be the effects of exogenous economic shocks. If these are similar for the different countries in the area then it is suitable as an OCA. To an extent this is a circular argument, since if exogenous shocks have similar effects on different countries then they will have no reason to change the existing mutual exchange rates.

N.M.Maskay[7], basing his estimation on the idea that shock absorption capacity combines the net influence of several criteria, examines the South Asian region. He concludes that the SAARC member countries are not suitable as an OCA.[8] On the other hand, his statistics also show that Nepal and India are not suitable, while there is actually no desire by either to change the existing pegged plus exchange rate system.

The above analysis indicates that the balance of advantages and disadvantages in trade, investment, development and facing exogenous shocks for a group of countries that decide to adopt a single currency is full of ambiguities. If anything the disadvantages weigh more heavily; while those aspects that are termed advantages turn out on closer examination to be ways of minimizing the disadvantages. As we shall see, the widely advertised price stability, low deficits, low levels of government debt and low interest rates, are actually essential measures to reduce the disadvantages in the management of a single currency area rather than positive advantages or required pre-conditions for entering into one.

Economic theory – the Mundell-Fleming model

Mundell's more important theory (the citation of the Bank of Sweden does mention the OCA since the Nobel prize was given to him in 1999, the year of the Euro) now goes under the name of the Mundell-Fleming model[9]; this is the one operationalized in the context of the management of the Euro.

High and rapid capital mobility is assumed, which is reasonable and actually prevails in the conditions of Europe (and, increasingly, the whole developed world). At the same time the response of the economy to a deficit/surplus leading to currency depreciation/appreciation in terms of income and demand is assumed to be slower.

Under a fixed exchange rate system if there is monetary expansion there will be more imports in the medium term; in the short term domestic interest rates will be reduced and there will be a capital outflow which should come to a stop only when the resulting upward pressure on interest rates brings into being a new equilibrium. But in order to maintain the fixed exchange rate the central bank will have to purchase domestic currency and this in effect will reverse the increase in money supply, so that a policy of monetary expansion under fixed exchange rates will be ineffective. In other words the central bank loses control of the money supply in such a system, and open market money operations are useless. However, if there is fiscal expansion, that is, if government spending increases, this will be effective, for capital would flow inwards in response to higher interest rates until there is sufficient additional capital for a new equilibrium; since depreciation is not a possibility the additional demand created by the expansion cannot be controlled by that means. This applies also to areas with a single currency, where capital mobility is complete, and the effects of monetary expansion cannot be confined regionally.

The reverse is true if exchange rates are flexible. Here monetary expansion will lead to a fall in interest rates as well as an expansion of domestic demand. The first will lead to an outflow of capital and of course pressure for depreciation, while the second leads to a balance of payments deficit, which points, at a somewhat later date, in the same direction. So monetary expansion (or contraction with the reverse results) is doubly effective. On the other hand, fiscal expansion leads to a rise in the rate of interest, so that there is an inflow of capital leading to appreciation; but it also leads to a rise in demand leading to deterioration in the balance of payments and pressure for depreciation. The two opposite tendencies cancel each other out.

This was a path breaking introduction of dynamic models to describe the key factors which influence monetary and fiscal changes in an open economy; and it not only came to represent the core of modern international macro-economics, but to be taken aboard the policy making apparatus of fiscal and monetary authorities and the IMF. In fact without it the Euro would have been difficult or impossible to manage.

In brief, then, monetary policy is linked to external balance and fiscal policy to internal balance.

This, coincidentally, accords well with the political compulsions of a single currency, which would ensure that fiscal responsibility or powers cannot be given to any central authority. The Mundell – Fleming model says that we *should not* give fiscal authority to a central institution thus giving economic substance to a political imperative. In the EU it was clear from the start that none of those joining the Eurozone would agree to surrender their autonomy to raise taxes, to use the revenues from such taxes for income redistribution or any other income equalization measures. The participating countries did not mind losing control of monetary measures; these would not have been effective anyway; and the central bank has taken them over for the management of the external balance.

The European Central Bank (ECB) is the decision making body in the Eurozone on all monetary matters. It has the sole prerogative for the creation of money; and the central banks of the member countries carry out day to day money market and foreign exchange operations, under the general guidelines of the ECB. Three things are done for money management: annual money targets are published so that business and the public know that the inflation rates are based on a realistic calculation – the maximum annual growth is not more than four and a half per cent; a target inflation rate is published, usually less than two per cent; and there is monitoring of an internally developed mix of other indicators, which are not published, but are used to issue warnings when the rate of inflation is about to be exceeded.

Attached to the goal of price stability is the size of each member country's deficit and debt, the first not to exceed three per cent of GDP, the second sixty per cent. Large deficits increase inflationary expectations, undermine both consumer and investor confidence, and could eventually lead to pressure for the devaluation of the Euro. Debt has been more difficult to control; almost every member country has more than sixty per cent, some twice as much. Since money creation is not in their hands this places a limit on profligacy; and if a member is well below the limit it can use fiscal means for economic adjustments.

Price stability is the primary objective of the European central banks. But this is not prominent in the literature as a pre-condition for an OCA. However, the EU had mandated it as a necessary condition for being able to join the Eurozone, partly for reasons connected with the strength and international prestige of the Euro. What is actually needed is only that the member countries should have rates of inflation, which are close together, since if some of them have different rates, people will switch to buying goods from the cheaper areas and no corrective will be available except fiscal measures. Low inflation rates have been specified for growth rather for the single currency as such. Low inflation has three consequences: that small differences in the prices of the factors of production and goods are not swamped out by high inflation, so the market can respond to such small differences with sensitivity, leading to better growth; that expectations of continued low inflation lead to low interest rates which benefit investment and growth; and that the beneficial impact on consumer credit and spending would be an additional factor for growth.

It will probably be difficult for South Asia to achieve such low rates of inflation. However, inflation has been brought under control to reach an average level of about four to five per cent; provided there is reasonable uniformity across the region, this pre-requisite for growth within a single currency area could perhaps be met. It is quite unrealistic to expect that in the foreseeable future South Asian economies will get anywhere near the figures for deficit and debt that the Eurozone has set.

Advantages

The Euro, introduction of which led to much of the discussion in South Asia on this subject, has certain incontrovertible advantages. In our region these advantages will hardly exist, or not exist at all for the time being.

For one, the cost of intra-area foreign exchange transactions is eliminated. Within the Eurozone trade accounts for roughly sixty per cent of the total trade of the member countries, so the cost saving is high. The economies being open, one can confidently predict that intra-Eurozone trade will continue to diversify and grow.

South Asian countries do not trade much with each other; the figure is about two per cent of world trade for India, the same for Pakistan. It is higher in the case of Nepal because of its high trade with India. Bangladesh and Sri Lanka have also become large markets for Indian goods, and hence the figures are higher, but still nowhere near even fifty per cent. Here it may be noted that the usual base for projections, which are the aggregated figures for trade within the region and of the region with the rest of the world, are largely irrelevant. Trade in South Asia comprises a differentiated collection of bilateral trade relations between India and its neighbours, it is not multilateral trade; in comparison trade between those neighbours is insignificant. And this collection has different rules. While this is not the place to go into details, three things can be said to illustrate the point. First, India's exports to the region (as percentage of total) have been growing; its imports from it are contracting, so that almost two decades after SAARC began, India's trade with the region remains at the same percentage of its total trade, and while its figures for trade with the rest of the world are growing, it remains the least open of the regional economies. India does not trade much within the region; not does it look like becoming an open economy.

Second, within the intra-regional trade different factors govern the figures for different states, including political factors, which are important in the case of Pakistan, also Nepal and Bangladesh; third, and in similar vein, the international trade of the region as a whole is not subject to generalizations. It is unwise to predict the future growth of trade within the region or of the region with the rest of the world on economic considerations, or to conclude that there will at some time be significant advantages from savings in intra-area foreign exchange transactions.

The costs of cross border payments for trade, and of hedging operations to safeguard against exchange rate fluctuations are eliminated in the Eurozone. For South Asia the same argument applies.

There is some saving in the management of several foreign currency accounts. In the Eurozone the French franc, the German mark, the Italian lira and so on were regularly used to designate trade. In South Asia there is no such trade since all of it is carried out through a vehicle currency like the dollar or now the Euro (even the Asian Clearing Union, set up for the specific purpose of trade between Asian countries, is hardly being used for the purpose). Hence, there will be little saving on this account.

Price transparency is another advantage, since consumers and business can more easily and quickly compare prices and arrive at better buying and business decisions. This also applies to travel and tourism; across all these areas competition will become more robust. In South Asia, for reasons given there will be little advantage on this account.

The major advantage, and the real reason for the Euro, is the enhanced position of Europe on the world economic stage. The Euro has proved its strength as a vehicle currency, as one playing a major role (and catching up with the dollar) as a currency to borrow in, issue international securities, hold ones reserves and designate international trade. Its financial markets are liquid, and both wide and deep enough to be a rival to those of the dollar. This also leads to the profits from seigniorage, meaning being able to borrow short term at low rates of interest and then lend long term at higher rates.

With the proved strength of the Euro, the position of the EU or Eurozone in organizations like the IMF and World Bank and WTO, indeed all multilateral trade and finance organizations, has improved. The EU had considerable economic clout even before 1999, and the five and a half years since then have shown that the single currency has reinforced that position, especially where economic rivalry with the US is concerned.

For any South Asian single currency these advantages of a strong international presence will not exist. The whole of South Asia has, for example, a 3.879% share in the votes of the IMF.

Monetary cooperation in South Asia

The benefits of international monetary and financial cooperation for growth and stability have been well recognised. It is, however, necessary to distinguish between cooperation which is general or global, that between a region and the rest of the world and that within a region; and, in the latter case, within a single currency area and one with flexible exchange rates.

The SAARC member countries do not trade much with each other, as has been pointed out above. Hence, the impact of devaluation in one country, to take one example, would not affect intra-regional trade. However, where the products of that country are in competition with that of another internationally, this would adversely affect the world exports of the other. This could happen as a result of monetary expansion; but the other ancillary effects of such expansion, like an outflow of capital and a deterioration in the balance of payments, would not have much effect on the other regional countries.

There is, therefore, little intra-regional incentive for monetary cooperation in the region. Nevertheless, in common with other developing countries there is an incentive for taking similar positions in matters of international trade. The markets for leather, tea, garments, are of interest to several countries in the region. Strictly speaking this would generate cooperation only in trade policy, and such cooperation is an ongoing process within the WTO fora. Trade and monetary matters are, of course, linked, but this link is, in the case of South Asia, with their major trading partners who are in the developed world. It is unrealistic to believe that SAARC can have any say in, for instance, decisions about monetary expansion in any of their major trading partners, for their trade is too small with the latter for there to be any negotiating strength.

Nevertheless it is to be welcomed that the SAARCFINANCE network was set up by the 1998 Colombo summit.[10] This comprises central bank governors and finance secretaries of the region, who generally meet on the sidelines of the annual World Bank and IMF gatherings. The SAARC summit at Islamabad formalized the acceptance of this body in the official regional process of cooperation. This is a beginning that looks towards a long future where intra-regional trade expands, the economies of the member countries develop a similar level of diversification and more trade and financial exchanges with each other and with the rest of the world, so that monetary cooperation becomes increasingly important to all of them.

Some suggestions for pooling part of the external reserves of the region have been made. These include the setting up of a reserve bank to handle such a pool; a bond fund, which would help finance regional investments; or a contingency fund on the lines of the Chiang Mai initiative. It is true that the external position of the four largest countries in the region, if compared to their external debt, can give cause for concern, despite repeated announcements in India, for instance, about how comfortable is the position. There is not, in the region, in other words, that substantial excess of reserves over debt that could give practical shape to such schemes, nor is there the political will. Even in ASEAN, where both political and economic cooperation is much older and has progressed much further than in South Asia, the 1997 crisis did not find any common emergency measures by the group to meet the situation. Indeed, for months after the crisis began, the leaders of the region did not even meet to talk about the situation; and subsequently they found it possible to publicly blame each other for it.

Despite this, it is the very fact that such cooperation is being talked about that gives enough reason to continue. Exchange of information about exchange rate policy, about whether there would be any use to think about target based or instrument based cooperation in the future, research into the effects of monetary changes in one economy on another, even if very small, would all contribute in the long run to better understanding.

Another idea is that of a parallel currency, that while the ground for a single currency is inadequate, in the meanwhile a parallel currency with a mutually acceptable name could soon be put into operation.[11] Since member states individual currencies continue this would be politically more acceptable. The parallel intra-regional currency would be used as a unit of account for trade and financial transactions within the region, so that over time banks, traders, and others get used to dealing in and accepting it. The idea is that members could also pledge to a reserve fund in this parallel currency, which could be used in a manner similar to the SDR of the IMF. And, over the years, member states central banks, which would jointly control the currency, will learn to stabilize its value in international markets and vis a vis the individual currencies of the members. Macro-monetary harmonization could be initiated in stages for this purpose. Separately, the other pre-conditions such as creation of a single market and expanded facilities for intra-regional financial flows would be put in place.

Once the pre-conditions are met, it is thought, such a parallel currency can grow in relation to, and over a period replace national currencies to become the single currency.

For the present conditions are clearly not suitable for such a move, neither governments nor officials are talking about it[12] and the only reason this is being talked about elsewhere is that Robert Mundell mentioned it. If such a currency is convertible it will simply mean that all the reserves, which are now in one drawer, will be put into two, one smaller and one bigger. Obviously, none of the regional countries are going to surrender control over either, meaning that the currency will be like a common fund for the region in name only, with control over it in the hands of the different countries.

Those who trade within the region will not use it, for it would only complicate their account books. Presumable its exchange rate will be fixed against some combination of hard currencies, which will lead to more complications, since if any SAARC member state should change its exchange rate with the dollar or Euro, that of the parallel currency will have also have to be changed. Incentives will have to be given for its use, the consolation being that since trade and investment within the region are low not much will have to be paid out in such incentives.

It is likely that discussion of a more general nature about monetary and financial cooperation, in however rudimentary a form, offers the best alternative for the time being.

It needs to be emphasised that all such proposals for cooperation carry a political message. Even if they are not feasible for implementation in the near future, the very fact that they are made, even more so if they are discussed at official level, signals a willingness on the part of civil society and governments in South Asia to examine a wide range of possibilities in the hope that some of them may in the long run, or the very long run, lead to intensified cooperation. It is this light that they are to be welcomed.

References

1 R.Dornbusch, "Expectations and Exchange Rate Dynamics", *Journal of Political Economy*, vol. 84, 1976, pp.1161-1176.

2 Zany Minton Beddoes, "From EMU to AMU?, The Case for Regional Currencies", *Foreign Affairs*, July/August 1999, vol.78, no.4, p.8.

3 Alan S. Blinder, "Eight Steps to a New Financial Order", *Foreign Affairs*, September/October 1999, vol.78, no.5, p.54.

4 R.A. Mundell, "A Theory of Optimum Currency Areas", *American Economic Review*, vol. 51, 1961, pp. 657-664.

5 R.I.Mckinnon, "Optimum Currency Areas", *American Economic Review*, vol. 53, 1963, pp. 717-724.

6 P.B.Kenen, "The Theory of Optimum Currency Areas: An Eclectic View", in R.A.Mundell and A.K.Swoboda, (ed.), *Monetary Problems of International Economy*, Chicago: University of Chicago Press, 1969.

7 Nephil Matangi Maskay, "South Asian Monetary Integration in Light of the Optimum Currency area Criterion of Patterns of Shocks", *South Asia Economic Journal*, vol. 2, 2001, pp. 203-219.

8 But N.C.Saxena finds that some groups may be suitable under the supply shocks argument. See "Is the Euro a Role Model For

Asia?", mimeo, University of Pittsburgh, cited in Sweta Chaman Saxena and Mirza Allim Baig, "Monetary Cooperation in South Asia", RIS discussion paper no. 71, 2004, p.10.

9 R.A.Mundell, "The Appropriate Use of Monetary and Fiscal Policy for Internal and External Stability", IMF Staff Papers, vol.9, 1962, pp.70-79; and R.A.Mundell, "Capital Mobility and Stabilization Policy Under Fixed and Floating Exchange Rates", *Canadian Journal of Economic and Political Science*, vol.29, 1963, pp. 475-485. Marcus Fleming, who was Deputy Director of the research department of the IMF for many years, including the period when Mundell was affiliated there and wrote his paper, also contributed to the theory, a contribution generally considered less significant than that of Mundell. J.M.Fleming, "Domestic Financial Policies Under Fixed and Floating Exchange Rates", in IMF Staff Papers, vol.9, 1962, pp. 369-380.

10 See Amit Dasgupta and Nephil Matangi Maskay, "Financial Policy Cooperation in SAARC: A First Step towards Greater Monetary Integration in South Asia", *South Asia Economic Journal*, vol.4, no.1, 2003, p. 138.

11 The suggestion was made by Mundell. See Saxena and Baig, no.8, p.22. It is there suggested that a parallel currency can help in promoting cooperation in trade and investment by funding provision of regional public goods; and there will be seigniorage therefrom.

12 It is worth remarking that while the former Prime Minister of India talked about a common currency and open borders in South Asia at a December 2003 Hindustan Times Leadership Initiative, neither of these suggestions is being taken as a realizable target in the foreseeable future by other SAARC member states, or by officials in India.

SECTION-V

PROSPECTS FOR A SOUTH ASIAN COMMUNITY

13

Imagining South Asia in a Unipolar World

CK Lal

Even though the term 'South Asia' has become quite popular over last few years, its meaning is not clear as yet. Is it a mere geographical expression, or does it have any root in history or relevance for the future? These questions challenge the meaning and purpose of the expression requiring a new construction rather than a mere 'reconstruction'. But imagining a South Asian identity is difficult precisely because it appears to be so obvious.

First, it needs to be clarified whether South Asia is in need of a regional identity or not; and if yes, the reason that has necessitated its manufacture. Second, there is a lot of confusion about several conflicting names that the people of South Asia are faced with. Some refer to the region as 'India', alluding perhaps to the Indic civilisation of the past. The 'Southern Asia' appendage is a legacy of Cold War rivalry for spheres of influence. The 'Subcontinent' is the favourite term of market analysts and media planners. South Asia encompasses all these connotations, and yet, emerges as an inclusive and secular expression capable of reflecting the aspirations of a common future slowly emerging in this geographical region of the world.

Once the question of necessity and the importance of its expression in an inclusive term are agreed upon, the challenges of 'imagining' begin. Due to the success of investments made in the creation of national identities over the last century, loyalties to the 'imagined communities' are raw and strong. A regional imagining has to be done without appearing to be challenging sub-regional 'national' identities. There is an urgent need to make haste, but slowly. Areas of commonalities have to be identified, the steps to be taken in order to accelerate their progress, tools need to be formulated—in short, a careful deliberation is warranted.

This paper posits that the rise of the hyperpower, and the emergence of a unipolar world where the US eagle casts a long shadow, has made the manufacture of a strong regional identity necessary. The safest name for such a regional identity is 'South Asia' as it is future, rather than past, oriented; hence it raises hopes instead of fears. The paper stresses the importance of thinking big—nothing less than a South Asian Union sometime in future—but beginning small by creating confidence building measures through the creation of non-controversial common cultural institutions.

1. Introduction

There are three ways of looking at the self—perception, presentation and reflection—how we see ourselves, how we want others to see us, and then how the image is reflected back to us from those who see us with their own 'eyes' informed as much by our effort as their own biases. South Asians look at themselves in many ways, but none of them are either purely individualistic or collectivist. It is very difficult to be exact about the hierarchy of self-identity of South Asians. Nevertheless, some generalisations are necessary and possible.

Individual South Asian is a progeny of a certain family, member of certain clan or caste through which s/he belongs to a community of region, faith, religion, language, culture or civilisation. The political affiliation to a party or an ideology is seldom important enough to figure in self-description.

The national identity, despite its fatal attraction, is the creation of the state. It is not the identity that comes first to the mind when defining the self to another. No Assamese introduces his/herself to a Tamil as a fellow Indian while in the Indian territory; and among Tamils themselves introduction will probably begin inside Tamil Nadu with "I am from Madurai" leading to "an Iyengar priest" or whatever.

Location and birth are thus two important markers of identity. This probably explains the controversy over the foreign origin, bad Hindi and non-Hindu faith of Sonia Gandhi in 2004 parliamentary elections in India. Imagining a non-Bangla speaker non-Muslim as a premier of Bangladesh is even more difficult.

The "Southasian" identity is too vague and confusing for South Asians themselves—the canvass is too big and its complexities too diverse to attract people in search of identities as certainties. Enormous investments have been made by the states to manufacture 'imagined communities', even then they are not as yet strong enough to withstand the centrifugal forces of other competing identities as often expressed in several struggles for regional autonomy or independence that keep cropping up all over South Asia.

Once faced with an 'outsider' while still inside the region, however, people tend to congregate around their political identities. In Sri Lanka, a Tamil from Chennai is as much of an Indian as an Awadhiya from Gorakhpur. The second layer of resistance to a common regional identity is thus political.

At the third level, resistance to a common identity weakens. Nepali Diaspora in Canada appreciates the advantages of Peace and Friendship Treaty of 1950 between India and Nepal (which gives citizen's right to their residents in each other's countries) far more than their compatriots back home because the former see opportunities where as the later are obsessed with its challenges. People from Manipur, Manipal, Makwanpur, Shimla and Sialkot discover commonalities among themselves while in Scandinavia, which they never knew, existed. It is at this level, between the nationalities and the global citizenship, that a regional identity needs to be imagined and then invented.

2. Imperatives for a Regional Identity

Potential is one thing, but possibility requires that there is a certain need for such an identity. Do South Asians need a regional identity? This question has been vexing the dreamers of South Asian Association for Regional Cooperation (SAARC) for quite some time. Despite consistent effort of nearly two decades now, this regional organisation has failed to take off. It appears that the national identities themselves within the region are too fluid to allow a regional identity to emerge where its components are comfortable about their places in it. With the disintegration of former Soviet Union, however, there has been a perceptible change in the ground reality. The post-Taliban Afghanistan has shown that now there is an eagle in the South Asian room that even an Elephant like India can not afford to ignore.

The unipolar world order has necessitated multiple centres. If absolute power corrupts absolutely, it is in the long-term interest of 'the power' itself to encourage multi-centrality. Perhaps that is the reason the US is consciously engaging itself more and more with New Delhi. But terms of such engagements are inherently hegemonic. The power loves client states doing its bidding to maintain the status quo. For a tolerant regionalism to emerge, initiative needs to be taken from within the region itself.

There are some very important reasons that warrant the imagination of South Asian solidarity, some of them are discussed below.

(a) Strategic

Unlike Soviet Union that relied on local elite in its client states, the unipolar order of US hegemony is dominated by its overbearing presence. Sometimes, the presence is direct, as in Afghanistan. At some other places, Nepal and Pakistan for example, US 'advisors' are power-centres in their own right. In more complex places like India and Sri Lanka, the entire range of Gramsci's hegemonic tools—intellectual, moral and political—are used to manufacture public opinion that perpetuates its hold.

Some of the characteristics of US hegemony are:

- US depends upon persons rather than the process to execute its will. Is it Hamid Karzai, General Musharraf or King Gyanendra, the concept of 'our man' dictates the priority of US policies. Such an approach is inimical to the evolution of democratic polity. To balance it, a regional solidarity of shared values is necessary. The arrogance of "He may be a bastard, but he is our bastard" can only be fought with a regional ideology that does away with the necessity of having political 'bastards'. Person-centred politics of the United States of America is perhaps responsible for the mindset in Washington where rulers of South Asia have to either confirm or run the risk of facing instability all the time.

- It is not just an accident that the two 'major non-NATO' allies of US in Asia are Israel and Pakistan. Despite the lifestyles portrayed by *MTV* and *Baywatch*, American society is one of the most fanatically religious in the world. It finds a bigoted regime easier to deal with, perhaps that was the reason it got so well with the Hindutva establishment in New Delhi. But South Asia needs to become avowedly secular if this region is to emerge out of the self-perpetuating cycle of religious conflicts. South Asian solidarity around a secular polity could be a powerful antidote to the American policy of exploiting religious differences to suit its political agenda.
- From Pol Pot to Zia-ul-Haq and from Marcos to Osama Bin Laden, the most abhorrent adherents of abusive politics in Asia have been nurtured by US policies. Democracy—at least some form of it—within and dictatorship abroad has been a consistent policy of all American administrations. This is based on an assumption that theirs is blessed nation while all others are accursed ones. If South Asia were to emerge as a haven of democratic order, US will be forced to renounce its favourite game of pitting one dictator against another all over the world. In time, though it may take a long time, South Asia may even emerge as a new ideological counterweight to the hegemonic designs of US.

(b) Economic justification

Apart from long-term strategically important reasons, there is a very strong tactical logic for imagining a unified South Asian region: economically, its regions that progress, not nations or states. From Burmese jungles to the foothills of Hindukush and from the dry plateau of Tibet to the lush greenery of Sri Lanka, there is something of a celestial unity—the monsoon, food habits, life styles, aspirations and beliefs are so similar that it can easily sustain an interdependent economic unit. This unit can give birth to economic enterprises small enough to adapt to local needs but big enough to compete with US-dominated multinational corporations bent upon subjugating the world to a unitary cola-culture.

(c) Political

A region as similar—and dissimilar—as South Asia can not even survive, let alone prosper, if it were to replicate the unitary political practices of the US, a state that "assimilated" immigrants to acquire the population after it was formed. This region has to probably learn more from Europe. The Chinese have successfully adopted the American model of production because they share a similar unitary political culture ruthlessly cultivated by powerful emperors, the last of them being Mao himself. South Asia has to emphasise pluralism instead and build institutions of coordination.

(d) Social

Social harmony, religious tolerance and common roots of South Asia are celebrated, but the region lacks institutions to support this diversity. However, institution comes up only when the underlying unity in the diversity is recognised and all possible social links are imagined. Before a South Asian community can be invented, it is important to imagine the kind of South Asians necessary to support it.

(e) Cultural

It has become acceptable to suggest that culture is evolving as the most powerful tool of political as well as economic hegemony. *Fox News, Bold and the Beautiful, Coca Cola, McDonald* and *Microsoft* are widely recognised as names that are creating US-like islands everywhere in the world. In the short term, there is no escaping their fatal lure. But to keep an alternative lifestyle alive that may one day emerge as an independent choice, it has become necessary to manufacture plurality of local cultures.

In the formulation of Benedict Anderson, nations exist as "imagined political communities". A nation is imagined because the members of even the smallest nation will never know most of their fellow-members, meet them, or even hear of them, yet in the minds of each lives an image of their communion. Anderson credits newspapers and novels for the rise of such an imagination. Television, internet, and not-for-profit organisations have begun to give rise to regional consciousness. But a full-fledged 'imagination' needs planned effort, more so because massive investments are being made to create a counter-imagination of US hegemony.

3. Conceptual confusion

There is a lot of confusion in the minds of people of South Asia themselves about what exactly is their region. A Pakistani being reproached with "What kind of South Asian you are!"[1] Myths and legends come to be shared only when there is an acceptance of shared identity. Hence, the game of naming is not as innocent as it appears. Lot of attention needs to be paid to come up with a name that is inclusive, recognisable, but not offensive to any of the groups.

In an attempt to clear the confusion by the process of elimination, some likely names need to be discussed.

(a) India

Had it not been appropriated by the post-1947 regime in New Delhi, it would have survived as an identifying marker, much like the Arabs, and included Afghanistan and Burma due to the shared history of British colonialism. Tibet too would have been part of it as the Roof of the World has always been an inalienable component of the "Indian" civilisation. But Jawahar Lal Nehru appropriated this name for his Bharat. These days, the word India is a synonym of Bharat, a country with New Delhi as its capital city. Any suggestion to use this name for the entire region is likely to invite the charges of hegemonic designs.

(b) Subcontinent

The subcontinent is a popular term even now, but it leaves out Sri Lanka and Tibet and has no religious, historic, or cultural connotations. It is basically a terminology of the market.

(c) Southern Asia

'Middle-East' had London as the centre of gravity; Southern Asia assumes that the 'real' Asia of power politics is China, and Beijing its epicentre. It is a geo-strategic expression, based on the carving out of spheres of influence during the cold war years. It is being re-invented by the defence establishment of India to pose it in opposition to the rising tide of Chinese influence. But for the rest of the region, the southern adjective has very little appeal. Beijing and New Delhi bureaucrats may fancy that they have swapped each other's recognition of Sikkim and Tibet, but other countries are unlikely to accept their contention of the Hindukush-Himalaya being a demarcation of civilisation fault-line. To take but just one example, Nepali territory extends beyond the Himalayas and there is no reason for the Burmese to accept a regional identity that assumes an unidentified point of reference to arrive at an adjective.

(d) South Asia

This term sounds dry, but least unacceptable to most of South Asians precisely for that reason. This expression has no colonial or geo-strategic baggage, and has neither been celebrated nor denounced. An identity around this expression can easily be 'imagined' to suit the needs of present and future generations.
In short, this term is:

- Geographical
- With little or no historical baggage
- Secular
- No economic connotations and
- Inclusive

But it needs to be 'imagined', before it can be 'invented', and then 'manufactured'. Perhaps the spirit of *Ekushe* — "democracy, pluralism, and multiculturalism"— can be a base for the imagination to emerge?

4. Challenges of creating a new identity

However, creating a new identity, even though at a secondary or a tertiary level, is a huge challenge. Massive investment has been made in creating national identities. Thousands have died to create and defend national honour. Imagination of any new regional identity needs to incorporate, not negate, these achievements.

In popular imagination, market and coercive power implicate each other. Concentration on 'soft power'—academia, media, arts and literature—is needed, but this fails to produce immediate results. Hence the hesitation on part of the political leaders whose attention span is never longer than the terms of their offices. Something tangible needs to be 'constructed' to get their commitment and maintain it.

In order to address these challenges, the SAARC process needs to be revitalised to make this moribund organisation meaningful. These steps should include, but not be limited to:

- Financial: Commitment of certain percentage of national budgets of member countries for the South Asian Commonwealth.
- Economic: Creation of institutions like South Asian Airlines Consortium and South Asian Bank is an idea whose time has come. There can be a common South Asian Currency that can work concurrently with individual national currencies for a while. Adoption of Common South Asian School curricula needs to begin so that changing schools within the region is easy. There would be little resistance to a Common South Asian Centre for the study of Climate change.
- Cultural: It is quite unlikely that anyone would object to a South Asian Academy of Arts and Music. Poets, writers and academicians from the region can meet more often under its aegis.
- Social: South Asian University or Centre of Advanced Studies and South Asian forums of several professional organisations need to be formalised. Some of it already exists, but more institutions and instruments need to be imagined.
- Political: Politics are by its very nature contentious. But few would object to the creation of a South Asian Parliament of Cultures or a common South Asian Passport for Eminent Citizens of South Asia.

It is apparent that the tool to implement these visions has to be a revitalised SAARC. Unfortunately, this organisation has very little except a permanent secretariat at its disposal and even this outfit is lead by career diplomats on rotation from different member countries. So the process of imagination has to begin by rethinking the composition, authority and responsibility of the regional grouping.

South Asia has several new neighbours—US in Afghanistan, China in Tibet and Norway in Sri Lanka. All of them may have benevolent intentions for all one knows. But they shall not remain so forever if the people of the region do not create solidarity of their own in the collective imagination.

Reference

1. S. Akbar Zaidi, a Karachi-based social scientist, was actually asked this question in New Delhi for not knowing who Draupadi was for not knowing who the Pandavas were, or who exactly Shakuni was, has every reason to look at the politics of definition with some scepticism. See http://www.dawn.com/2002/09/09/op.htm#2

14

South Asian Union: Vision, Mission and Agenda

B. Ramesh Babu

The vast subcontinent of South Asia, stretching from the Himalayas in the north and the Indian Ocean in the south, is a natural geographical region. After the end of the British empire, for a variety of historical and political reasons, Afghanistan and Myanmar (Burma) went out of the orbit of South Asia. The region today comprises of seven states, namely India, Pakistan, Bangladesh, Nepal, Sri Lanka, Bhutan, and Maldives. By its sheer size, population, scale of the economy, relative advance in science and technology, India is the colossus of the region. It is the dominant power by far. Another peculiarity of South Asia is that India separates, keeps apart, all its neighbours form one another. All of them have common borders with India and the later has border and other disputes with all of them. Nonc of India's neighbours share borders with one another. They feel isolated and are afraid of the giant next door. There is nothing India can do about its being very big and more powerful in all respects. But it can and should choose not to act like the proverbial "Big Brother!" The dominant country need not dominate. It can and should instead choose to lead the region in a cooperative venture to fight poverty, deprivation and misery. The quarter of mankind that lives in the region is way down on the Human Development Index of the UN. This is the biggest challenge confronting India and the region. The South Asian states should learn to lead by example.

To attain the long-term goal of a South Asian Union, in which the member states are at peace with themselves and at peace with each other, calls for bold leadership from India.

We should have a 'vision' of a cooperative South Asia, commit ourselves to the 'mission' and evolve a shared and practical 'agenda' to translate the goal into a reality. This paper is essentially an effort in prescription, an intellectual mode and avocation with which Indians are most comfortable! Focus of the paper is on what the government of India, top policy makers, elected leaders, captains of business and industry, academics, NGOs, above all the attentive public and the people as a whole—should do.

The Vision

Despite the prolonged exertions of the governments and leaders of the seven states comprising South Asia, the region ranks among the poorest in the world. There is no need to substantiate this miserable reality with statistics. The reasons are numerous and a great deal is written diagnosing the malaise. There is also a great deal of literature on what India should do, what Bangladesh should do and so on. However, most of these prescriptions are conceived in narrow conflictual terms within the nation state paradigm and as zero sum games vis-à-vis other nations. One nation could gain only at the expense of the others. Such conventional and negative frameworks of thought and action have become so habitual that they are seen as "natural." That is the way the world works, they say. It is high time that nations and individuals get out of such inherited shackles of thought and seek new, cooperative and creative perspectives on the conduct of international relations. We in India should take the lead in launching a paradigm shift in the way we visualize and deal with the economic and social backwardness of the region. We must learn to look at the region as a whole, as a single unit for planning, legitimization and implementation through institutions that are inter-governmental, transnational and regional.

Though there is much talk about the radical transformation of the world in the post Cold War era (especially globalization), the mental moulds of even international relations experts (not to speak of public officials, elected leaders, and the 'informed' public), remain riveted to the rigid state-centric frameworks inherited over the long history of pervasive distrust among nations. Consequently, international conflict is seen as inevitable, endemic and naturally ordained. By definition, therefore, chaos is the norm and anarchy is the rule in world politics.

In South Asia we have the added burden of the long legacy of mutual suspicion and hostility among the seven states. What we need instead is a vision of a new South Asia thriving with growing inter-national cooperation, discarding the tradition of inter-governmental conflicts. To begin with, there is an urgent need to envision a South Asian Union in which the 'seven sisters' are at peace with themselves and with one another and also with the neighbouring regions of Southeast Asia, West Asia and the world at large. How does the vision of a peaceful South Asia committed to work for a cooperative dispensation seem and feel? It seems eminently desirable and feels beautiful. Both the cerebral and the emotional (the head and the heart) are integral to the whole and both are equally significant. The new vision of a better future for the vast population of South Asia should be converted into a 'mission.' This, in turn, should be parceled into a clear, time bound, and specific 'agenda.' The redeeming purpose of intellect is to devise practical steps to achieve ideal objectives.

The Mission

If South Asia is viewed as one socio-economic unit for regional planning, leaders and specialists can come up with macro strategies of development for the sub-continent as a whole and for the uplift of all its inhabitants. We must recognize the fact that the states of the region have also grown with the times (like most others elsewhere in the world) and are ready to discard inherited and outdated notions and ideological constructs of the past. Liberalization, privatization and globalization have come into play in much of the region (like the world over). The ongoing transformation brings in much needed flexibility of approach in adopting appropriate strategies and in devising the necessary institutions. However, it is crucial to recognize and remember that blind and imitative privatization of the liberal capitalist variety being foisted on the world by the US and the World Bank that marginalizes the poor and the unskilled, and ignores the concerns and interests of the rural and urban masses is to be eschewed like plague. The 2004 Lok Sabha and Assembly elections in India have given a clear warning in this regard. Leaders and officials that do not heed the warning will do so at their own peril.

As a first step, the people, public officials, leaders and the governments can and should be educated about the enormous opportunities missed, losses suffered and time lost as a result of *the lack of cooperation for over a half century* among the states in South Asia. Even by the most conservative estimates the 'costs' of the senseless hostility and protracted unwillingness to cooperate are staggering indeed. These can and should be constructed statistically and given the widest possible publicity and in a manner that is easily understood by the common people of South Asia. The political and social costs of the legacy of hostility and mutual suspicion are even more staggering.

The next step is to 'rescue' the South Asian governments from the sterile and negative mindsets of the past. This mission can and should be accomplished by scholars and men of goodwill in partnership with the media and the concerned NGOs. This campaign of education should be aimed at the leaders as well as the public. This is no doubt a gigantic task. But, it is less difficult now than a few years earlier. Latest indications show that the informed and attentive public as well as the proverbial "man in the street" are (in their own uncomplicated way) far ahead of the governments and the elected leaders in India (and Pakistan, Nepal etc.) Ordinary people of South Asia are able to see that their destiny and welfare are deeply interlinked. Moreover, unlike their governments and the big leaders, the people need not and do not worry about losing face! Elected leaders and governments also see the logic of the situation, but are unwilling to risk acknowledging in public the transformed and still evolving environment in favour of cooperation for mutual benefit. Narrow patriotism and chauvinistic rhetoric seem so comfortably risk free! But they damage the cause of the material betterment and social progress of the vast masses living in the region.

In this context the compelling historical analogy of the Cold War era and the lessons that were *not* learned deserve to be recalled, however briefly. Seen from the perspective of the mankind as a whole, the negativistic, sterile and chilling strategic concept of Mutual Assured Destruction, aptly called MAD, skewed the whole international system for over a half century. While the Big Two indulged in the most wasteful, brazen and immoral race of piling up more and more deadly weapons on top of their already sky high arsenals, the rest of the world was forced to live on the edge of nuclear holocaust. During the entire era the presidents of the United States were not merely an avowed champions of anti-communism, but also its unacknowledged prisoners! Their only option was to be more aggressively anti-communist than the rivals in the public arena. To be accused of being soft on communism spelled disaster and political death. The immobilizing impact of the no holds barred US-Soviet confrontation worldwide was equally pernicious on the Russian side as well. The blind hatred between the two super powers and their allies that gripped the world was nothing less than madness and hysteria. The consequential waste of intellectual and emotional energies and the material resources was colossal, beyond imagination indeed. What obtains in the Indo-Pakistan equation is not at all dissimilar. Only the scale of resources and talent wasted are smaller, not its utter stupidity! While the two 'patriotic' governments in South Asia indulged in nuclear one-upmanship and saber rattling, the poor masses of the two nations (and the rest of the region) are condemned to a life of deprivation, poverty and misery. The US is forced to intervene every now and then, however reluctantly, to literally drag the two warring neighbours from each other's throat and avert a potential nuclear disaster. Government of India (and that of Pakistan, Bangladesh, Sri Lanka and Nepal) needs to be 'rescued' from the equally compelling and misplaced 'patriotism' and the immobilizing predicament they are in and believe they are in.

Time is ripe to launch a sustained campaign to 'educate' the government of India, the elected and other leaders of the country about the unwisdom of the protracted stalemate (and worse) with Pakistan and other South Asian states. It is also necessary to reassure them that the overwhelming majority of the people in India (and the other neighbouring states) realise the utter stupidity and futility of the three major wars and the fifty-year long Indo-Pak cold war. The costs of decades long hostility and mutual suspicion have added up to a 'hurting stalemate', which is preparing the ground for mending fences with the arch enemy. The escalation of the arms race especially since the nuclear blasts of May 1998 – one-upmanship on nuclear bombs, missiles, fissile materials – reinforces the rationale of this 'vision' and 'mission.' It enhances the urgency and relevance of mutual accommodation. If only there is no irresponsible talk of concessions given away and 'surrender' to the other side and if only there is prudent advocacy of cooperation for mutual benefit, things can and will improve dramatically. This will happen sooner than we imagined possible ten years ago. Unless cooperation and working for common benefit (i.e., playing non-zero-sum games) become positively desirable and politically (electorally) viable, the prevailing state of mutual suspicion and hostility cannot be overcome. In fact, now is the most opportune time for reconciliation and a fresh beginning. We must recognize and build on the fact that former prime minister Vajpayee's initiatives for peace with Pakistan did not become a contentious issue in the elections of 2004. Congress and all other parties were supportive because an overwhelming majority of the Indian people favoured peace and accommodation with Pakistan. The people had enough by way of hatred and hostility. They want to forget and bury the past. Moreover, the new generation wants to get along and go along and concentrate on material advancement and better life for themselves and their families.

If a meaningful campaign for Indo-Pakistan cooperation cannot be waged now, it can never be waged. The change of government in New Delhi did not adversely affect the composite dialogue process. The postponed dates for the meetings have been announced by mutual consent. Though the peace process with

Pakistan derailed more than once before, the present situation seems propitious and hopeful. Though India-Pakistan equation is of considerable significance for the progress of SAARC, it is necessary to isolate the pernicious impact of the bilateral relationship from the intra-regional relations in South Asia. The India-Sri Lanka and India-Nepal trade treaties are good pointers to what can and should be done.

The crucial next step is to devise specific activities, result oriented programmes, and policy oriented research projects with a view to move the vision and the mission forward from possibilities to actualities. One of the practical ways of doing this is to select one or two macro opportunities for cooperation (not merely resolving conflicts) involving two or more states in the region as challenges for delineating 'objective' strategies that are economically efficient and technologically viable. India, Nepal, Bangladesh and Bhutan should negotiate a long-term treaty for the development and utilization of the vast water resources and the limitless hydroelectric potential of the Himalayan region as a whole. (At the initial stage, political and other considerations should be kept aside. These will certainly come in at the later stages of obtaining the needed support and necessary approvals from the governments.)

Such initiatives for cooperation and material advancement of the people of the region should bring together technical experts, government officials, NGOs, media persons and scholars. To begin with the meetings and sessions for exchange of ideas can and should be held at informal level and move forward towards higher degrees of formal interaction among the states. Initially the focus should be on non-controversial areas like power generation and infrastructure development. Bigger and richer countries (i.e., India) must be willing and ready not to drive the hardest bargain vis-à-vis the poorer and weaker sister states. As mentioned earlier, the dominant country should choose not to dominate, nor should it give 'easy concessions' or 'surrender.' In this context the 'image' and appearances are as important as the reality. Otherwise the prospects of the very process of seeking cooperation for mutual benefit will be in jeopardy. India should lead for the economic and social advancement of the people of the whole region. Leadership is different from domination and the distinction is central to the cooperative and forward looking South Asian Union envisaged here. We should lead by example.

The Agenda

Once the vision of a South Asia charaterised by willing cooperation for mutual benefit and the mission of taking it forward towards a customs union, on to an economic union and ultimately to the South Asian Union are clear, the task of setting forth an agenda to achieve the goal is not too difficult. A set of initiatives and actions that India should take unilaterally, without waiting or even expecting reciprocity from the other states of South Asia.

1. India should begin by giving *concessional access* to its vast markets for the goods and services of all the six states (Afghanistan). How much concession to what products from which countries is to be worked out through mutual consultations between the governments, official experts, organizations representing trade, investment, labour and agriculture. The main principle is that the concessional duty benefits given should be real, not ornamental.
2. Government of India and Indian business and industry should and can invest in the neighbouring countries on a substantial scale. Mutual benefit and welfare of the masses should be the guiding spirit. Obviously, the capital invested should earn due return so that the surplus so generated becomes additional investment for the next round of development. The motive should not be profits only, profits at any cost. Capitalism, yes, but not mercenary capitalism as championed by the US. The basic and the fundamental lesson of the 2004 elections –don't ignore the poor, don't deprive the rural and urban masses the benefits of liberalization, privatization and globalization. In an electoral democracy marginalizing the marginalized (knowingly and/or unknowingly) leads to the 'throwing the rascals out.'
3. India should generously transfer technology to and share the advances it has made and continue to make in science,

technology, industry and agriculture with its immediate neighbours in South Asia. We have always condemned the advanced countries of the West for their callous failure in transferring technology to and sharing their knowledge with the developing and poor countries. Let us practice what we preach to others and show the world that sharing knowledge and innovation benefits everyone, including us.

4. Former prime minster Vajpayee announced aid of hundred million dollars to fund poverty alleviation programmes in the region, but outside India. The new government of prime minister Manmohan Singh should double or triple the aid offered. Even more important than the quantum of aid is India's lead and active participation in the formulation and implementation of the poverty alleviation programmes that are best suited to the needs of the people of South Asia.

5. On all bilateral disputes with all our neighbours in South Asia (including Kashmir), India should and can be more flexible and accommodative. In diplomacy it is not always best to drive the hardest bargain against other nations. The goal of diplomacy is to resolve disputes once and for all. This can be achieved only when disputes are settled amicably and with mutual consent. The disputants should not feel aggrieved or that they were given a raw deal. Then bitterness remains in the national consciousness and the resolve to do tit for tat lingers on, which in effect means that the dispute is not settled even if a treaty is signed between the parties concerned. Divisive disputes should be settled in such a way that all the parties gain in the bargain and it is equally important that it should appear to be so! Then, and then only all of us can move forward to concentrate on the present and future tasks on hand for the betterment of all the people. It is high time we consciously reject the western concepts of national security and mercenary sovereign state, which promote endless conflicts and *justify* not merely the *power* of the sovereign nation state but its *right* to dominate and exploit other states and peoples. Such perverted conceptions seem to say that the state has an *obligation* to dominate

and be always aggressive. The so-called national interests have degenerated into the self-interests of the ruling groups or the establishment, which are patently against the welfare of the common people of the country. (The US war of aggression on Iraq is the latest, if not the most grotesque, example of the power structure in command hijacking national interests for private gain. Bush and his cronies are the real beneficiaries, the racketeers, while the young soldiers are the sacrificial goats at the altar of the American flag!)

6. Economists and specialists in international trade will point out that the intra-regional trade of India is less than a miserable two per cent of our foreign trade. In a few years, this may increase at the most to a respectable four or five per cent. We all know that the economies of the seven sister states are essentially competitive and not complementary. All the former colonies were groomed to meet the needs and sub-serve the interests of the imperial powers in command for centuries. Since their independence these ex-colonies have struggled to diversify and acquire a broad spectrum of capabilities. Most of them (including India) are yet to become balanced and self-sufficient economies.

   Regional economic integration is a means to strengthen international competitiveness, enhance efficiencies, generate income and hence act as an engine of growth. The goal is not merely to promote intra-regional trade. Regional Trade Agreements (RTAs) promote cooperation, enhance South Asia's share in FDI flows and enable the region to make progress in restructuring industry on a pan-regional basis. The RTAs between India and Nepal (1996) and India and Sri Lanka (2001) have led to a lot of dynamism in intra-regional investment within the short period of their operation.

   The rationale of the approach advocated and the particular suggestions made is that man does not live by bread alone. The socio-cultural and political dividends of the policy of leading by example and choosing to eschew domination far outweigh the relatively meagre financial benefits flowing from regional economic integration in the immediate future.

7. In addition to implementing an agenda like the above, there is an urgent need to seek, nurture and effect an attitudinal change on the part of the governments, leaders and the peoples of South Asia. Here again we should lead by example. We should work closely with all those who share our vision of a new South Asia devoid of conflicts, and full of cooperation and goodwill. As mentioned earlier, we should launch a concerted campaign in India to turn the tide in favour of a South Asian Union. Obviously, the government of India, the state governments should take the initiative to launch a massive and sustained educative campaign on a long-term basis. But, that is not enough. Business, industry, labour unions, experts from all walks of life, intellectuals, artists, NGOs, private associations and individuals committed the cause of a peaceful and cooperative South Asia should do their part at all levels and in all possible ways. Only then we can ensure that the government of India (and other governments in the region) will stay committed to 'the mission' and remain true to 'the vision.'

8. One of the crucial constituents of this "Vision, Mission, and Agenda" is the planning and conducting of workshops/ training programmes specially designed for the middle level officials of the ministries dealing with external, economic, security and cultural affairs that are likely to be included in the negotiating teams and/or involved in the preparation of background papers for inter-country negotiations. This is a newly emerging sub-field called 'pre-negotiation' theory and practice.[1] The proposed workshops/training programmes to be conceptaulised and directed by committed scholars and seasoned senior diplomats, should zero in on specific issues of regional importance (involving India and at least two other countries); analyse in depth and identify opportunities for mutually beneficial cooperation. If the intention is to promote international cooperation in the region, even most contentious issues could be broken down into specific

constituents of convergence and divergence on a continuum ranging all the way from easily reconcilable to wholly irreconcilable points. We should select a contentious issue for this kind of close scrutiny. Then, we can begin with the limited constituents that are not in dispute, move on to areas in which broad agreement in principle is possible, then move forward to items on which agreement can be ironed out at the higher levels of bureaucracy and conclude with the points on which dispute settlement is possible only at the political level(s) at the top. Such a targeted search is not an easy task. But it helps in circumscribing the points of disagreement to their narrowest range. The next step is to concentrate on the areas of agreement so identified and work our way upward to the more difficult core issues of the dispute that require delicate handling at higher political levels. This way the content and the range of a particular controversy or dispute can be grasped clearly and its extent and intensity monitored. The process is bound to be laborious, but it helps us realize that in a majority of cases, the areas under dispute and their significance are far more limited than what the governments make them out to be in public, popular perceptions imagine them to be, and media pundits with their eye and now portray them to be (especially in living colour on the TV). By highlighting the large number of points of agreement within the contentious issue, the whole atmosphere of debate and the thrust of disputation between the governments and peoples of South Asia can be and will be transformed for the better. Findings of such in-depth exertions by the two or three sides of the disputants should be widely circulated in all the concerned states through the print and electronic media so that there is perceptible change in the environment and ethos of interaction among the governments and peoples of South Asia. From the negativism prevalent till recently we can and should transit to a more positive frame of mind in favour of cooperation for mutual benefit. This certainly is a better alternative than each of us blindly concentrating on our 'national interests' and 'national security' conceived in narrow conflictual terms and pursued as zero-sum games at the expense of one another.

9. Finally, the participants of the seminar should take the initiative to constitute a small committee of academics and media professionals to design a multi-media campaign in India to further "the vision, mission, and the agenda" for a South Asian Union. This should be conceived as a long-term project of say ten years duration.

Conclusion

"What South Asia faces today is not merely a crisis of development, but a threat to its real resource base, to its fragile ecological system, to its democratic structures and to life itself in the region. There is a systemic crisis. No individual South Asian country can solve these problems by itself and a major effort at regional cooperation would be required to complement national development strategies and the nation building efforts. The complexity and the magnitude of the problem have been underestimated by all concerned." So observes a systematic and penetrating study on the strategies needed for poverty eradication in South Asia released recently.[2]

The era of post cold war globalization has unmasked a number of critical inadequacies and failures of economic reforms carried out in tune with the liberal capitalist free market model championed and foisted by the US and the West on the rest of the world. The poor, the unskilled, the rural and urban masses, the youth and women, the minorities and the backward classes –i.e., the marginalized sections of the population— did not receive the benefits of liberalization, privatization and globalization. They have been left out, their concerns and problems have been ignored and they have been marginalized further. Such a reform process obviously cannot go on and should not be allowed to proceed further. The Indian voters said so in the most unambiguous manner available to them in an electoral democracy. Abandoning democracy is not on the cards and is simply unthinkable in India. The only option open to the rulers is to publicly favour "growth with a human face," which at best is a clumsy phrase and a wooly concept. If this is used as a rhetorical stratagem to ignore and side track the will of the people, the future of the country will be bleak and beyond redemption indeed.

In the altered context of the twenty first century, some early enthusiasts of globalization foresaw the 'End of the State.' But, we all know that the state is here to stay and that it will not oblige by doing a disappearing act voluntarily. We also know that we need the sovereign nation state for a long time to come, even if it is less of a sovereign than before and many states around the world are still involved in nation building while they as well as most other established nations are coming together to form regional international organizations. (The EU is the most striking example.) It is, therefore, too early to bid 'Farewell to the State.' However, it has become absolutely necessary to bid farewell to 'The Welfare State.'

The radically altered global political/ideological context calls for a new social contract between the state and the poor, the vast majority in all the countries of South Asia. In the world of today, the state has to shrink in some respects, but it has also to take on new responsibilities in some other vital areas. Business is not the business of the state, every one agrees. But it is very much the business of the state to take on the stupendous and very complex tasks of poverty alleviation and its eventual eradication; empowerment of people (including women and children); meeting the very basic needs of the people such as drinking water, minimum standards of sanitation, medical care and health and primary education for all. Above all we have to rethink and revamp the extant development strategies for the betterment of the vast majority of the people, who are currently left out and callously sidelined.

To build a contented (over time prosperous) and peaceful India, we need a peaceful and rapidly developing South Asian neighbourhood. This can be achieved only with the leadership of India that is willing and ready to share and cooperate with all the states in the region. In short, we need *"the vision, the mission, and the agenda!"*

References

1 Jay Rothman, *Developing Pre-Negotiation Theory and Practice*, Policy Studies, no. 29, Jerusalem: Hebrew University, 1989; and *A Pre-Negotiation Model: Theory and Training*, Policy Studies, no. 40, Jerusalem: Hebrew University, 1990. These two path- breaking studies deserve the attention of all IR scholars, especially because the adversaries chosen for the innovative experiment were Israel and Palestine.

2 Ponna Wignaraja and Susil Sirivardana (eds.), *Readings on Pro-Poor Planning Through social Mobilisation in South Asia: The Strategic Option for Poverty Eradication*, Vol. 1, New Delhi: Vikas Publishing House, 1998.

15

Envisaging the South Asian Resurgence: Systemic Imperatives for Regional Synergic Management

Manoj Soni

If South Asia were to be personified and if the region misses the present historic prospect of synergizing the regional energy of cooperation, the region would perhaps echo the same sentiments as those so painfully experienced and yet so beautifully expressed by Frost.

There are indeed two directions that exist as choices before the nations of South Asia. A direction towards synergy of comprehensive national energies which empower these nations and a direction of discord that could disintegrate their vary identity. And disintegration of identity, in the post-modernist sense, need not necessarily be synonymous with demise of physical existence. The rampant forces legitimizing the localization of alienation of people from their national roots could well deform the very fabric characterizing the distinctness of a given national society. It is not that such a choice has emerged before South Asia for the first time. The choice has always been there. What differentiates the scenario in the Uni-Centric Multi Polar world emerging in the aftermath of the Soviet Union's disintegration is that this emergent international systemic order is replete with imperatives which have the capability of transforming South Asia into a region of significance from its present state of a region of sympathy. Thus, the focus of this paper is on an optimistic attempt to analyze these imperatives and delineate a vision and strategy for the South Asian resurgence largely understood within the context of the South Asian Association for Regional Cooperation (SAARC).

How is South Asia situated in terms of international systemic structures shaping the world order in these formative years of the twenty first century? The answer to this question necessitates a response to a more primary question: How the international systemic structures shaping the present world order are knotted?

The present world order, is being shaped by Uni-Centric Multi Polar international systemic structure. In a sense, it is a strategic synthesis of the extremities of Uni-Polarity and Multi-Polarity. Concomitantly, such a structure has a unique characteristic of balancing the extreme predilections of both – Uni-Polarity and Multi-Polarity – which have shaped the international system in the preceding centuries.

A Uni-Centric Multi Polar structure facilitates, recognizes and even legitimizes the central role of a democratic nation-state with comprehensively unmatchable power configuration. At the same time, it necessarily accommodates multiple poles of power embodied as nation-states, international organizations and even international regimes, which have selective comparative advantage over the central power of the structure. A Uni-Centric Multi Polar structure positions the central power as a *sin qua non* for ensuring stability of the systemic structure and the ensuing international order. The multiple poles of power, in competitive collaboration with the central power, are deemed necessary for maintaining order in the system and source the wherewithal and direction for exploration, creation, protection, and expansion of wealth and power for use in primarily protecting each player's national interest and generally maintaining a favorable international order for the constituents of the structure. This structure does not allow any single actor or a sub-alliance of the constituents of the structure to run its / their independent writ over the system to alter its order fundamentally in its / their favour.

Today, the United States occupies the central role in the Uni-Centric Multi Polar structure and exhibits all the characteristics indicated in the just profiled conceptual framework of emergent international order. The European Union, Japan, China, Russia, India, the United Nations Organization, the World Trade Organization, the World Bank, the International Monetary Fund and the World Intellectual Property Organization constitute the multiple poles of power of that structure.

Having attempted to profile the systemic structures of the international order, let us once again take up the first question as to how South Asia is situated in terms of international systemic structures shaping the world order in these formative years of the twenty first century?

The simple answer could be that South Asia as a nuclear flashpoint region today has a repulsive bearing upon the emergent international order. But at the same time if India is recognized as a constituent of the Uni-Centric Multi Polar structure shaping the present world order, then South Asia could be perceived as having immense potential for emerging and being acknowledged as a vibrant, stable, and wealthy pole of power in the Uni-Centric Multi Polar configuration.

This potential of the world's most explosively precarious region is empowered by its geo-strategic location, the variety and abundance of its natural resources, the magnitude of its market, the vast array of its scientific and technical human-intellectual resources, the immeasurable wealth of its untapped intellectual property, the strength of its concordant cultural undercurrent and the most recently acquired firepower for mass extinction.

Unfortunately for billions of people of the region, all these ingredients of empowerment have been used, since decolonization, by a handful of leaders and their nations against the interests of South Asian people ironically under the garb of so called national interest. It is possible to argue that South Asia did have a historic opportunity for prudently realizing and streamlining its enormous power potential during the Cold War period, had it emerged as a sustainable leader of a formidable nonaligned block. But the forces of history and the imprint it leaves on the minds and actions of large masses of human being cannot, of course, be so easily glossed over or defied. Perhaps, it requires the more sublime nature of the human self to venture into attaining goals that are ultimately higher and beneficial to vast majority than a parochially myopic minority.

If the axiom of history repeating itself has any element of credence, then the unfolding of the pattern of the formation of international order shaped by the Uni-Centric Multi Polar structure, on one hand, provides strength to that credence and provides imperatives for South Asian resurgence, on the other. South Asia, once again, has a historic opportunity to reorganize and reorient its massive power and substantial potential for emerging as a credible pole of power by harmonizing its management of regional as well as international conduct either through institutionalized or conventionalized processes and policies.

Normatively speaking from the perspective of global interest, the emergent international order hinged upon the Uni-Centric Multi Polar structure can be stabilized, sustained and legitimized more reasonably if the nations of South Asia housing the largest mass of humanity, equipped with great resources and armed with the deadliest of weapons, is accorded a just role for protecting its national interest and realizing its regional aspirations. However, the brutish realities of politics do not favour favours for free even when stipulated by higher human values such as justice or even peace. Actors on the stage of world politics have to define their own roles and script their own acts on the basis of their capability – actual or potential.

At the same time, the systemic dynamics, in the larger interest of macro-dimensional order, have been known to be affording imperatives for hitherto dormant but potentially or actually capable actors, to integrate themselves with the systemic mainstream. The present systemic dynamics are endowed with such imperatives for South Asia, in view of the region actual power and potential capabilities. These imperatives in a way are sourced by the ingredients of the region's capabilities enlisted just a while ago, such as its geo-strategic location, the variety and abundance of its natural resources, the magnitude of its market, the vast array of its scientific and technical human-intellectual resources, the immeasurable wealth of its untapped intellectual property, the strength of its concordant cultural undercurrent and the most recently acquired firepower for mass extinction. The five decades succeeding decolonization of the South Asian nations have certainly changed the core of these nations, especially India and partly Pakistan; and can be ignored for long only at great systemic risk. Thus, the system, in the interest of its own strength and stability, would encourage a resurged South Asia to be a part of trouble-shooting team rather than letting it remain a trouble-making horde.

How could South Asia engage itself to this imperative? Or more importantly, *could* South Asia possibly engage itself to this systemic imperative?

The South Asian nation-states within the SAARC could commit themselves to restructuring three key areas of their national and regional conduct in order to be able to credibly and sustainably engage themselves to the systemic imperative. These areas are economics, security and governance. Author likes to profile a broad outline of a vision derived from selective focus on these areas for the South Asian resurgence and then attempt delineating a strategy for building synergy for its realization.

The first challenge before the South Asian nation-states is that of accelerating national economic development especially by protecting the national interests in trade and intellectual property, while rethinking regional economic cooperation.

Twenty first century is the century of mind. Innovation, its management and protection are the keys to sources of wealth. In this context, issues related to generation, valuation, protection and exploitation of intellectual property have become critically important all around the world and particularly for the developing economies. In the present day knowledge-driven world economy, intellectual property discourse is no longer a self-contained domain, rather, it is and could be a highly effective policy instrument with great bearing upon a wide range of national interests including security.

For instance, the discourse of intellectual property as an instrument of policy has a very special significance for the states of South Asia where there is abundance of untapped and unprotected traditional knowledge systems with huge economic potential. If the states of South Asia could deter the process of globalization from appropriating the elements of these collective traditional knowledge systems into proprietary knowledge for the commercial profit of the few powerful nations and corporations, they could reap rich dividends from their endeavors. In fact, this could be a battle for yet another kind of intellectual decolonization, but is a battle to be worth fighting and winning.

The second key area of concern is managing an evenhanded national and regional security environment. Historical rivalries, mutual distrust, apparent threat perceptions between and amongst the states of South Asia have bred the siblings of extremism and terrorism over the past three decades. In the vitiated environment of the present day, the task of building mutual trust is the most complex, particularly between the long-standing traditional rivals – India and Pakistan. The problem is further complicated by differing perceptions about India by its regional neighbours. While India sees itself as primarily a South Asian power, its neighbours view and often interpret India's conduct as that of a regional hegemony.

Sir Claude Auchinleck, one of the last British Commanders of the Indian Army, had lamented the partition of India from a strategic point of view. The partition, as believed by him, fragmented the strategic entity of the Indian subcontinent, which otherwise had a substantial bearing upon the equations on the regions' and even the world's strategic dynamics. The heroic task before the present day and may be the future generation of statespersons of South Asia would be to regain or recreate that strategic identity within and without the region. That is perhaps the most daunting of all regional security management challenges.

Any attempt at redesigning the process and pattern of governance within the South Asian states towards a more legitimate, accountable and just form, if successful, could itself become a very powerful catalyst for bringing about both the above profiled and many more crucial turnarounds. This is an area of prime concern for not only the billions of citizens of the South Asian states, but, is also a concern for the security and stability of international system. Non-democratic regimes, in past, have tended to degenerate into breeding grounds for violent convulsions and fundamentalist thinking and ultimately deform into rogue states. With the imminent danger of inadequately safeguarded lethal capabilities for mass extinction within reach of unscrupulous individuals and organizations, the stakes for survival, security and stability of not just the region but the world at large are very high. The abuse of fundamental human rights, the instances of state atrocities, the unprincipled pursuit of power, the unethical modes of exploiting national resources for unjust personal and parochial purposes and the farcical nature and functioning of so called democratic institutions are also areas of grave civil crisis in all the states of South Asia, without exception. Without a determined, well-equipped and penetratively effective overhauling rectification of the process and pattern of governance, the South Asian states would suffer a grave loss of credibility within the international society of civilized nation-states. It is equally appreciable that such a rectification and redesigning cannot be achieved merely by legal and legislative compulsions. It needs more of refined political will, a sublime civic culture and a sense of belonging, responsibility and pride in every citizen towards his / her state. A well conceived and effectively implemented education system and timely and decent employment opportunities are the proven keys to such ethical empowerment of the large masses.

Finally, delineate a strategy for realizing the vision of a resurged South Asia as informed by the above three key areas. For the purpose of this paper author likes to call this strategy as South Asian Regional Synergic Management, which is adapted from the discourses by Ken Blachard, John Carlos and Alan Radolph who are amongst the leading international management consultants. What is South Asian Regional Synergic Management?

Regional Synergic Management may be understood as a cutting edge strategy that provides for both the strategic advantage that states are seeking and the opportunity that its citizens are seeking. It is the means of involving the actors in the region as partners in determining the course for the region's success or for that matter, failure. While giving these partners the authority and responsibility to make important decisions in the overall interest of the region to which their own interests are linked is a key structural aspect of the Regional Synergic Management, it is not the whole picture. The real essence of the Regional Synergic Management comes from creating avenues, processes and platforms for releasing the knowledge, experience and motivational power that is already in these actors but is being severely underutilized.

The key to the strategy of the Regional Synergic Management in South Asia is empowerment of the key actors – empowerment by information sharing, empowerment by creating autonomies through boundaries and empowerment by letting the teams become hierarchy.

The first key to empowerment is information sharing. Information sharing between and amongst the actors of South Asia, especially the states is a crucially missing link for sustaining mutual trust. People without information seldom act responsibly, or act at all. When information is shared through a consensually agreed process the concerned actors are almost compelled to act with responsibility as they feel included and trusted.

The second key to empowerment in the strategy of the Regional Synergic Management is creating such structures which are intended to inform partners – the actors – about the range within which they can act with autonomy. This is what is creating autonomy through boundaries. For instance, the boundaries in the Regional Synergic Management strategy take the form of vision statements, collaborative goals and decision-making rules. Within the ranges set by those boundaries the actors can determine what to do and how to do it. As the empowerment process unfolds, the range of structures can widen and deepen to allow the actors greater degrees of autonomy, control and responsibility.

The third crucial key that should work in conformity with the two keys outlined above is letting teams of actors becoming hierarchy. Most of the complex decisions of managing cooperation in such a diverse region as South Asia naturally require input from a collection of sources which need to be transformed into team efforts for desired success. The bottom line is that teams are more effective than individuals tightly positioned in hierarchy to mange complex situations successfully. The team with its synergic effort offers greater knowledge as well as a mechanism of support. These teams are not supposed to be just recommending ideas; rather, they are to make and implement decisions and are to be held accountable for results.

For the sake of convenience of understanding and scope of this paper, if we restrict our analysis to the dynamics of South Asia, even then there are remarkable parallels between these vivacious human interactions and the master's play. Both are cosmic and complex. The characters are sometimes heroic; at other times they are petty. The action is always dramatic and often tragic. As with any good play, the audience is drawn into action at the Globe, the London theatre where Shakespeare staged his plays. Similarly, the regional and global theatre of politics draws us all in. Indeed, we are seated on the stage, no matter how remote the action may seem or how much we may want to ignore it. Like it or not we, the South Asians and the world, are stuck with each other and the progress of the play between us will take a course depending upon our choice of one of those two roads that were referred in the beginning of this paper, viz., a road towards synergy of comprehensive national energies which empower our nations and a direction of discord that could disintegrate our vary identity – a choice that the coming generation and not we will either enjoy, endure or regret.

16

Resurrecting Maritime South Asia: Critical Perspectives on the 21st Century

Sanjay Chaturvedi

Introduction

What implies by *'resurrecting' maritime South Asia* for the purposes of this paper is the revival and rejuvenation of maritime mindsets and perspectives, which, despite a long-standing history, have gradually been eroded and marginalized. It is good to be reminded, at the very outset, how the ancient Indian Ocean 'world' of maritime trade and commerce, sustained and strengthened by human-cultural flows and intercourse at regional and sub-regional levels, was deranged by the imperial-colonial metropolitan economies and further destroyed by the cold war ideological geopolitics of alliances in the Indian Ocean region. Such geo-strategic alliances often worked at cross-purposes and effectively undermined the prospects for cooperation among the littorals states.

As the twenty first century unfolds, the imperatives of shared and comprehensive maritime security demand and deserve a truly multilateral, multi-level, and multi-sectoral effort and coalition among state and non-state actors in South Asia. Against the backdrop of innovative and maritime geographies introduced by the third United Nations Convention on the Law of the Sea (UNCLOS III), both the state and non-state actors in South Asia would be increasingly compelled to address wide-ranging concerns such as the ecologically sustainable development and management of mineral and marine resources, securing energy supplies and sea-lanes of communication, combating illegal immigration by sea and transnational crime (including piracy), managing maritime disasters, conserving marine eco-systems and protecting coastal communities and their habitats.

The paper argues and illustrates that geographical (re) imaginations and geopolitical imperatives of maritime South Asia can be approached far more meaningfully through a map centred on the south-polar projection. It also argues that the SAARC, which sadly lacks a maritime focus at present, ought to be at the forefront of mapping and building a new maritime architecture of regional and sub-regional cooperation in the Indian Ocean, especially with regard to the Arabian Sea and Bay of Bengal.

The paper begins with a brief overview of the trans-oceanic, commercial-cultural flows in the Indian Ocean region (IOR) over centuries, and how such mobile geographies were being undermined by the imperial-colonial geopolitics and its pursuit for primacy both on land and at sea. This would be followed by a brief comment on the cold war variety of geopolitics and its implications for the IOR. The argument then becomes that we need to revision South Asia in terms of fast multiplying, multifaceted dimensions of maritime (in) security. The concluding section, while briefly reflecting on the nature and scope of some of the issue-areas that could possibly constitute the agenda of an inclusive South Asian oceanic dialogue in the twenty first century, addresses the problems and prospects of forging new strategic alliances among SAARC members on the one hand, and between SAARC and Indian Ocean Rim Association for Regional Cooperation (IOR-ARC) in pursuit of shared maritime security and prosperity in the region.

Maritime South Asia: A Geo-historical Perspective on the Indian Ocean

It is a truism that the waters of the world form one vast expanse. Whereas the commons sense geographical understanding of the Indian Ocean is that it is the smallest of the three oceans, spanning the southern hemisphere from the Cape of Good Hope (Southern Africa) to the Cape Leeuwin (Western Australia), and divided into two almost eqúal halves by the Indian peninsula. As K. M. Panikkar once wrote, "the oneness of the sea is an obvious geographic fact, although... later scientific achievements have made it possible to bring large areas of oceanic surface under the control of land powers and thus to convert them into closed seas." [1] "From this point of view", said Panikkar,

...the geographical structure of Indian Ocean is particularly important. For the most part its area is walled off on three sides by land, with the southern side of Asia forming a roof over it. The continent of Africa constitutes the western wall, while Burma, Malaya and the insular continuations protect the eastern side. The vital feature which differentiates the Indian Ocean from the Pacific and the Atlantic is not the two sides but the sub-continent of India which just out far into the sea for a thousand miles to its tapering end at Cape Comorin...Considered geographically the Indian Ocean in its main area, in spite of the vastness of its surface and the oceanic character of its currents and winds has some of the features of a landlocked sea. Another important feature of this Ocean is the distribution of islands and archipelagos near its continental shores or in its vastness...The bays and the bights of the Indian Ocean require special consideration.[2]

It is in the human consciousness of 'landlocked' geographical structure of the Indian Ocean that the geo-cultural moorings and geopolitical impulses of a futuristic South Asian dialogue on peace and cooperation are historically rooted.

It is useful to be reminded that the Indian Ocean region was the home of the world's first urban civilization, and the centre of the first sophisticated commercial and maritime activities.[3] The Indian Ocean enabled the peoples on its shore to exchange and share a range of cultural values and economic activities. What emerged from and merged into this process was the Indian Ocean 'world' in its own right, the essential unity of which was determined by, what Braudel called, the *longue dure'e* or the long-term rhythms and patterns of long-distance maritime trade. It was an area, which included an enormous range of cultural and economic practices dictated, driven and defined by its unique maritime trading system, which provided the peoples of that 'world' with an economic unity and certain cultural commonalties which set them apart from the peoples of contiguous 'worlds' such as the Mediterranean and East Asia. Cultural commonalties were made possible by trade linkages, which facilitated the diffusion as well as fusion of religious and cultural systems such as Hinduism, Buddhism and Islam across the Ocean.

Any history of Indian Ocean must, therefore, as pointed by Kenneth McPherson[4], focus on the communities who have used that ocean and the forces that historically shaped their relationship with the sea. He argues that the history of the modern world can only be understood by examining the component parts from which it is constructed and not by partitioning human history into the studies of 'them' and 'us'. Such a history shows beyond all doubt that regional histories of mobility and flows are the foundation of global history and provide yet another means of discovering how our ancestors related to and interacted with one another and shaped the world in which they lived.

Five millennia ago the Indian Ocean connected the world's earliest urban civilizations—Mesopotamia and the Indus valley—in a web of maritime flows, which dealt in luxury commodities. Even after the Indus valley civilization ceased to exist some 3500 years ago, a resurgence of maritime trade paralleled the spread of settled farming and the development of urban life in the Ganges valley and the dry zone of northern Sri Lanka. By the middle of the first millennium BC, Peninsular India, Sri Lanka and the Maldives were closely linked parts of an extensive coastal trading network. While agriculture was the major prop, which underpinned all states in South Asia, in parts of the subcontinent and Sri Lanka maritime trade generated revenue through levies and dues on markets and harbours and provided means of converting local farm produce into luxury commodities and precious metals. In this way access to sea and the creation of coastal markets and harbours was on the determining factors in the formation of many coastal states in South Asia, most particularly, along the Malabar, Coromandal and Orissa coasts and in Sri Lanka too. The expansion of markets across South Asia not only led to quickening of the pace of economic activity but also encouraged the expansion of technological and cultural practices. Throughout South Asia, ruling groups absorbed and adapted aspects of the urban civilization, which was re-emerging in the Ganges valley.

In the Deccan too, in the wake of the decline of Mauryan empire, the Satavahana dynasty (c.50 B.C- c. A.D 225), rulers took a keen interest in maritime trade with the Arabian Sea and the Bay of Bengal through ports on the west coast of India such as Sopara, Bankot (Mandagora) and Malvan (Ernnaoboas) and on the east coast such as Masulipatnam. These ports were visited by ships from Egypt and the Persian gulf crewed by Egyptians, Arabs and the Persians. Thus, by the time the present era dawned, sailors and merchants from Egypt, the Red Sea, the Persian gulf and the South Asia thronged ports around the Arabian Sea from the Horns of Africa to sail as far as South as the Tanzania coast. To the eastern half of the Indian Ocean, centered upon the Bay of Bengal, was the exclusive domain of merchants and mariners from South and South East Asia.

The eastward mobility of South Asian merchants and mariners facilitated –and was in turn facilitated by – the spread of South Asian culture and religion into South East Asia. Throughout this area, from Irrawaddy valley of Burma to coast of Vietnam, where the spread of settled farming communities was giving birth to more complex social and economic organization, South Asian cultural and religious forms were adopted. Thus from the times when the Romans dominated the Mediterranean and much of the Middle East to the collapse the great Arab empire in the thirteenth century AD, South Asia remained the centre of the maritime trade network linking the Arabian Sea and the Bay of Bengal.

Since there existed a civilizational inter-cultural labyrinth, there never arose a point of conflict among Indian Ocean littorals;

all races, religions, learnt to live together, knowing fully well that in peace and trade they were optimizing their benefits. In the Western Indian Ocean, for instance, flows and interactions of this nature resulted in a 'composite culture', making it an area of 'high solidarity'.[5] How and why was the inter-Asian trade network disrupted, or rather, subordinated to European needs? Was it a consequence of the imperialist domination of Asia and Africa during the nineteenth century? Or was the imperialist domination itself was an end product of the stagnation and decay which had been at work in Asian societies for a long time? There appear to be no final answers regarding internal and external causations.

Classical Maritime Geopolitics: Pursuit of Primacy

The nineteenth century Europe produced a geopolitical maritime thinking aimed at 'mastering' the oceans, the most outstanding spokesman of which was one of America's best known and most influential naval officers, Alfred Thayer Mahan (1840-1915). Mahan attached more importance to sea power than any of his contemporary geopoliticians. His classic, *The Influence of Sea Power Upon History 1660-1783*, which appeared in 1890, was a profound analysis of the correlation between the sea and the state power.[6] His cherished and passionately pleaded dream was an enduring Anglo-American alliance as the key to the mastery of the world. Mahan held that sea-transported power and the command of the seas were the dominant form of power that generated economic strength and prosperity of a people, and constituted the decisive factor in international politics. Future world power, accordingly, must rest on control of the seas; mere land powers, howsoever large, were destined to decline and decay.

A contemporary of Mahan, Sir Halford J Mackinder (1861-1947), heavily emphasized land power, while pronouncing that with man's exploration of the globe –including those of the oceans– the world had become 'a closed political system'. In the emerging close international system, advances in transport technology rendered the idea of world domination, for the first time, a viable political proposition. Mackinder's key proposition was that the history of the world had been shaped by the eternal conflict between the landsmen and seamen. In the northern and interior portion of Eurasia lay an area inaccessible to sea power and capable of becoming the spring and seat of a land power of phenomenal capability–the Heartland. Mackinder held that the heartland power using its resources for building a strong agricultural-industrial economy, could dominate most of the 'World-Island' (the term he used for the composite of Eurasia and Africa); he presumed that the endowment of the area with its rich resource base was capable of sustaining a 'world power'.[7]

According to K.M. Panikkar, "Mackinder...thought equally in terms of the Eurasian continent and consequently the Indian Ocean was considered only a link area of "The World Island" of which the only effective political boundaries were the Atlantic and the Pacific". This imperial vision, along with the discourse supporting it, portrayed national security in terms of territorial expansion, advocated the development of colonies as signs of national health, privileged the European state as the key factor in analysis and inflated beyond all reasonable proportions the overall supremacy of the European, later 'Western' culture.

With the arrival of Europeans the economic boundaries of the Indian Ocean world expanded to encompass direct linkages with European and American markets. Until the late seventeenth century, however, these extra-regional linkages did not fundamentally alter the 'long-term rhythms' of life in the Indian Ocean. But from the eighteenth century European capitalism, first commercial and then industrial, began to drastically alter patterns of indigenous economic, cultural and political life. The indigenous long-term forces, which had shaped the history and cultures of the Indian Ocean world were overwhelmed, and It was integrated as a region into global system whose long-term cultural and economic rhythms were fundamentally influenced by the industrialized nations of Europe and North America. The eighteenth century also marked the beginning of the process of integration of Indian Ocean into the bitterly contested arena of world geopolitics.

The Cold War Geopolitics

It was typical of the cold war discourse that singular attributes of a particular place were subordinated to its perceived position in the abstract spaces of the grand strategy.[8] It was 'friendly' or 'threatening', 'ours' or 'theirs'. This homogenization of global space made the details of local geography unimportant or 'trivial'. In the reductionist strategic thinking of the cold war planners, the chief 'value' of marine space and resources was, thus, judged primarily in the context of grand strategies and counter-strategies.

Once subjected to the hegemonic conflict between the two superpowers, hooked on to the cold war geopolitical discourse and entangled in its containment militarism, maritime perceptions and policies of the Indian Ocean littoral states came to be dominated –and distorted– by confrontation, the arms race, divided security and conflict lines. The Cold War geo-strategy transformed the political geography of the Indian Ocean into a military geography.[9] The presence of oil in Western Indian Ocean, the sea lanes to the Suez and around South Africa made control of the straits —Bab-el-Mandab and Hormuz— and of South Africa as prime targets of super power rivalry in Egypt, Somalia, Kenya, Mauritius etc. Nuclearlization of oceans kept pace, though in a less blatant manner, with the spread of nuclear weapons on land, though it varied from ocean to ocean.[10]

The post-Cold War Indian Ocean and South Asia: Towards a New Regionalism?

The post-cold war geopolitical realities in the Indian Ocean region are more complex and compelling than ever before,[11] certainly far more intricate than the weapon supplies and systems in the area might suggest. And they pose as serious a threat, if not more, to the 'national' security of the countries of the region broadly defined. What Mary Kaldor[12] has described as 'new' wars in a global era of organized violence also has a maritime dimension. The wide spectrum of such threats includes attempted coup involving foreign mercenaries, various forms of terrorism that include hijacking, mining, sabotage operations vis-à-vis shore-based and sea-based installations, illegal trafficking in arms and narcotics, and off late piracy.

Among numerous constraints encountered in containing and eliminating such threats, is the fact that only a few among the twenty nine littoral states and six island territories of the IOR have the necessary naval and coast guard capability for the surveillance of their vast maritime zones and the coastline. Whereas piracy attacks are common throughout South East Asia, the Singapore straits and the whole area in the vicinity of Singapore territorial waters are said to be extremely dangerous. [13]

The challenge of de-territorialised threats...

De-territorialised threats of the kind mentioned above seriously undermine the pursuit of economic growth and commercial interdependencies, and hence cannot be left entirely at the discretion or disposal of state actors and governments. Combating transnational crime calls not only for high levels of intergovernmental cooperation and commitment; also essential is the creation of more economic opportunities, through international cooperation among state and non-state actors at both bilateral and multilateral levels, in the Indian Ocean's economically deprived sub-regions.

The Indian Ocean littoral is also host to an increasingly complex geopolitical economy of organized violence, with various terrorist hubs (LTTE in Sri Lanka, Al Qaeda in Yemen, Somalia, Singapore and Pakistan, Abu Sayyaf in the Philippines, Free Aceh Movement in Indonesia). Arguably, the centre of gravity of terrorism at sea is currently located in the Asia-Pacific region. Among the two dozen-odd terrorist groups identified as having engaged in maritime terrorism, at least nine are currently active - five of these operate in the Indian Ocean. This situation is further complicated by the regional presence of Asia's two principal illicit opium production areas, the Golden Crescent (Afghanistan-Iran-Pakistan) and the Golden Triangle (Myanmar-Laos-Thailand), and high seas piracy.

...and strategic competition

The growing militarisation and nuclearisation of the Indian Ocean region is but the latest in a series of developments reflecting the numerous strategic rivalries converging in this theatre.[14] Here, traditional major sea powers such as the United Sates, Russia, Britain are not on the decline, while new sea powers such as Japan, China and India (around ninety seven per cent of the latter's trade is sea-borne), whose growing maritime interests and naval capabilities cannot be ignored, are on the rise.

In a vastly transformed world, the United States is unquestionably the most dominant power in the Indian Ocean and is likely to remain engaged in the region on several counts: the war on terrorism, safety and security of sea-lanes, markets and energy security imperatives. China, with its growing economic and trade contacts in the Indian Ocean littoral, is also likely to pay increasing attention to the region - particularly to ensure uninterrupted access for strategic and commercial purposes.

Towards A new and adaptive regionalism!

Since mid-1990s one finds ascendance of a vision of 'commonality', and the beginning of a new phase in the regional diplomacy of the littoral countries of the IOR. The most talked about regional initiative is the so-called Indian Ocean Rim-Association for Regional Cooperation (IOR-ARC) established in 1997. Current moves towards the development of a cross-cultural, regional dialogue across the Indian Ocean have to be viewed in the context of changes in the global great power structure, and sweeping structural reforms of the international economic order imposed by the "hegemony of trans-national liberalism."[15] Yet, many policy-makers and foreign policy analysts, both inside and outside the IOR, have been slow to recognize, let alone anticipate, the emerging regional and sub-regional geopolitical reconfigurations. A critical glance at a map of the post-Cold War Indian Ocean region suggests a set of geopolitical equations and flows that can not be explained by classical geopolitical doctrines. For instance, this map emphasizes the location of the world economy's energy suppliers. If globalization is shorthand for a world economy undergoing increased integration of production, finance, and trade, then IOR's resources (ninety eight per cent of the world's diamonds, sixty six per cent of the oil reserves, sixty per cent of uranium, five per cent of rubber, forty per cent of gold) are the crucible of globalization for both the developed and the developing countries.

The fusion of India's 'Look East' policy (against growing dissatisfaction with the painfully slow progress of the SAARC) with

Australia's 'Look West' policy, combined with post-apartheid South Africa's need for a regional identity and the widely perceived need to respond effectively to the challenge of globalization, resulted in the fairly enthusiastic launch of the IOR-ARC in 1997. The IOR-ARC initially had fourteen member countries (Australia, Indonesia, India, Sri Lanka, Singapore, Malaysia, Oman, Yemen, Kenya, Tanzania, South Africa, Mozambique, Mauritius, and Madagascar). In 1999, this expanded to nineteen countries (with Thailand, Bangladesh, Seychelles, United Arab Emirates and Iran). In addition, there are five dialogue partners (Egypt, Japan, China, UK and France) and one observer (Indian Ocean Tourism Organization). Australia, India and South Africa appear to be the three key players.

Although not explicitly stated in the IOR-ARC charter, and despite arguments made both for and against, 'open regionalism' was eventually adopted as the organization's guiding principle. (Essentially, open regionalism does not bind member countries to any commitments, is based on voluntary action, and decisions are taken on the basis of consensus.) This perhaps was not surprising, given the commitment of the leading economies in the region, including Australia, to the World Trade Organization.

But as early as 1998, the IOR-ARC, seen by many as complementary to existing regional organizations such as APEC, the EU and NAFTA, had lost its direction as well as momentum. There are at least two key reasons for this:

- First, as a tripartite institutional arrangement (comprising business, academics and officials) imposed from above, without an established background of regional cooperation among either business or academic groups, the IOR-ARC appears to be lacking meaningful roots within the region. There is, therefore, a pressing need to cultivate both academic and business interest in the IOR-ARC, which at present is exercising minimal influence among member countries.
- Second, the pro-active role and enthusiasm of Indian business organizations such as Federation of Indian Chambers of Commerce and Industries (FICCI) and Confederation of Indian Industries (CII) and their

counterparts in Oman has not been matched by the business interest from other countries, including Australia, Singapore and South Africa. An uncritical acceptance of the APEC model to begin with, combined with a relative neglect of realities specific to the Indian Ocean region – where bilateralism remains restricted mainly to certain sub-regions – has led to a situation where expectations are not matched by an overarching vision, political will, or the necessary building blocks.

It is time to restructure and reorient the IOR-ARC along the lines of a *new* regionalism, dictated and driven by functional cooperation in sectors marked by growing convergence of interests among states and corporate world (for example, securing energy flows and safeguarding Sea Lanes of Communication (SLOCs)) and willing to adapt to new realities.

The current inward-looking, autonomy-seeking, geopolitically driven, Euro-centric style of regionalism, so typical of the 1950s and 1960s, is likely to further reinforce a 'govern-mentality' that is exclusively concerned with institution building. Instead, what the Indian Ocean demands and deserves, in my view, is an *adaptive* regionalism, which is outward-looking, and based on broadly conceived, flexible, market-sensitive, functional-sectoral cooperation. What is of critical importance here is not so much a commonly accepted *definition* of an Indian Ocean 'region' as an acknowledgement of the fact that the Indian Ocean is part of the world-ocean, and lacking inclusive networks of cooperation willing and able to *confront* uncertainty, *promote* confidence-building and *incorporate* uncertainty.

Human-Environmental Security and Climate Change

The well-founded knowledge that the Indian Ocean is the repository of fabulous resources is a significant geopolitical reality in the area. At the same time, most of the Indian Ocean region, with a few exceptions, is in desperate need of rapid economic development to meet the basic needs of its burgeoning population through harnessing of available resources. It is estimated that by now around seventy five per cent of Latin America's population, forty two per cent of Africa's and thirty seven per cent of Asia's is urbanized. Soon, if not already, out of as many as twenty five mega cities with a population of over nine million, fifteen would be coastal cities – with as many as ten in the Indian Ocean alone—which comes to about forty per cent of all mega cities. Whereas five out of these ten happen to be in South Asia.

Among the ten largest urban areas within 160 km of the coast, two are in India: Bombay (12.6 million) and kolkata (10.9 million). South Asian states are yet to think collectively as to how to deal with these mega cites in relation to the oceans. Both intra-state and inter-state cooperation is called for at the level of preventing the environmental degradation and the corresponding need to preserve the marine ecosystems from both the land-based and sea-based sources of pollution. In many coastal regions of South Asia, population and development pressures, as well as human activities further inland are combining to degrade and destroy marine habitat, threaten marine wildlife and alter coastal marine ecosystem. The seas are being polluted mindlessly through the dumping of refuse and dangerous wastes from land. The mega-city of Bombay alone dumps at least one million tons of untreated urban sewage into the sea every day.

Most interactions between human activities and the marine environment are best observed, measured and managed at the grass-roots level, by those directly affected. This applies especially to coastal communities–considered to be at special risk because of their isolation, fragile resource base, and often, poorer levels of education and health— and calls for an alternative to state-centred, highly centralized and bureaucratized approaches to growth-centred ocean development. One critical distinction between growth-centred and community-based development is that "the former routinely subordinates the needs of people to those of the production system while the latter seeks consistently to subordinate the needs of the production system to those of people."[16] Addressing the needs of the poor coastal communities and the ecosystems in South Asia's fragile coastal areas requires taking a long-term perspective, forming new partnerships with local communities and national stakeholders, continuously involving government, and fostering the ongoing commitment of all stakeholders. Such imperatives are likely to acquire greater urgency due to climate change.

Climate impacts on coastal zones of Asia include accelerated sea-level rise and more frequent and severe storm events. Large populations in coastal areas of Southeast and South Asia are vulnerable to pressure from unsustainable resource use and environmental degradation. These areas are already subject to numerous climate change-related stresses, including loss of coastal mangroves that act as major environmental determinants of coastal fisheries. Major delta areas of South Asia are likely to be subjected to stresses associated with sea-level rise, changes in water regimes, saltwater intrusion, siltation, and land loss. Low-lying coastal cities are likely to be at the forefront of impacts. The cities of Karachi, Mumbai and Dhaka– have already witnessed significant environmental stresses in recent years.

Degradation has taken place in the sensitive coastal areas of the sub-continent. Except in the forested areas of India's western coast and the coastal desert of Pakistan, the coastal landscape is largely altered, indicating a decline in the integrity of coastal ecosystems.

While the coastal areas of South Asia harbour some of the richest and most diverse marine and coastal habitats, and species in Asia, many of these valuable species are now endangered and threatened. These seas also provide an important resource for coastal communities, especially where a substantial portion of the population is either vulnerable or living in poverty. In many instances these communities depend on these resources, not simply to make a living but for survival. Increasing levels of resource exploitation have had the effect that costal zones and watersheds are being increasingly being converted for agriculture and urban development, resulting in direct pressures on coastal areas from elevated nutrient levels.

Sea-level rise increases the risk of coastal flooding if the other factors determining flood risk remain the same. Recent estimates are that twenty one per cent of the world' s population live within thirty kilometer of the coast and these populations are growing at twice the global trend. Consequently, increases in flood risk could have significant human impacts. The new Hadley Centre climate model[17] predicts a global rise in sea level of twety one cm by the 2050s due to rise in greenhouse gases from human activities. This estimate includes direct prediction of thermal expansion combined with estimates of land-based ice-melt, using a model developed by the University of Utrecht driven by the predicted climate change; an improvement on earlier estimates. Sea-level rise will not be the same everywhere; in some areas it could be up to twice this global mean, in other areas relatively little; later estimates of coastal impacts will include this variation.

With constant protection and no further sea-level rise, the model predicts an increase in the annual number of people at risk of flooding from ten million people in 1990 to thirty two million people in the 2050s; taking into account sea-level rise this increases to seventy eight million, i.e. an extra forty six million people at risk. *Three quarters of these people are concentrated in a few vulnerable regions, particularly South and South East Asia*, where there are many densely populated deltas, and West Africa, where the coastal population is growing rapidly. In addition, there are relatively large increases in the numbers of people at risk in all the regions comprised of small islands: the Caribbean, the Indian Ocean and the Pacific Ocean.

With evolving coastal protection and no sea-level rise, the number of people at risk amounts to some twenty seven million people by the 2050s; when the effects of sea-level rise are included, this rises to fifty million people, i.e. an additional twenty three million people. The same six regions contain most of these people, but *under this scenario the majority are concentrated in one region: South Asia*. The areas with many small islands again experience large relative increases in the number of people at risk. While adaptation is feasible in many of these vulnerable areas, it will involve long-term planning and substantial costs.

It is a truism that the dependence of South Asian countries on the Indian Ocean is multiple and total. But most of them have followed a sectoral approach to ocean development with various ministries concerned focusing on certain aspects of coastal zone management or resource development. Needless to say perhaps, these countries must get moving towards an integrated ocean management system that emphasizes in particular the need for comprehensiveness, coherence, consistency and cost-effectiveness in the formulation and implementation of ocean related policies.[18] Lacking still in South Asia are appropriate sustainable development models for fisheries, robust strategies for managing increasingly diverse and sometimes conflicting ocean uses in the face of poverty and population pressures on the coastal zone; and adequate means to disseminate ocean-related sustainable development technologies. There is still a 'management by crisis' mentality associated with the ocean use and an emphasis on conventional security that often works against sustainable development.

Securing the Sea Lanes of Communication

Strategically located between Africa, the Southern Ocean, Asia and Australia, the Indian Ocean encompasses shortest and most economical international SLOCs between the Pacific Ocean and the Middle East and Europe used by more than 300,000 tankers carrying about fifteen billion barrels of oil annually. Four critically important access waterways are the Suez Canal (Egypt), Bab el Mandeb (Dijbouti-Yemen), Strait of Hormuz (Iran-Oman), and Strait of Malacca (Indonesia and Malaysia). More than 9.5 million barrels of oil pass through the Strait of Malacca daily. Substantial volumes of international long distance maritime goods from the Persian Gulf, Africa, Asia and Europe pass through these SLOCs. Against the backdrop of global economic integration gaining momentum, and with more than half of the world's annual merchant fleet tonnage passing through the Straits of Malacca, Sunda and Lombok that connect the Indian Ocean to the Pacific, the Indian Ocean accounts for the carriage of the highest tonnage of goods. While most of the eastbound goods are made up of bulk crude oil, the bulk of the westbound goods are mainly made up of manufactured goods.

While the volume of global trade moving on the major maritime routes through the Indian Ocean is already impressive, it can expect to grow even more so in the future. The reason for that growth is that the route favours the use of much larger containerized vessels (8,000 TEU and above) operating between key hub ports.

While maritime trade grew at roughly three per cent per year in the 1990s, containerized trade grew at over eight per cent. The number of full containers ships internationally is predicted to more than double in this decade. To accommodate that growth larger vessels will be utilized and the preferred route for such vessels is the Indian Ocean.

While the major maritime trade route through the Indian Ocean is of increasing importance to the global economy, it funnels trade through vulnerable 'strategic choke points' at the eastern and western exits as well as the strait of Hormuz for traffic entering or exiting the Persian gulf. Credible threats to those choke points could severely disrupt maritime trade, increase costs and impact the health of the global economy. Freedom of the seas and particularly the free flow of commerce and maintaining the safety and security of the major maritime trade route that connects East Asia, Europe and East Coast are of critical (inter)national importance.

Threats to sea lane security in the IO have and would continue to come mainly from pirates, terrorists and other criminals sponsored by militia or insurgents.[19] For reasons like traffic congestion, navigational constraints and the presence of economically deprived communities particularly along the coastal areas on the Indonesian side of the waterway, the Malacca and Singapore straits are likely to remain a favourite venue for piracy activities. Concerns, bordering urgency, regarding the impact of sea robberies in the straits on economy and the potential risks to lives, properties as well as environmental damage, cannot be addressed through installation of coastal maritime surveillance radar chains along the entire coast of straits and deployment of more patrol boats alone. Long-term effective measures require regional and sub-regional agendas for dialogue as well as action.

What is also likely to make the SLOCs contested sites is that maritime rights continue to be an issue of contention between maritime powers and smaller littoral states.[20] Whereas the former are concerned with the threats of 'creeping jurisdictions' by littoral states on SLOCs accessibility, the latter are becoming increasingly anxious over 'creeping security jurisdiction' of the maritime powers especially over the high seas. However, the common interest of both the maritime powers and the littoral states in the security of SLOCs dictates regional importance of their cooperation to ensure that security.

A testimony in a congressional hearing, in May 2004, by the top US military officer in the Asia Pacific region, Admiral Thomas Fargo, to the effect that American counter terrorism forces might be deployed in the Malacca strait has evoked sharp reaction from both Indonesia and Malaysia, the two Indian Ocean countries separated by the strait. Since under international law security of the strait is their joint responsibility, both countries see the US proposal as an infringement of their sovereignty. Furthermore, both countries claim they were not consulted about the plan.

Subsequently, it has been clarified by the US government that Fargo's testimony was not a 'policy' statement but one of many components of a Regional Maritime Security Initiative (RMSI) soon to be discussed with Asian nations. Be that as it may, the US lead initiative to 'combat the transnational threats of maritime piracy and terrorism in the Malacca and Singapore straits by introducing mechanisms for information sharing and cooperation on law enforcement operations' is well on it way. Another objective of the RMSI is said to be to monitor, identify and intercept suspected vessels and activities in national and international waters. In order to do so, it is told that a large naval force is needed and the US, as the world's only super power, is one of the few countries with the capability to contribute to operational success there.

Maritime Confidence Building Measures in South Asia

Having identified above just a couple of issue-areas where a new regional architecture of maritime cooperation could possibly be built, it is important to briefly reflect on a relatively neglected issue of maritime confidence building measures in South Asia. One recent exception to this 'tradition' of neglect is the study of Commander Rajesh Pendharkar[21], where he forcefully argues that, "in the present context of Indo-Pakistani relations, maritime CBMs could prove to be path-breakers for overall military CBMs and conflict resolution in the regions."[22] '"Maritime CBMs", argues Pendharkar, "may succeed where other forms of CBMs have failed for following reasons"

(a) Since the maritime realm has been the least contentious of the three dimensions of military conflict, it may be easier to engage in meaningful CBMs.

(b) The Indo-Pakistani obligation to the international community to ensure the safety of neutral trade through the region could be seen as an opportunity to cooperate.

(c) There is a wide scope of non-contentious issues upon which maritime cooperation may be achieved, such as the search and rescue operations (SAR) maritime disaster management, protection of the maritime environment, preventing of arms trading, and the interdiction of smuggling and the narcotics trade. International conventions, in fact, make maritime cooperation in these areas mandatory.

(d) The character of the naval forces themselves make it possible to cooperate in a manner detached from political wrangling between the two states.[23]

Commander Pendharkar is quite right in pointing out that both bilateral and multilateral fora offer particular strengths and weaknesses in building maritime cooperation. He, therefore, proposes a two-pronged approach to maritime confidence building measures in the region. According to him, a multilateral framework could be put in place around a search and rescue agreement and regional maritime security management between the coastal states of the Arabian Sea. An additional advantage of participating in such a multilateral arrangement, where international precedents have already been codified, would be that "Indian and Pakistani navies should be able to break the ice and build enough confidence to proceed to a bilateral framework."[24] Whereas, a bilateral framework, in order to facilitate a continued engagement mechanism between India and Pakistan, could be built around an 'Incidents at Sea agreement'. Such an agreement, to quote Pendharkar,

...could lead to regular consultative talks and the creation of Maritime Risk Reduction Centres (MRRCs) for exchange of

notifications and incident related information intended to prevent escalation during crises. The agreement could also pave the way for establishing a Joint Activity Zone along the disputed maritime boundary wherein fishermen of both sides could operate free from fear of apprehension and without being drawn into political battles. Both sides could also undertake joint scientific explorations to ascertain the true quality and quantity of mineral resources in which the sea bed of the disputed zone is believed by some to be rich. Such a measure would not only provide an impetus for cooperation, but the results of joint exploration would bring facts, rather than beliefs, to the conflict resolution team.[25]

There is no reason why such bilateral arrangements could not be worked out between other South Asian countries, leading eventually to a wider regional network of proposed Maritime Risk Reduction Centres and Joint Activity Zones. The idea, is *worthy* of serious consideration by both the analysts and the policy makers in South Asia in every sense of the term. Also because such a network of MRRCs could also address the issue of the security of sea lanes of communication and thereby provide a South Asian 'response' to the proposed RMSI by the US.

Conclusion: Looking Ahead

In this paper, a modest attempt is made to demonstrate that the multifaceted challenge of maritime security can be met more effectively through the paradigm of a new geopolitics; a geopolitics that (a) contests the imperialist legacy of international maritime relations; (b) reclaims peaceful, co-operative, trade-based, maritime geopolitical traditions; (c) abandons the illusion of having 'mastered' the oceans in favour of a growing appreciation of finite capacity of the marine environment to endure and assimilate human-induced changes; (d) champions the cause of securing a peaceful, socially just and environmentally sustainable order for the oceans through patient negotiations and consensus, rather than by domination or use of force; and (e) articulates the concept of comprehensive ecological-human maritime security.

India's foreign policy today – both bilateral and multilateral – is marked to a large extent by unprecedented pragmatism and proactive thrust as well as a growing ascendance of geo-economic over geopolitical considerations. A 'new' mapping of the Indian Ocean region by India's political and economic elite, especially in the context of the nation's 'Look East' policy, is well under way - a process that is likely to bring about a change in India's image of itself *vis-à-vis* the rest of the world. There are positive indications that India is both able and willing to question its own 'land-centric' mindset and engage far more actively with issues related to maritime security broadly defined. There is also a growing appreciation that such issues straddle the traditional 'civilian-military' divide –where the responsibility for the former is assigned to the independent civilian ministries/departments and agencies, and the latter to ministry of defense and armed forces –and, therefore, demand a new institutional landscape as well as higher levels of coordination.

Against the backdrop of growing regional militarisation, the diffuse complexities of terrorism, insecurities related to energy flows and environmental degradation, the idea of broadening the scope of the IOR-ARC as an Indian Ocean-centric architecture of maritime cooperation, based on adaptive regionalism, and achieved through both bilateral and sub-regional initiatives, deserves the critical attention of both state and non-state actors with a stake in the region. The new challenge calls for burden-sharing and joint responsibility between governments and the corporate world to help defuse mutual suspicions, conflicts and rivalries. South Asian states have a central and critical role to play in the rejuvenation of the IOR-ARC. Together, they could impart a badly needed vision[26] as well as agenda for dialogue and action to this one and only experiment in Indian Ocean regional cooperation.

It has been argued recently by McPherson[27] that, both SAARC and IORARC need an injection of enthusiasm and expanded agendas for multilateral cooperation. According to him, despite the fact that the Indian Ocean itself is vital to the member states of both organizations, neither has focused on maritime issues. The Indian Ocean, he says:

"may provide a new agenda to strengthen the basis for cooperation and cooperative action on the part of SAARC...a shift

in focus to include maritime issues may present an opportunity to break the logjam facing both organizations. They both need to establish new agendas to further the process of developing cooperation, and the Indian Ocean provides a range of vital issues that will profoundly affect all the region's inhabitants in the coming century." [28]

Such ideas, are worthy of some serious consideration.

In order to meet the threats mentioned above as well as fully exploit the opportunities offered by the geo-economics of corporate globalization, the Southern Asian Rim as a whole needs to be re-imagined as encompassing not only 'spaces of places' but also 'spaces of flows'. Such a perspective challenges the conventional geographical scale and requires foreign policy, military and commercial establishments in South Asia to reorient themselves. With both state and non-state actors looking for definitions and certainties in a period that is itself struggling to find answers to the issues related to identity, boundaries and sovereignty[29] need to be handled by the intellectuals and institutions of statecraft on the subcontinent within a much larger *oceanic* vision.

Given that ocean and seas are a very different medium – with high seas providing direct and open access across long distances –each member state of SAARC is, in fact, a maritime neighbour of the other. Even land-locked Nepal has a stake in the maritime geopolitical economy of the Indian Ocean. What the subcontinent needs is a South Asian maritime solidarity based on the principle of equity, which in turn can be achieved through a wide ranging, multicultural South Asian oceanic dialogue. Such a dialogue, in order to qualify as 'humane' would be expected to display special sensitivity to the needs and requirements of groups and individuals who are disadvantaged by geography (landlocked states regions and communities), by economic and social circumstances and by their adherence to traditional methods of resource exploitation.

The geopolitical context and geographical coordinates for 'locating' such a dialogue will have to somewhat unconventional. In order to qualify as map-makers in their own right, South Asians demand and deserve new geographical imaginations and geopolitical visions. While continental perspectives centered on – and oriented towards –historically privileged 'North' remain important, the promise and potential of resurrecting maritime South Asia is best approached and realized through a world map of flows and mobility centred on south-polar projection.

References

1. K. M. Panikkar, *India and the Indian Ocean*, Bombay: George Allen & Unwin (India) Private Limited, 1971.
2. *Ibid.*
3. Satish Chandra (ed.), *The Indian Ocean: Explorations in History, Commerce and Politics*, New Delhi: Sage, 1987.
4. K. Macpherson, "Indian Ocean: A History of People and the Sea", in Holder Fuber, Sinnappah Arasaratnam (ed.), *Maritime India*, New York: Oxford University Press, 2004.
5. C. Verlinden, "The Indian Ocean: The Ancient Period and the Middle Ages", in Chandra, n.3, pp.12-27.
6. G.R Sloan, *Geopolitics in United States Strategic Policy, 1890-1987*, Brighton: Wheatsheaf Books, 1988, pp. 87-95.
7. Parker, W. H., *Mackinder: Geography as an Aid to Statecraft*, Oxford: Clarendon Press, 1982.
8. See Sloan, n.6.
9. R.B. Rais, *The Indian Ocean and the Super Powers*, New Delhi: Vistaar Publications, 1987.
10. M. Zuberi, "Nuclear Ocean", *Journal of Indian Ocean Studies*, Vol. 10, no.1, 2002, pp. 1-14.
11. P.V. Rao (ed.), *India and the Indian Ocean: In the Twilight of Millennium: Essays in the Honour of Professor Satish Chandra* Delhi: South Asian Publishers, 2003 D. Rumley & S. Chaturvedi (eds.), *Geopolitical Orientations, Regionalism and Security in the Indian Ocean*, New Delhi: South Asian Publishers, 2004.
12. M. Kaldor, *New and Old Wars: Organized Violence in a Global Era*, London: Polity Press, 1999.
13. J.S.Gill, "Sea Piracy –A Review in International Law and Shipbased Operations Steps", *Journal of Indian Ocean Studies*, vol. 19, no.1, 2002. pp.81-90.

14. D Berlin, "Indian Ocean Redux-Arms, Bases and Re-emergence of Strategic Rivalry", *Journal of Indian Ocean Studies*, vol. 10, no. 2002, pp.26-45.

15. Agnew, J. and S. Corbridge, *Mastering Space: Hegemony, Territory and International Political Economy*, London: Routledge, 1995.

16. D.C.Korten and G. Carner, "Planning Fraemworks for People-centred Development", in D.C. Korten and R. Klauss (eds.), *People-centred Development: Contributions Toward Theory and Planning Frameworks*, West Hartford: Kumarian Press, 1984, p.201.

17. Hedley Centre , http://www.metoffice.com/research/hadleycentre/pubs/brochures/B1998/coastal.html

18. A. Vallega, A, *Sustainable Ocean Governance: A Geographical Perspective,* London: Routledge, 2001; L. Juda and R.H. Burroughs, "The Prospects for Comprehensive Ocean Management", *Marine Policy*, vol.14, no.1,1990, pp.23-35.

19. V. Sakhuja, "Contemporary Piracy: Terrorism and Disorder at Sea: Challenges for Sea Lane Security in the Indian Ocean" in Rumley and Chaturvedi, n.11, pp.269-281.

20. M. Taib Bin Yassin, "Security of Shipping in the Straits of Malacca (SOM): Is UN Mandated Petrol the Answer?" Paper presented at the second annual conference of the Indian Ocean Research Group, Tehran, February 2004.

21. R. Pendharkar, *The Lahore Declaration and Beyond: Maritime Confidence Building Measures in South Asia*, Occasional Paper no. 51, Washington D.C.: The Henry L. Stimson Centre, 2003.

22. *Ibid.*

23. *Ibid.*

24. *Ibid.*

25. *Ibid.*

26. S.Kelegama, "Indian Ocean Regionalism: Is there a Future?" *Economic and Political Weekly*, vol. 37, no. 25, 22 June 2002, pp. 2422-2425.

27. See MacPherson, n.4.

28. *Ibid.*

29. J.A. Camilleri and J. Falk, *The End of Sovereignty? The Politics of a Shrinking and Fragmenting World*, Aldershot: Edward Elgar, 1992.

Bibliography

Ahmad, Ishtiaq, *Nuclear Non-Proliferation Issues in South Asia*, Islamabad: Islamabad Council of World Affairs, 1996.

Ahmad, Q.K., "SAARC: Envisioning the Future", *South Asian Survey,* Vol. 9, no. 2, July/December 2002, pp.187-200.

Ahmed, Imtiaz, *Memories of a Genocidal Partition: the Haunting Tales of Victims, Witnesses and Perpetrator*, Colombo: Regional Centre for Strategic Studies, 2002.

Ahmed, Mutahir, "Confidence-Building Measures Between Pakistan and India: an Argument for Change", *Contemporary South Asia*, Vol.7, no.2, July 1998, pp.137-45.

Ahsan, Abul, "The Evolving Context of Regional Cooperation in South Asia", *South Asian Survey*, Vol.3, no.1 & 2, January/ December, 1996, pp. 47-52.

Alagh, Yoginder K., "Technology and Development in South Asia: Some Perspectives", *South Asian Survey*, Vol.2, no.1, January/June 1995, pp.1-24.

Ali, Karamat, "Labour Movement in South Asia: Implications for SAARC", *South Asian Survey*, Vol.2, no.1, January/June 1995, pp.25-32.

Anderson, Michael R. and Sumit Guha, (eds.), *Changing Concepts of Rights and Justice in South Asia*, Delhi: Oxford University Press, 1998.

Babu, B. Ramesh (ed.), *Globalization and the South Asian State*, New Delhi: South Asian Publishers, 1998.

Bajpai, Kanti, "Security and SAARC", *South Asian Survey*, Vol.3, nos.1 & 2, January/December 1996 pp. 295-308.

_____, "Crisis and Conflict in South Asia after September 11, 2001", *South Asian Survey,* Vol. 10, no.2, July/December 2003, pp.197-214.

Banerjee, Dipankar, "Southern Asia after the Cold War", *South Asian Survey*, Vol. 2, no.2, July/December, 1995, pp.163-72.

_____. "Towards Comprehensive and Cooperative Security in South Asia", *South Asian Survey,* Vol.6, no. 2, July/December 1999, pp. 305-18.

_____(ed.), *CBMs in South Asia : Potential and Possibilities*, Colombo: Regional Centre for Strategic Studies, 2000.

_____(ed), *Security in South Asia: Comprehensive and Cooperative*, New Delhi: Manas Publications, 1999.

_____(ed), *Security Studies in South Asia: Change and Challenges*, Delhi: Manohar Publishers, 2000.

_____(ed), South *Asia At Gun Point: Small Arms and Light Weapons Proliferation*, Colombo: Regional Centre for Strategic Studies, 2000.

_____(ed), *South Asian Security Futures: A Dialogue of Directors Regional Strategic Studies Institutes*, Colombo: Regional Centre for Strategic Studies, 2002.

_____and Robert Muggah, *Small Arms And Human Insecurity: Reviewing Participatory Research in South Asia*, Colombo: Regional Centre for Strategic Studies, 2002.

Baral, Lok Raj, "Reconstruction of South Asia: A Precondition for SAARC", *South Asian Survey,* Vol.10, no.1, January/June 2003, pp. 71-84.

_____,"SAARC:The Problem of Becoming a Community", *South Asian Survey,* Vol.6, no.2, July/December 1999, pp. 241-58.

_____, Bastiampillai, and Others, *Governance and Defence Spending: Views from South Asia*, Colombo: Regional Centre for Strategic Studies, 2001.

Basrur, Rajesh M., *India's External Relations: A Theoretical Analysis*, New Delhi: Commonwealth Publishers, 2000.

_____(ed.), *Security in the New Millennium: Views From South Asia*, New Delhi: India Research Press, 2001.

_____and Hasan-Askari, Rizvi, "Nuclear Terrorism and South Asia," *Occasional Paper*, 25, Albuquerque, NM Cooperative Monitoring Center, Sandia National Laboratories, February 2003.

Bastiampillai, Bertram, "SAARC: A Decade Later", *South Asian Survey*, Vol.3, nos.1 & 2, January/ December, 1996, pp.219-28.

Bates, Crispin, *Community, Empire and Migration: South Asians In Diaspora*, Hyderabad: Orient Longman, 2000.

Bayly, C.A. ,*Origins of Nationality in South Asia : Patriotism and Ethical Government in the Making of Modern India*, Delhi: Oxford University Press, 1998.

——Beddoes, Zany Minton, "From EMU to AMU?, The Case for Regional Currencies', *Foreign Affairs*, Vol.78, no.4, July/ August 1999, pp.8-13.

Behera, Ajay Darshan, *Politics of Violence and Development in South Asia*, Colombo: Regional Centre for Strategic Studies, 1999.

Behera, Navnita Chadha and Others, *Beyond Boundaries: A Report on the State of Non-Official Dialogues on Peace, Security & Cooperation in South Asia*, Canada, Ontario: University of Toronto-York University, 1997.

Berlin, D., "Indian Ocean Redux-Arms, Bases and Re-Emergence of Strategic Rivalry", Journal *of Indian Ocean Studies*, vol.10, no.1, April 2002, pp.26-45.

Bhasin, Kamla, "Gender Workshops with Men in South Asia: Experiences and Reflections", *Convergence*, Vol. 29, no.1, 1996, pp.40-60.

Bhardwaj, Arjun and Delwar, Hossain, *Globalization and Multinational Corporations in South Asia: Towards Building a Partnership for Sustainable Development*, Colombo: Regional Centre for Strategic Studies, 2001.

Bhagwati, J., "Regionalism and Multilateralism: An Overview", in De Melo, J. and A. Panagariya (eds.), *New Dimensions in Regional Integration*, UK: Cambridge University Press, 1993.

Bhattacharya, K. Swapan, "Interface between Trade and Sustainability in South Asia", South *Asian Survey,* Vol. 8, no.1, January/June 2001, pp.37-66.

Bhopal, Kalwant, "Researching South Asian Women: Issues of Sameness and Difference in the Research Process", *Journal of Gender Studies,* Vol.10, no.3, November 2001, pp.279-86.

Bhuyan, Ayubur R., "Regional Cooperation in South Asia: Outlook and Prospects under SAPTA", *South Asian Survey*, Vol.3, nos.1 & 2, January/December 1996, pp.197-218.

Bidwai, Praful and Achin Vanaik, *South Asia On A Short Fuse: Nuclear Politics And The Future of Global Disarmament*, New Delhi: Oxford University Press, 1999.

Bjorkman, James Warner (ed.), *Fundamentalism, Revivalists and Violence in South Asia*, New Delhi : Manohar, 1988.

Blinder, Alan S., "Eight Steps to a New Financial Order", *Foreign Affairs*, Vol.78, no.5, September/October 1999, p.54-67.

Bose, Sumantra, *Kashmir: Roots of Conflict, Paths To Peace*, New Delhi: Vistaar Publications, 2003.

Brar, Bhupinder, "SAARC: If Functionalism has Failed, Will Realism Works?", *South Asian Survey,* Vol.10, no.1, January/June 2003, pp. 31-42.

_____, "South Asia: A Region of States or a Region of Regions", *South Asian Survey,* Vol.6, no.1, January/June 1999, pp. 89-98.

Brass, Paul R. and Achin Vanaik (eds.), *Competing Nationalisms in South Asia: Essays for Asghar Ali Engineer*, Hyderabad: Orient Longman, 2002.

Brichieri-Colombi, Stephen and Robert W. Bradnock, "Geopolitics, Water and Development in South Asia: Cooperative Development in the Ganges—Brahmaputra Delta", *The Geographical Journal*, Vol.169, no.1, March 2003, pp.43-64.

Brodie, Henry and Phillips Talbot, (eds.), *South Asia in the World Today*, Chicago: University of Chicago Press, 1950.

Buzan, Barry, Rizvi, and Others, *South Asian Insecurity And The Great Powers*, Hampshire: Macmillan, 1986.

Chadda, Maya, *Building Democracy in South Asia: India, Nepal, Pakistan*, New Delhi: Vistaar Publications, 2000.

Chari, P. R, *Perspectives on National Security in South Asia: in Search of a New Paradigm*, New Delhi: Manohar Publications, 1999.

Chari, P. R. and Ayesha, Siddiqa-Agha, *Defence Expenditure in South Asia: India and Pakistan*, Colombo: Regional Centre for Strategic Studies, 2000.

Chari, P.R and Others, *Nuclear Non-Proliferation in India and Pakistan : South Asian Perspectives*, New Delhi: Manohar, 1996.

Chary, Srinivas, "South Asia Approaches the Millennium: Reexamining National Security", *The Journal of Asian Studies,* vol.55, no.3, August 1996, pp.773-74.

Chatterjee, Indrani, *Unfamiliar Relations: Family and History in South Asia*, Delhi: Permanent Black, 2004.

Chaturvedi, Sanjay, "Common Security? Geopolitics, Development, South Asia and the Indian Ocean", Third *World Quarterly*, vol.19, no.4, December 1998, pp.701-24.

Chaudhury, Anasua and Basu, Ray, *Energy Crisis and Sub-regional Cooperation in South Asia*, Colombo: Regional Centre for Strategic Studies, 2000.

Chaudhry, Ghaffar M., "Abolishing Poverty and Hunger: A South Asian Perspective", *Contemporary South Asia*, vol.5, no.3, November 1996, pp.253-61.

Cheema, Pervaiz Iqbal, "SAARC Needs Revamping", *South Asian Survey,* vol.3, nos.1 &2, January/December 1996, pp. 309-20.

——— and Jasjit, Singh, *Defence Expenditure in South Asia: An overview*, Colombo: Regional Centre for Strategic Studies, 2000.

Chellaney, Brahma, "Fighting Terrorism in Southern Asia: The Lessons of History", *International Security,* vol. 26, no.3, December 2001, pp.94-116.

_____, "South Asia's Passage to Nuclear Power", *International Security,* vol.16, no.1, Summer 1991, pp.43-72.

Chenoy, Anuradha M., "Women in the South Asian Conflict Zones", *South Asian Survey,* vol.11, no.1, January/June, 2004, pp. 35-48.

Chishti, Sumitra, "The Decision-Making in the World Trade Organization and South Asian Countries", *South Asian Survey,* vol.9, no.2, July/December 2002, pp. 219-38.

Cohen, Stephen P., *The Security of South Asia: American and Asian Perspectives*, Urbana: University of Illinois Press, 1987.

————, "South Asia: The Origins of War and the conditions for Peace", *South Asian Survey,* vol.4, no.1, January/June 1997, pp. 25-46.

Colombage, S.S., "Payments and Monetary Cooperation in South Asia : Developments and Perspectives", *South Asian Survey*, vol.2, no.2, July/December 1995, pp.213-24.

Crunden, Robert M. and Others, *New Perspectives on America and South Asia*, Delhi: Chanakya, 1984.

Das, Debendra Kumar and V.R. Panchamukhi, *SAARC: Regional Co-operation and Development, Perspectives, Problems, Policies*, New Delhi: Deep & Deep Publications, 1995.

Dash, Kishore C., "Domestic Support, Weak Governments, and Regional Cooperation: a Case Study of South Asia", *Contemporary South Asia*, vol.6, no.1, March 1997, pp.57-77.

_____, "The Challenge of Regionalism in South Asia", International *Politics*, vol.38, no.2, June 2001, pp.201-28.

_____, "The Political Economy of Regional Cooperation in South Asia," *Pacific Affairs*, vol.69, no.2, Summer 1996, pp.185-209.

De Mel, Lal, "Competitive Advantage through Human Resource Development: An Opportunity for South Asia", *South Asian Survey,* vol.9, no.1, January/June 2002, pp.17-22.

De Rosa D.N., and K. Govindan, *Agriculture, Trade and Regionalism in South Asia: A 2020 Vision for Food, Agriculture and Environment*, Washington, D.C.: International Food Policy Research Institute, 1997.

De Silva, K.M., "The European Community and ASEAN: Lessons for SAARC", *South Asian Survey,* Vol. 6, no.2, July/December 1999, pp. 271-82.

Deb Kaushik, and Ankush Malhotra, "Lessons in Urban Transport in South Asia", *South Asian Survey,* Vol. 7, no.1, January/June 2000, pp.113-30.

Dixit, J.N., "Prospects of South Asian Cooperation in the Transformed World–Post – 11 September", *South Asian Survey*, vol.10, no.1, January/June 2003, pp. 43-56.

_____ "The Future of Security in South Asia", *South Asian Survey*, vol. 8, no.1, January/June 2001, pp.125-33.

Dornbusch, Rudiger, "Expectations and Exchange Rate Dynamics", *Journal of Political Economy*, vol. 84, no.6, 1976, pp.1161-76.

Dubey, Muchkund and Nancy Jetly, *South Asia and its Eastern Neighbours*, New Delhi: Konark Publishers, 1999.

Elsenhans, Hartmut, "European Integration: Limited Automatisms and Implications for SAARC", *South Asian Survey,* vol. 4, no.2, July/December 1997, pp. 235-58.

Etienne, Gilbert, "Agricultural Policies and Development in South Asia", *South Asian Survey,* vol.4, no.1, January/June 1997, pp. 95-108.

Fleming, J.M., "Domestic Financial Policies Under Fixed and Floating Exchange Rates", *IMF Staff Papers*, vol. 9, March 1962, pp. 369-80

Ganguly, Rajat, *Kin State Intervention in Ethnic Conflicts: Lessons from South Asia*, New Delhi: Sage Publications, 1998.

Ganguly, Sumit, *Conflict Unending: India-Pakistan Tensions Since 1947*, New Delhi: Oxford University Press, 2002.

Ganguly, Sumit, and Ted Greenwood (eds.), *Mending Fences: Confidence and Security-Building Measures in South Asia*, Boulder: Westview Press, 1996.

Gill, K. P. S., *Terror and Containment Perspectives of India's Internal Security*, New Delhi: Gyan Publishing House, 2001.

Gill, K. P. S. and Ajai Sahni, *The Global Threat of Terror: Ideological, Material & Political Linkages*, New Delhi: Bulwark Books, 2002.

Ghosh, Partha S., *Cooperation and Conflict in South Asia*, New Delhi: Manohar Publications,1989.

Gonsalves, Eric and Jetly, N. (eds.), *The Dynamics of South Asia: Regional Cooperation and SAARC*, New Delhi: Sage Publications, 1999.

Gujral, I.K., "South Asia – Co-Existence of Conflict and Cooperation", *South Asian Survey*, vol.3, nos.1-2, January/December 1996, pp.255-58.

Gunaratna, Rohan, *Inside Al Qaeda: Global Network of Terror*, New York: Columbia University Press, 2002.

Gunatillake, Godfrey, "The Cultural Dimension of the South Asian Community", *South Asian Survey,* vol. 8, no.1, January/June 2001, pp.107-16.

Gupta, S.P., William E. James, and Robert K. Mc Cleery (eds.), *South Asia as a Dynamic Partner*, New Delhi]: Macmillan, 1994.

Gustavsson, Jakob, "How Should We Study Foreign Policy Change?" *Cooperation and Conflict*, vol.34, no.1, March 1999, pp.73-95.

Haider, Zaglul, "Crises of Regional Cooperation in South Asia," *Security Dialogue*, vol.32, no.4, December 2001, pp.423-37.

Hasan, Mubashir, "Towards a New Vision for South Asia", *South Asian Survey,* vol.4, no.1, January/June 1997, pp.5-12.

Hasina, Sheikh, "Human Development, Poverty Alleviation and Peace in South Asia", *South Asian Survey*, vol.10, no.1, January/June 2003, pp. 5-12.

Hassan, M.K., "Is SAARC a Viable Economic Block? Evidence from Gravity Model", *Journal of Asian Economics*, vol. 12, no.2, Summer 2001, pp. 263-90.

Hays, Peter L. and Others, *Countering the Proliferation and Use of Weapons of Mass Destruction*, New York: Mcgraw-Hill, 1998.

Hellmann, Donald C., *Southern Asia: The Politics of Poverty & Peace: Critical Choices for Americans*, Lexington, Mass: Lexington Books, 1976.

Henderson, Harry, *Global Terrorism: The Complete Reference Guide*, Mumbai: Jaico Publishing House, 2003.

Hewitt, Vernon, *The New International Politics of South Asia*, Manchester: Manchester University Press, 1997.

Huge, James F. and Gideon Rose, *How Did This Happen?: Terrorism and the New War*, New York: Public Affairs, 2001.

Husain, Syed Anwar, "The Road Ahead for SAARC", *South Asian Survey,* vol.6, no.2, July/December 1999, pp. 231-40.

Hussain, Ross Masood, "New Directions for SAARC: A View from Pakistan", *South Asian Survey,* vol.10, no.1, January/June 2003, pp. 57-70.

_____,"Promotion of Inter-Government, Inter-People and Inter-Institutional Understanding in South Asia", *South Asian Survey*, vol.2, no.2, July/December 1995, pp.185-200.

_____, "SAARC 1985-1995,Review and Analysis of Progress", *South Asian Survey*, vol.3, nos.1-2, January/December 1996, pp. 9-24.

Hye, Sayed A., "Human Resources in South Asia: The Region's Advantage and its Development from SAARC Perspective, *South Asian Survey,* vol.9, no.1, January/June 2002, pp.23-34.

Iftekharuzzaman, *Regional Economic Trends and South Asian Security*, New Delhi: Manohar, 1997.

Jain, B.M., *Nuclear Politics in South Asia : In Search of an Alternative Paradigm*, Jaipur: Rawat Publications, 1994.

Jain, Purnendra C., *Distant Asian Neighbours: Japan and South Asia*, New Delhi: Sterling Publishers Pvt. Ltd., 1996.

Jalal, Ayesha, *Democracy and Authoritarianism in South Asia: A Comparative and Historical Perspective*, New Delhi: Cambridge University Press, 1995.

Jayasekera, P.V.J. , *Security Dilemma of a Small State*, New Delhi: South Asian Publishers, 1992.

Jayawardena, L., and Others, *Indo-Sri Lanka Economic Cooperation: Facilitating Trade Expansion through a Reciprocal Preference Scheme*, Study Group Series No. 9, UNU/WIDER,1993.

Jervis, Robert, *Perception and Misperception in International Politics*, Princeton, NJ: Princeton University Press, 1976.

Joeck, Neil, *Maintaining Nuclear Stability in South Asia*, Oxford: Oxford University Press, 1997.

Joy, P.A. and Saeed, M., *SAARC: Trade and Development*, New Delhi: Deep & Deep Publications, 1995.

Kadirgamar, Lakshman, "South Asian Cooperation in the Twenty–first Century: Opportunities and Challenges", *South Asian Survey,* vol.5, no.1, January/June 1998, pp.27-38.

Kahol, Yudhishtar, *SAARC: Through the New Millennium*, New Delhi: Anmol Publications Pvt. Ltd., 2003.

Karuppaswamy, M., "Information Technology and Infrastructure Development: The South Asian Context", *South Asian Survey,* vol.7, no.1, January/June 2000, pp.37-42.

Katsouris, Andreas and Daniel Goure, "Strategic Crossroads in South Asia: The Potential Roles for Missile Defense", *Comparative Strategy*, vol.18, no.2, April/June 1999, pp.173-89.

Kayathwal, Mukesh Kumar, *Security and Foreign Policy in South Asia*, Jaipur: Pointer Publishers, 1999.

Kelegama, Saman, "SAPTA and its Future", in Gonsalves, Eric and N. Jetly (eds.), *The Dynamics of South Asia: Regional Cooperation and SAARC*, New Delhi: Sage Publications, 1999.

_____, "A Need for a New Direction for SAARC: An Economic Perspective", *South Asian Survey,* vol.9, no.2, July/December 2002, pp.171-86.

_____, "SAARC – From Association to Community: A Small Country Economic Perspective", *South Asian Survey,* vol.6, no.2, July/December 1999, pp. 259-70.

_____, "SAPTA and Its Future", *South Asian Survey*, vol.3, no.1 & 2, January/ December, 1996, pp.155-72.

Khan, Ali Ashraf, "South Asian Potential for Global Competitive Advantage", *South Asian Survey,* vol.9, no.1, January/June 2002, pp. 13-6.

Khatri, Sridhar K., "The Politics of Becoming a Community: Stages and Prerequisites", *South Asian Survey,* vol.6, no.2, July/December 1999, pp. 197-230.

_____ "Security Issues in South Asia: A Nepalese Perspective", *South Asian Survey*, vol.2, no.1, January/June 1995, pp.101-10.

———(ed.), *Regional Security in South Asia*, Kathmandu: Centre for Nepal and Asian Studies, Tribhuvan University, 1987.

Khosla, I.P., "Constructing the South Asian Community", *South Asian Survey,* vol.6, no.2, July/December 1999, pp. 181-96.

_____ "SAARC and India: An Overview", *South Asian Survey,* vol.6, no.1, January/June 1999, pp. 9-22.

Khuhro, Hamida, "South Asia: Recognising the Realities of a Fractured Past and a Global Future", *South Asian Survey,* vol.8, no.2, July/December 2001, pp.185-94.

Kodikara, Shelton U., *External Compulsions of South Asian Politics*, New Delhi: Sage Publications *India Pvt. Ltd.*, 1993.

_____, *South Asian Strategic Issues: Sri Lankan Perspectives*, New Delhi: Sage Publications, 1990.

Krepon, Michael and Amit Sevak, *Crisis Prevention, Confidence Building and Reconciliation in South Asia*, New Delhi: Manohar Publications, 1996.

Kukreja, Veena, *Civil-Military Relations in South Asia: Pakistan, Bangladesh and India*, New Delhi: Sage Publications, 1991.

Kumar, Nagesh and Chadha Alka, "Exploiting the Potential of Information and Communication Technologies for Development in South Asia", *South Asian Survey*, vol.9, no.2, July/December 2002, pp.201-18.

Lahiri-Dutt, Kuntala, "A New Bond: Coal in the Energy Sector in South Asia", *South Asian Survey,* vol.7, no.1, January/June 2000, pp.131-41.

Lall, K.B., "Regional Cooperation in South Asia: Some Reflections", *South Asian Survey,* vol.6, no.1, January/June 1999, pp. 7-8.

Lama, Mahendra P., "Economic Reforms and the Energy Sector in South Asia: Scope for Cross-border Power Trade", *South Asian Survey,* vol.7, no.1, January/June 2000, pp. 3-24.

———, "Integrating the Tea Sector in South Asia: New Opportunities in the Global Market", *South Asian Survey,* vol. 8, no.1, January/June 2001, pp.67-96.

_____, "SAARC Integrated Programme of Action: Towards More Effective Cooperation", *South Asian Survey,* vol.5, no.1, January/June 1998, pp.39-56.

Lavakare, P. J "Science and Technology in SAARC: Aspirations, Achievements and Hopes", *South Asian Survey*, vol.3, nos.1-2, January/December 1996 pp.123-34.

Lawrence, Ziring, *The Subcontinent In World Politics : India, its Neighbors, and the Great Powers* New York: Praeger, 1982.

Lehr, Peter, "The Dynamics of South Asia: Regional Cooperation and SAARC", *Contemporary South Asia*, vol.9, no.1, March 2000, pp. 92-93.

Leonard Weiss, "Pakistan: It's Deja Vu All Over Again," *Bulletin of the Atomic Scientists*, vol.60, no.3, May/June 2004, pp. 52-59.

Lewis, R Barry, "The Winds of Change: Buddhism and the Maritime Links of Early South Asia", *The Journal of Asian Studies,* vol.55, no.4, November 1996, pp.1045-46.

Lyon, Peter, "South Asia and the Geostrategics of the 1990s", *Contemporary South Asia*, vol.1, no.1, March 1992, pp.25-39.

Mallick, Ross, *Development, Ethnicity and Human Rights in South Asia*, New Delhi: Sage Publications, 1998.

Mehrotra, L.L. Chopra, H.S. Kueck, and W. Gert, *SAARC 2000 and Beyond,* New Delhi: Omega Scientific Publishers, 1996.

Mekenkamp, Monique and Others, *Searching for Peace in Central and South Asia: An Overview of Conflict Prevention and Peace Building Activities*, Boulder: Lynne Rienner Publishers, 2003.

Mishra, R.C., *Security In South Asia: Cross Border Analysis*, Delhi: Authors Press, 2000.

—————, McKinnon, Ronald I., "Optimum Currency Areas" *American Economic Review*, vol. 53, no.4, November 1963, pp.717-24.

McPherson, Kenneth, "SAARC and an Indian Ocean Dialogue", *South Asian Survey,* vol.3, No.1 & 2, January/December 1996, pp. 321-26.

_____, "SAARC and the Indian Ocean", *South Asian Survey,* vol.9, no.2, July/December 2002, pp. 251-62.

Maass, Citha D., "South Asia: Drawn Between Cooperation and Conflict", *South Asian Survey*, vol.3, nos.1-2, January/December, 1996, pp.259-76.

Maley, William, "The 'War Against Terrorism' in South Asia", *Contemporary South Asia*, vol.12, no.2, June 2003, pp.203-17.

Malik, Iftikhar H., "Ethnicity and Contemporary South Asian Politics", *Round Table*, no. 322, April 1992, pp.203-14.

Malik, Mohan, "The Stability of Nuclear Deterrence in South Asia: The Clash between State and Antistate Actors", *Asian Affairs: An American Review*, vol.30, no.3, Fall 2003, pp.177-99.

Mallick, Ross, "Cooperation Among Antagonists: Regional Integration and Security in South Asia", Contemporary *South Asia*, vol.2, no.1, March 1993, pp.33-45.

Maskay, Nephil Matangi, "South Asian Monetary Integration in Light of the Optimum Currency area Criterion of Patterns of Shocks", *South Asia Economic Journal*, vol.2, no.2, July/December 2001, pp.203-19.

Mehrota, L.L., "SAARC and the Informatics Revolution", *South Asian Survey*, vol.3, nos.1-2, January/December 1996, pp. 101-122.

_____ "The Security Environment in South Asia", *South Asian Survey*, vol.2, no.2, July/December 1995, pp.173-84.

Mehta, Pratap Bhanu, "Ethnicity, Nationalism and Violence in South Asia", *Pacific Affairs*, vol.1, no.3, Fall 1998, pp.377-96.

_____ "A View From South Asia", *Foreign Policy*, no.137, July/Aug 2003, pp.37-8.

Mehta, Rajesh, K. Swapan Bhattacharya and "SAPTA I, SAPTA II and SAFTA: Impact on India's Imports", *South Asian Survey,* vol.4, no.2, July/December 1997, pp.259-76.

Mendis, Vernon L.B., "Perspectives on SAARC", *South Asian Survey*, vol.3, No.1 & 2, January /December 1996, pp. 33-46.

Mohan, C. Raja, "A Paradigm Shift toward South Asia?", *Washington Quarterly,* vol.26, no.1, Winter 2002, pp.141-56.

Morshed, A.K.H., "SAARC on its Tenth Birthday", *South Asian Survey*, vol.3, nos.1-2, January /December 1996, pp. 53-8.

Mukherjee, Neela, "SAARC Countries, Regional Trade in Services and WTO, Issues and Prospects", *South Asian Survey*, vol.9, no.2, July/December 2002, pp. 239-50.

Mukherji, I. N., "Charting a Free Trade Area in South Asia: Instruments and Modalities", a paper presented at the second conference of the South Asia Network of Economic Research Institutes (SANEI), August 2000, pp.26-29.

_____, "India's Trade and Investment Linkages with Nepal: Some Reflections", *South Asian Survey*, vol.5, no.2, July-December 1998, pp.183-97.

_____, "South Asian Preferential Trading Arrangement: India's Role", *South Asian Survey,* vol.6, no.1, January/June 1999, pp. 23-38.

Mundell, Robert A.,"The Appropriate Use of Monetary and Fiscal Policy for Internal and External Stability", *IMF Staff Papers*, vol.9, March 1962, pp.70-79.

_____ "Capital Mobility and Stabilization Policy under Fixed and Floating Exchange Rates", *Canadian Journal of Economic and Political Science*, vol.29, November 1963, pp. 475-85.

_____ "A Theory of Optimum Currency Areas", *American Economic Review*, vol. 51, no.4, November 1961, pp.657-64.

Muni, S.D., "Problem Areas in India's Neighbourhood Policy", *South Asian Survey,* vol. 10, no.2, July/December 2003, pp.185-96.

_____ "Regionalism Beyond the Regions: South Asia Outside SAARC", *South Asian Survey,* vol.3, nos.1-2, January/ December 1996, pp. 327-38.

Muni, S.D.(ed)., *Understanding South Asia: Essays in the Memory of Late Professor (Mrs.) Urmila Phadnis*, New Delhi: South Asian Publishers, 1994.

——— and Lok Raj Baral, *Refugees and Regional Security in South Asia*, Delhi: Konark Publishers, 1966.

Murty, Radhakrishna, K., "Proximate Determinants of Population Growth in the SAARC Region", *South Asian Survey*, vol.2, no.1, January/June 1995, pp.33-40.

Naik, Niaz A., "SAARC – From Association to Community: Prospects and Problems", *South Asian Survey,* vol.6, no.2, July/December 1999, pp. 333-43.

Nasr, S.V.R., "The Rise of Sunni Militancy in Pakistan: The Changing Role of Islamism and the Ulema in Society and Politics," *Modern Asian Studies*, vol.34, no.1, January 2000, pp.139-80.

Naqash, Nasir A., *SAARC: Challenges and Opportunities*, New Delhi: Ashish Publishing House, 1994.

Nuruzzaman, M.D., "SAARC and Subregional Co-operation: Domestic Politics and Foreign Policies in South Asia", *Contemporary South Asia*, vol.8, no.3, November 1999, pp.311-22.

Oommen, T.K., "State Versus Nation in South Asia: Linking Language and Governance", *South Asian Survey*, vol.9, no.2, July/December 2002, pp. 275-86.

______, "State Versus Nation: Linking Culture and Governance in South Asia", *South Asian Survey,* vol.8, no.2, July/December 2001, pp. 213-18.

Pachauri, R.K., "Energy and Environment in the Context of SAARC", *South Asian Survey,* vol.4, no.2, July/December 1997, pp.295-308.

Panagariya, A., "Trade Liberalization in South Asia: Recent Liberalization and Future Agenda", *The World Economy*, vol.22, no.3, May 1999, pp.353-78.

Pandian, S.G., "Moving South Asia's Economies Beyond the Indo-Pakistan Paradigm in the South Asian Regional Association for Cooperation", *Contemporary South Asia*, vol.11, no.3, November 2002, pp.329-44.

Paranjpe, Shrikant, "Development of order in South Asia: Towards a South Asian Association for Regional Cooperation Parliament", Contemporary *South Asia*, vol.11, no.3, November 2002, pp.345-56.

Pendharkar, R.,*The Lahore Declaration and Beyond: Maritime Confidence Building Measures in South Asia*, Washington, D.C.: The Henry L. Smitson Centre, 2003.

Phadnis, Urmila, *Ethnicity and Nation-Building in South Asia*, New Delhi: Sage Publications, 1989.

Pigato, M., and Others, *South Asia's Integration into the World Economy*, Washington, D.C: World Bank, 1997.

Prasad, Bimal, "Prospects for Greater Cooperation in South Asia: The Political Dimensions", *South Asian Survey*, vol.3, nos.1-2, January/December 1996, pp.277-86.

Qadir, Shaukat, "The Concept of International Terrorism: an Interim Study of South Asia", *Round Table*, no.360, July 2001, pp.333-43.

Rafique, Najam, "SAARC – From Conflicting Cultures to Cooperatives Community", *South Asian Survey,* vol.6, no.2, July/December 1999, pp. 319-32.

Rahman, Atiur, "Imperatives for Regional cooperation in South Asia: Creating an Environment for Sharing Experiences of Knowledge-based Development", *South Asian Survey,* vol.7, no.2, July/December 2000, pp.209-26.

Rahman, Waliur, "Culture, Tradition and Modernisation in South Asia", *South Asian Survey,* vol.8, no.2, July/December 2001, pp. 203-12.

Raipuria, Kalyan, "SAARC in the New Millennium: Need for Financial Vision", *South Asian Survey,* vol. 8, no.1, January/ June 2001, pp.17-36.

Rais, Rasul Bakhsh, "Integration and Community Formation in South Asia: Need for Institutions, Norms and Values", *South Asian Survey,* vol.8, no.2, July/December 2001, pp.219-28.

Rajain, Arpit, "Promoting Cooperation through Growth Triangles and Quadrangles in South Asia", *South Asian Survey,* vol.6, no.1, January/June 1999, pp. 63-74.

Raje, Vasundhar, "Bulding Regional Cooperation: India's Role", *South Asian Survey,* vol.6, no.1, January/June 1999, pp. 3-6.

Raju, A. Subramanyam, *Third-Generation Indian Perceptions Of The Kashmir Issue*, Colombo, Sri Lanka : Regional Centre for Strategic Studies, 2001.

———, "Energy Cooperation in South Asia", in Sanjay Chaturvedi & Dennis Rumely (ed), *Energy Security and the Indian Ocean Region*, New Delhi: South Asian Publishers, 2005, pp.190-203.

_____ (ed.), *Nuclear India: Problems and Perspectives*, New Delhi, Colorado: South Asian Publishers, International Academic Publishers, 2000.

_____(ed.), *Terrorism in South Asia: Views From India*, New Delhi, Singapore: India Research Press, Marshall Cavendish Publishers, 2004.

——— and Keethaponcalan, *Maritime Cooperation between India and Sri Lanka*, New Delhi: Manohar Publishers,2006.

Ramana, M.V. Reddy and Rammanohar, C., *Prisoners of the Nuclear Dream*, Hyderabad: Orient Longman, 2003.

Rana, A.P., "'New Directions' in the Study of SAARC: Evaluating the Bases of Regional Cooperation in South Asia", *South Asian Survey*, vol.10, no.1, January/June 2003, pp.13-30.

_____,"South Asian Cooperation after the Cold War: Coping with the International Dimension", *South Asian Survey,* vol.6, no.1, January/June 1999, pp. 99-107.

Randall L. Schweller, "Bandwagoning for Profit: Bringing the Revisionist State Back," *International Security*, vol.19, no.1, Summer 1994, pp.72-107.

Rasheed, Sajjadur K.D., "Transport Infrastructure Development in Bangladesh: Potential for Regional Cooperation", *South Asian Survey,* vol.7, no.1, January/June 2000, pp.43-54.

Ray, Aswini K., "Democratic Modernisation in Segmented South Asia and the Role of Civil Society in Regional Cooperation", *South Asian Survey,* vol.8, no.2, July/December 2001, pp.229-36.

Reed, Ananya Mukherje, "Regionalization in South Asia: Theory and Praxis", *Pacific Affairs*, vol.70, no.2, Summer 1997, pp.235-51.

Rizvi, Gowher, *South Asia in a Changing International Order*, New Delhi: Sage Publications, 1993.

Roy-Chaudhury, Rahul, "The Maritime Dimension: Ports, Shipping and Shipbuilding", *South Asian Survey,* vol.7, no.1, January/June 2000, pp.99-112.

Rubinoff, Arthur G., "The Multilateral Implications of Ethno-nationalist Violence in South Asia", *South Asian Survey,* vol.7, no.2, July/December 2000, pp.273-93.

Rupesinghe, Kumar and Khawar Mumtaz (eds.), *Internal Conflicts in South Asia*, Thousand Oaks: Sage Publications, 1996.

Saberwal, Satish, "Ethnicity and Social Order: South Asia Today", *Contemporary South Asia*, vol.2, no.1, March 2001, pp.23-34.

Sabur, A.K.M. Abdus, "Management of Intra-Group conflicts in SAARC: The Relevance of ASEAN Experiences", *South Asian Survey*, vol.10, no.1, January/June 2003, pp. 85-100.

Saigol, Tariq Saeed, "Salient Features of Pakistan's Trade with India", *Economic Review*, vol. 27, no.11, November 1996, pp.22-23.

Schulz, J.J., "Riding the Nuclear Tiger: The Search for Security in South", Arms *Control Today*, vol.23, no.5 June 1993, pp.3-8.

Shaha, Rishikesh, "Human rights and SAARC", *South Asian Survey*, vol.3, nos.1-2, January /December 1996, pp.287-94.

Sahadevan, P., *Coping with Disorder: Strategies to End Internal Wars in South Asia,* Colombo: Regional Centre for Strategic Studies, 2000.

Sahai, Shashi B., *South Asia: From Freedom to Terrorism*, New Delhi: Gyan Publishing House, 1998.

Sharma, Suman, *India and SAARC*, New Delhi: Gyan Publishing House, 2001.

Shatri, Amita, "Regional Powers and Small State Security: India and Sri Lanka, 1977- 90", *The Journal of Asian Studies,* vol.56, no.1, February 1997, pp.225-26.

Samaddar, Ranabir, *Cannons into Ploughshares: Militarization and Prospects of Peace in South Asia*, New Delhi: Lancer Publishers, 1995.

Siddiqi, Toufiq A., "India-Pakistan Cooperation on Energy and Environment: To Enhance Security", *Asian Survey*, vol.35, March 1995, pp.280-90.

Sidhu, Waheguru Pal Singh, "Terrible Tuesday and Terrorism in South Asia", *South Asian Survey,* vol. 10, no.2, July/ December 2003, pp.215-30.

Silwal, Y.K., "SAARC, The First Decade", *South Asian Survey*, vol.3, nos.1-2, January /December 1996, pp. 25-32.

Singh, Jagtar, "South Asia in the Global Electronic Village: Issues and Implications", *Resource Sharing & Information Networks,* vol.14, no.2, December 1999, pp.73-84.

Singh, Tarlok, "Organization of South Asian Policy Studies", *South Asian Survey*, vol.3, nos.1-2, January/December 1996, pp. 67-70.

Sobhan, Rehman, "Aid and Governance in South Asia", *South Asian Survey*, vol.3, nos.1-2, January/ December 1996 pp.245-51.

_____, "Prioritising Justice in South Asia's Development", *South Asian Survey,* vol. 8, no.1, January/June 2001, pp.3-16.

_____, "Regional Cooperation in South Asia: A Quest for Identity", *South Asian Survey,* vol.5, no.1, January/June 1998, pp.3-26.

Srinivasan, T.N., *Developing Countries and the Multilateral Trading System: From the GATT to the Uruguay Round and the Future*, Delhi: Oxford University Press, 1998.

———, *Regional Trading Arrangements and Beyond: Exploring Some Options for South Asia – Theory, Empirics and Policy, Report* No:142, Washington: World Bank, 1994.

———(ed.), *Trade, Finance and Investment in South Asia*, New Delhi: Social Sciences Press, 2001.

Stein, Burton and Sanjay Subrahmanyam (eds.), *Institutions and Economic Change in South Asia*, Delhi: Oxford University Press, 1996.

Stobdan, P., "Regional Issues in Central Asia: Implications for South Asia", *South Asian Survey,* vol.5, no.2, January/June 1998, pp.245-64.

Synnott, Hilary, *The Causes And Consequences Of South Asia's Nuclear Tests*, Oxford: Oxford University Press, 1999.

Tellis, Ashley J., *India's Emerging Nuclear Posture: Between Recessed Deterrent and ReadyArsenal*, New Delhi: Oxford University Press, 2001.

Thapa, Surya Bahadur, "The Future of South Asian Cooperation: A Partnership for the Twenty-first Century", *South Asian Survey,* vol.6, no.2, July/December 1999, pp. 173-80.

Thapliyal, Sangeeta, "Potential for Cooperation in South Asia: The Need for a Sub-Regional Approach", *South Asian Survey,* vol.6, no.1, January/June 1999, pp. 51-62.

Thomas, Raju G.C., *South Asian Security in the 1990s*, London: Brassey's, 1993.

Thomas S. Kuhn, *The Structure of Scientific Revolutions*, Chicago and London: University of Chicago Press, 1970.

Upadhyaya, S.K., "The Future of SAARC Depends on Economic Cooperation", *South Asian Survey*, vol.3, nos. 1 & 2, January/December 1996, pp.151-54.

Uppal, Joginder S., *Economic Development in South Asia*, New York: St. Martin's Press, 1977.

Vohra, N.N., "Cooperating for good Governance in South Asia", *South Asian Survey,* vol.7, no.2, July/December 2000, pp.169-74.

Wadhva, Charan D., "Assessing SAARC Preferential Trading Arrangement (SAPTA)", *South Asian Survey*, vol.3, nos.1-2, January/December 1996, pp.173-96.

_____, "Some Reflections on the Interlinkages between Regional Economic Cooperation and Cultural Interaction", *South Asian Survey*, vol.3, nos.1-2, January/December 1996, pp.135-48.

Waqif, Arif A., "Civil Service Capacity for Regional Cooperation: Some Comparative Aspects in the EU and SAARC Regions", *South Asian Survey,* vol.6, no.1, January/June 1999, pp. 75-88.

_____, "A Conceptual Approach to National and Regional Harmonisation for Employment Generation and Poverty Alleviation", *South Asian Survey*, vol.2, no.2, July/December 1995, pp.201-12.

_____, "GATT-1994 and South Asian Region Cooperation: A Survey of Issues and Approaches", *South Asian Survey*, vol.3, nos.1-2, January/ December 1996, pp.229-44.

———(ed.), *South Asian Cooperation in Industry, Energy and Technology*, New Delhi: Sage Publications, 1987.

Waslekar, Sundeep, *A Handbook for Conflict Resolution in South Asia*, New Delhi: Konark Publishers, 1996.

Weerakoon, Dushni., "Globalisation and South Asia: The Role of Foreign Direct Investment in Economic Development", *South Asian Survey,* vol.11, no.1, January/June 2004, pp. 3-20.

_____, "Indo-Sri Lanka Free Trade Agreement: How Free is it?", *Economic and Political Weekly,* vol.36, no.8, 24 February 2001, pp.627-29.

———and J. Wijayasiri, *Regional Economic Cooperation in South Asia: A Sri Lankan Perspective*, Colombo: Institute of Policy Studies, 2001.

Wignaraja, Ponna, "The Intellectual Quest in SAARC: Potential for a Unique Partnership in Moving Towards a South Asian Community", *South Asian Survey*, vol.3, nos.1 -2, January/ December 1996, pp. 71-90.

Wignaraja, Ponna and Akmal Hussain (eds.), *The Challenge in South Asia : Development, Democracy and Regional Cooperation*, New Delhi: Sage Publications, 1989.

——— and Susil Sirivardana, *Readings on Pro-Poor Planning Through Social Mobilisation in South Asia: The Strategic*

Option for Poverty Eradication, vol. I, New Delhi: Vikas Publishing House, 1998.

Wilson, A. Jeyaratnam, "The Foreign Policies of India's Immediate Neighbours: A Reflective Interpretation", *Journal of Asian & African Studies*, vol.25, no.1, January/April 1990, pp.42-59.

_____, "The politics of Ethnicity and Ethno-Nationalisms in South Asia, *Contemporary South Asia*, vol.2, no.3, November 1993, pp.327-33.

Zaki, I.H, "SAARC: Beyond the First Decade", *South Asian Survey*, vol.3, nos.1-2, January /December 1996, pp. 59-64.

Zimba, H.E. Lyonpo Yeshey, "A South Asian Panorama for the Twenty-first Century", *South Asian Survey,* vol.9, no.1, January/June 2002, p 3–12.

Zuberi, M., "Nuclear Ocean", *Journal of Indian Ocean Studies*, vol.10, no.1, April 2002, pp.1-14.

Compiled by Ann Kumaraswamy, Librarian, Indo-American Centre for International Studies, Hyderabad. 500007.

Index

D

E

F

G

H

N

O

S

U

V